"Get Beethoven!"

About the Author

Paul Cassidy was born in Derry in 1959. He has spent his entire working life with the Brodsky Quartet. Together they have played over 3000 concerts in more than 60 countries and made in excess of 70 recordings. Paul is a prolific arranger. In addition to his countless works for strings, he has collaborated with Elvis Costello, Bjork, Sting and many other eminent composers. Examples of these can be found on Brodsky albums such as; Petits Fours, Moodswings and The Juliet Letters, also on Bjork's Family Tree.

"Get Beethoven!" is Paul's first book, though a second, a fun-filled account of his forty years in the Brodsky Quartet, is due for release in autumn 2021 to coincide with that group's 50th anniversary. He lives in London with his wife, Jacqueline (cellist and founder member of the Brodsky Quartet) and their two daughters, Holly and Celia.

For further information, including a selection of photographs to accompany this book, please visit; www.paulcassidy.eu

"Get Beethoven!"

Paul Cassidy

Matador
9 Priory Business Park,
Wistow Road, Kibworth Beauchamp,
Leicestershire. LE8 0RX
Tel: 0116 279 2299
Email: books@troubador.co.uk
Web: www.troubador.co.uk/matador
Twitter: @matadorbooks

ISBN 978 1838593 421

British Library Cataloguing in Publication Data.
A catalogue record for this book is available from the British Library.

Typeset in 11pt Sabon by Troubador Publishing Ltd, Leicester, UK

Matador is an imprint of Troubador Publishing Ltd

Contents

1

Altnagelvin

I have no memory pre-Altnagelvin.

Alt na nGealbhan or 'height of the sparrows' is the impossibly romantic name given to Derry's very own… house of fear. No doubt the original village of the same name was worthy of such an evocative title, standing as it did, pride of place, overlooking lovely Derry on the banks of the Foyle but the high-rise brick and glass cuckoo which installed itself there in the spring of 1960 certainly was not. Gorging itself on the poor, unsuspecting local community, it grew to an unhealthy eleven stories, an out-and-out skyscraper by Derry standards. It remains to this day the city's tallest building, perched there aloft, keeping its beady eyes peeled for any folk showing signs of weakness, who might help satisfy its insatiable appetite.

This is where I found myself, aged three. Oh, how heavenly my first three years of life must have been. You see, unusually for a baby, I was apparently the apple of everyone's eye, the centre of attention. I'm afraid there's no denying it, according to my family folklore, rather like the cuckoo over in the Waterside, I came along and ousted my big brother from his number-one spot, effectively ruining his life for evermore. I went and got born for goodness' sake, an appallingly devious plan never before hatched in the history of mankind, all designed with the sole purpose of destroying his utopian existence. Imagine the shock then of, from one day to the next, being ripped from that adored, mollycoddled, cotton-wool existence and finding oneself in a rotting environment where cotton-wool took on a very different aspect. Suddenly, life was completely alien; the lights, sounds, surfaces, people… one's very being, both physically and

mentally, was thrown into shock. The fear factor was overwhelming…
and that smell!!

Sixth floor, right-hand corner window of Altnagelvin Hospital,
that was me. You could see it clearly from the road. No one could have
prepared me for that trauma. My sister Joan took me there and left me.
Mum couldn't do it.

"Sure, your daddy called every day," they always say.

In reality, he used to show up very late on the odd Sunday night causing
a bit of a commotion with the staff, stay for a brief moment, then be gone.

I had inherited a hip condition known as Perthes. The only real
treatment in those days was complete rest, no problem for a three-year-
old boy, right! I found myself in the polio ward and in time befriended
another unfortunate waif by the name of Martin Rush. We quickly
became firm friends and partners in crime, wreaking as much havoc as we
possibly could, wandering off round the hospital, playing games. We'd
often be found in the canteen seeing what goodies we could scrounge, or
if we had the stomach for it, in A&E to see the bloodied drunks being
wheeled in after a night on the town. Once we were caught in the ladies'
ward in the middle of the night. We were only four years old remember,
yet on this occasion, the charming ward matron decided to teach us a
lesson. I'm not sure what happened to Martin, but I was thrown into
an electricity generator room whereupon the lights were switched off
and the door locked shut. The noise in there was overpowering and
terrifying. It was pitch black. My efforts to open the door were in vain,
my tiny fists banging on that huge iron wedge, futile. Cried out, I sunk
to the floor and covered my ears. I'd say I was left alone in there for a
good hour.

When I was finally retrieved, I was marched back to my bed where
a traction device had been erected and I was duly strapped in. Our few
innocent distractions had been suspended indefinitely. Imagine if, instead
of crouching in fear, I had gone blindly searching for a light switch, I could
have electrocuted myself, set fire to the whole building, or both.

I consider myself very fortunate in that during my time there, there
were no operations or unpleasant procedures, just countless X-rays and
enforced bed rest. The whole experience drove me crazy however and after
eighteen months or so I was literally climbing the walls. My mum and the
staff finally agreed on a plan to take me home, on condition that a bed

be placed in the kitchen for me. The kitchen was the hub of the house and a place where I could be monitored. This would have seemed like heaven but for the fact that they nevertheless insisted on encasing me, all the way from my chest to the toes of my left foot, in plaster of Paris. Oh, the itching!!

This lasted a year, at which point I was deemed well enough to move onto the next step, a rather fetching calliper/boot arrangement. Though uncomfortable and unsightly, this meant I could begin my life again. I'll never forget the feeling of freedom, getting rid of that infernal plaster and letting the fresh air at my body. I ran round and round our house laughing and singing, as happy as the day's long. The day of my final release would be another year hence. I lost touch with my mate Martin but I'm sorry to relate that his bad luck continued. I heard he was shot dead, up in Creggan in the early '70s.

2

Mum and Dad

My dad, like so many Irish men of that era, boarded a ship bound for New York, aged twenty. The youngest of ten, he started life in a two-room cottage with earthen floors, in a place called the Bankhead, which overlooked the Swilly Port of Buncrana. Unfortunately, he could not have arrived in the Big Apple at a worse time. He used to tell a story of walking along one of the avenues to work early one morning and hearing a terrifying crashing sound. There followed some commotion up ahead, and gradually, as he approached the scene, he realised that the noise had been some poor man throwing himself off a tall building, his body ripping through one of those characteristic awnings before exploding on the pavement below. It was 1929.

In the half a dozen years he spent there, in what must have been an extremely alien environment for him, he did what he could to survive. He worked in bars, hotels and as a bellhop in apartment buildings. He got involved in the whole prohibition scene and even gained his licence as a boxing promoter, one of his great lifelong passions, the other being horses.

Perhaps it was this brush with prohibition that influenced the rather extraordinary decision he took immediately upon his return to Ireland in 1933. The ship pulled into Derry at the foot of Baronet Street. At the top of Baronet Street on the Strand Road, Derry's main drag, stood a most inconsequential hostelry with a 'For Sale' sign. It consisted of one small room selling only whiskey, and stout from clay bottles. It had no toilet... he bought it!

It proved to be a pretty shrewd move. Bit by bit he added to it, buying the next house and then the next. In the Second World War, Derry became the number one port in the Battle of the Atlantic (the German Navy would subsequently surrender on the Foyle not a mile from the pub door). Navies from all over parked their crafts at the end of Baronet Street. Sea legs found dry land; dry throats found Joe Cassidy's Railway Bar. By the time I came along, this establishment had grown into a magnificent landmark gin-palace on three floors.

A certain Dr Cavanagh from Greencastle, a charming little fishing port at the mouth of Lough Foyle, had opened a GP practice just up the road from the Railway Bar. He and his wife were a busy couple with a growing family and an increasing need for a nanny. But where would they find the perfect girl to look after their brood? The doctor said he would start by asking around the village just in case… boy was their luck in. Not 200 yards up the road from the Cavanaghs on the crossroads of Drumaweir stood another landmark, Browne's Cottage. It had been in the Browne family for well over 200 years and it was a place where people liked to congregate, stop and have a chat. Within that delightful, classic-style thatched cottage there lived an angel, a young lady with the sunniest disposition; the youngest of seven children, she was warm, kind, happy, hard-working and able. The Cavanaghs' prayers were answered. They say that, when she reluctantly boarded the old Lough Swilly bus to take up her new post in the big smoke, her Botticelli golden curls bouncing on her waist, she was a vision of beauty n'ere seen before in those parts. She had just turned eighteen; her name was Celia.

Not long after acquiring the pub, my dad took the brazen decision to avail himself of one of those new-fangled automobiles. At a time when most people were using the pony and trap and you could count the cars in Northern Ireland on the fingers of one hand, this acquisition showed a man with ideas and ambition. Even if his foray into the New World hadn't been a resounding success, he was certainly showing a pioneering spirit right here on the banks of the Foyle. I bet that car came in handy when he was trying to catch the eye of the enchanting *cailín* who had lately captured his attention and was befuddling his mind. He found himself spending more and more time, when he should have been pouring drinks and entertaining his customers, standing by the door, hoping to strike up a conversation as she passed, pushing prams or playing games with the young Cavanaghs. I guess the little darling of Drumaweir didn't stand much of a chance up against the charms of the boy from the Bankhead with his fancy suit, easy American drawl, budding business and that purring Austin with the walnut dash and leather seats.

Joseph and Celia fell in love and were married in Ballybrack Church with a bit of a shindig in Drumaweir Cottage itself, after the service. There was no such thing as a fancy wedding dress or a romantic honeymoon. Instead they moved into less than salubrious digs above the still tiny Railway Bar.

3

The Family

The couple's offspring began with Helen on 13.09.37 and finished with me on 13.09.59. Whether or not this is a reflection of my mum's fastidious nature or my dad's clinical eye for detail I'm not sure, but he did manage to bring his own life to a close on the very same date – 13.09.93.

As I mentioned, my dad was the youngest of ten and my mum the youngest of seven; together their children's roll call reads like this (those of a nervous disposition, look away now):

Helen	13.9.37
Bridget	16.11.38
John	19.12.39
Mark	17.5.41
Margaret	29.6.42
Mary	18.4.44
William	11.6.45
Joe	17.2.47
Bernadette	17.4.48
Joan	31.3.49
Peter	4.9.50
Rose	25.9.51
Clare	23.2.53
Denis	16.5.54
Andrew	10.7.58
Paul	13.9.59

You see how, once again, that innate sense of symmetry is at work; eight boys, eight girls. We know of at least three miscarriages, so basically my mum was pregnant from the age of nineteen to forty-three. One of the boys died early on in life, William was simply lactose-intolerant and tragically died in his mother's arms, aged six weeks. Andrew's demise on the other hand was less clear-cut and there remains a veil of uncertainty over it, in some quarters, to this day. More of that anon.

By 1954, Mr and Mrs Cassidy were about to welcome child number fourteen into the world. Though, with the success of the pub, they had progressed to a very fine town house, a short walk from the premises, this brood needed somewhere serious to live. Somewhere which offered lots of space inside and out. At that time, the citizens of NI found themselves in an apartheid situation. People of the Green persuasion were not encouraged to have a proper education, good job, fancy car or adequate housing. Despite making up something like 98 per cent of the population of Derry, the Catholic Nationalists were very poorly treated. Usually, when a house like Kebroyde came up for sale, it wouldn't even go on the market. Word would get out and an appropriate buyer would be found privately. On this occasion however the vendor, a certain Mrs Biggar, decided that the house would go to private auction with sealed bids, highest bid wins. This suited my dad. He was a betting man anyway (50p accumulators were his favourites) but when it came to this house, he was determined not to miss it.

Kebroyde was a majestic place, the last of a set of ten such houses on the road north out of Derry towards Donegal and the Inishowen Peninsula. Though a proper, no-nonsense Victorian pile from the outside, internally it only had the usual layout of four bedrooms, three reception rooms etc. However, it also boasted an extraordinarily grand hallway, flanked with huge stained-glass windows, a wonderful mahogany staircase, enormous kitchen, utility room, pantry, walk-in cold store, servants' quarters, and a loft space that, if properly utilised, could have nearly doubled the living area. It sat in more than an acre of stunning garden, mostly walled. There was a summer house, tennis court, kennels, stables, greenhouse, potting shed, garage, vegetable garden, orchard, oh and did I mention, a three-bedroomed house out back for the gardener. My dad put everything he had into that brown envelope and nervously awaited the outcome.

The town house where they lived was adequate; well built, clean, warm and fully functioning, but they had seen the promised land. Those majestic square rooms, that mighty kitchen, big enough even for them to all sit and eat, the storage areas, the garden… it was altogether dreamy. Imagine the hysteria therefore when Papa Bear's bet came up trumps. He'd beaten the odds, his was the highest bid and it had been accepted. His great gamble had paid off; he'd managed it. Kebroyde was to be the new Cassidy home.

On the morning he received the miraculous news, a huge weight had been lifted from his shoulders. He had secured something truly special for himself, his wife and family, and he tootled off to work with a spring in his step. The Railway Bar was an establishment in which both denominations were welcome, my dad was very happy to help quench the thirst of all persuasions. On this day, not unlike many others, a select group of wealthy Protestant businessmen came in for their liquid lunch. Instead of ordering the usual G&Ts or whiskey sodas however, the conversation went something like this:

"So, Joe, we hear you've bought Kebroyde."

"Yes indeed gentlemen. Isn't that just wonderful news."

"Hmmm, well you may feel it's wonderful Joe, but you know as well as we do, you cannot possibly buy Kebroyde. I mean, it's ludicrous to imagine you could actually live out there on the Culmore Road."

"Oh, you think so, do you?"

"Well of course Joe. Now, we've known each other a long time. Let's stop this nonsense, and you tell us how much it'll cost to change your mind," said the portly gent, producing a cheque book from his inside jacket pocket and placing it on the counter.

"Now then gentlemen, I want to make it very clear. I bought that house fair and square. My family and I are absolutely thrilled to have acquired it and we fully intend to move in as soon as we possibly can."

"Just name your price, Joe."

"No amount of your money will change my mind on this, sir. Now what was it you wanted to drink?"

"We won't be drinking here today, or any other day from now on."

The cheque book was put away and as they turned to leave, one of them said to my dad;

"You fool, you'll never pay the rent!"

There and then, my dad vowed the only way he would ever leave Kebroyde thereafter was feet first, a vow he would come to realise.

In many ways, this reaction was painfully predictable from these quarters. What was less predictable but doubly painful was the fact that when, in the weeks to come, my family tried to move home, they couldn't find anyone willing to take on the job. One side, indignant and outraged that a Catholic family should move into such a property; the other, harbouring some kind of totally misplaced jealousy. Bizarrely, our own people, so used to being downtrodden, felt he was getting too big for his boots. Incredible though it may sound, the family moved themselves that country mile out the road. Using whatever they could find, from the car to wheelbarrows, prams and their own backs, they took what they could, bit by bit, until they were finally installed in the mighty Kebroyde.

4

Russell

As a consequence of all this Perthes business, school started comparatively late in life for me and I was seven years old when I rolled up to St Patrick's Primary School. Now, my parents had not named me Sioux, but at a time when I was still strapped into a calliper, and a certain cowboy was riding high in the movies, life had arranged for me to hobble into a playground full of budding comedians. I handed them a one-liner on a silver platter. Enter, Hopalong Cassidy! Add to this the bizarre fact that, as I made my tentative way across the tarmac playground, a flock of swans flew overhead and one of them singled me out for some special treatment; a dollop of good luck from on-high or further proof that a space cadet had arrived at school.

Whilst my designer paraphernalia robbed me of vitesse, finesse and agility, that boot did lend me the capability of delivering a formidable blow to the shins of anyone foolish enough to venture too close. My first teacher, the angelic Sister Katherine and I hit it off instantly but my time in the infants was, somewhat bewilderingly for me, brought to an abrupt end when, at milk time on day two, a knock came to the classroom door. I was called out and led, without explanation, through a maze of corridors to the 'big school'. PANIC!! Those lanolin floors polished to within an inch of their lives, those huge, heavily painted heating pipes, that canteen smell. Was this some kind of horrendous nightmare, did these deserted passages lead back to Altnagelvin...? My escort knocked on a heavy, wooden door marked 'Rm6'.

"Come in!" said a voice from inside.

"Mrs Farren, this is Paul, your new recruit," announced my guide.

"Hello Paul, you're very welcome," answered a very prim and proper Mrs Farren.

It appeared I was being moved to the 'big boys' for some unknown reason.

"I've prepared a place for you over here by the window next to your new desk partner. His name is Russell Whiteman," she continued.

Before I had even taken my seat, this boy, with a lion's mane for hair, whom I'd never set eyes on before that moment, grabbed me by the sleeve and whispered:

"You know, I went to the sun in a rocket yesterday."

"Wow. Didn't you burn up?" I asked, somewhat taken aback.

"Aw, not at all. You see, I was clever. I went up at night!"

I liked this guy, Russell.

Life at the big house was fairly mundane. My parents were getting on a bit when they had me. They must have, at that stage, been thoroughly weary of the whole kid thing. What could I possibly do to surprise them; they had the T-shirts. A year into my schooling I was finally released from my infernal shackles and could run around freely for the first time in nearly four years. By this stage Russell and I were best buddies and busy creating and living in our own imaginary world. Russell was one of five and lived a pleasant five-minute walk across a field from us. His mum Eileen was full-on Donegal stock but his dad, Ron, a florist, was a rare breed in those parts; he hailed from a place called… Yorkshire… far out, man!

In Russell I had found a soul mate. Without ever having to voice it, I think we instinctively recognised in each other a very particular similarity. We were both stubborn as mules and grindingly determined to plough our own furrow. Come what may, we would follow our instincts and daydream our way through life with no regard for rules or conventions. Annoying obstacles such as certain aspects of school or religion were deftly ignored or sidestepped in our pursuit of happiness. We were naturally attracted by the outdoors and lead a Davy Crockett-style existence in the beautiful countryside we had around us.

From an early age we started collecting birds' eggs and over a five- or six-year period amassed a wondrous collection of nearly one hundred different British birds from buzzard to bittern, guillemot to goldfinch. We thought nothing of scaling a derelict building in search of a jackdaw's, enormous pine trees for a rook's, cliff faces for a kittiwake's; often holding the eggs in our mouths for the even more scary descent back to terra firma. Perilous bogs or wetlands were treated with similar disdain if they housed our prize, the eggs of a snipe, reed-bunting or moorhen. This precious collection has lately come back into my hands, Russell having looked after it for many years; it now sits in pride of place in our sitting room in Cuíll, a recently procured hideaway on the spellbinding Isle of Doagh.

Hunting was the next passion to engulf us. We would fashion catapults from wire coat hangers and carefully chosen rubber bands, for smaller prey requiring pinpoint accuracy; a meticulously selected forked branch and car tubing for less delicate work. At first, we would simply use stones, or for special occasions, a marble, but later on we graduated to making our own ammunition. Lead 'bullets' were the rounds of choice. Late at night when my parents had gone to bed, we would assemble our utensils. Bits of lead from disused buildings would be melted down in a pot on the stove. We would drill small 6in holes lengthways into a plank of wood, pour in the molten lead, wait for it to cool, and with one expertly delivered blow using a hammer and chisel, the plank would split down the middle revealing our perfectly proportioned lengths of lead which could then be chopped into the desirable little balls, ready for use. In retrospect, one is horrified at the health and safety aspect of this caper. We used the same saucepans for our brew that my mum used for preparing vegetables or soups. Poor old Beethoven was plunged into deafness for less exposure.

Our playground was a magical tract of land that ran for about a mile along the river, not ten minutes from our house. Starting at the Sandbank in the south and finishing at Culmore Point in the north, it was known as the Shore. Most of this area had been the extended garden of a most impressive house called Brookhall, home of the McDevitt family until a great fire in the 1960s ravaged it, leaving only the outer stone shell. However, the fire had not damaged the stable block, greenhouse, walled gardens and orchards, all of which were still intact yet deserted. What a gift for two highly impressionable young boys. Our imaginations ran wild. This was all ours and we practically took up residence.

The next house along, going north was an equally fine property belonging to Commander Gilliland. Thankfully this glorious place had not been destroyed and was, on the contrary, resplendent in all its glory. It had the things you might expect from such a residence; a boathouse, a gatehouse, extensive gardens, stables, garages and so on, but the thing which made it stand out from the rest and the thing which most endeared it to us, was an extraordinary and rightfully renowned arboretum. This was an enchanted place, otherworldly and the absolute antithesis of the sort of landscape that surrounded it. Upon breaching its walled defences, one was immediately in awe somehow. The acoustic changed radically. An overwhelming quietude reigned there, and we spent a lot of time just lying prostrate among the impeccably maintained and often unique trees, luxuriating in the impossibly soft terrain and watching the outside world go by, carefree in our cocoon.

Finally, the most northerly section of our territory consisted of the grounds of yet another imposing property. This time it was the backyard of a convent school called Thornhill (all my sisters went to school here). This corner of our enclave had an almost sub-tropical feel. The ground fell away sharply to the river and in between the web of exquisitely manicured paths, the vegetation was so thick and lush that, once penetrated, one could disappear from prying eyes in an instant. At the heart of this heaven-sent Garden of Eden was an extensive bamboo plantation. Though we had a few dens dotted about the place, the one in the bamboos was undoubtedly the coolest. It was accessed via a perfectly placed overhanging branch. We would climb the tree, crawl out the branch and drop silently into the heart of the gently waving bamboos. It was here that we had hewn out a sizeable clearing, totally invisible to any passer-by. The floor, which was a foot deep in soft bamboo leaves, was super comfy and quiet. The space as a whole, warm as toast.

As I write I'm remembering another den up at McDevitt's. It was in the middle of a circular collection of holly trees whose centrepiece was a huge oak which, though still alive, was completely hollow. Here again, we made a clearing easily big enough to allow us to safely make a small fire. We could climb up the inside of the great tree to a vantage point where we could keep an eye out for unwelcome visitors or check the state of the incoming tide.

We had been drawn to the bamboos initially because they provided the perfect material for making bows, crossbows and arrows. Though somewhat crude in their manufacture, these weapons were surprisingly effective and, like the catapults, very personal. Our arrows carried names such as 'Swift' (me) or 'Flash' (Russell). We were so proud of them.

The third and final passion that was to engulf these two young boys was fishing. It swept us along like a tsunami and was by far the most enduring of our endeavours, so much so that Russell went on to make it his life's work. "What nasty, little murderous so-and-sos," I hear you exclaim. Birds' eggs, hunting and fishing. I can assure you, I've often thought the same thing myself, but you know, these activities were so normal back then, where I grew up. Life is strange, and often the people out there fishing and hunting are the very people who cherish and adore their quarry most. It's an endless frustration that one cannot indulge in these pursuits without the inevitable result.

In a desperate attempt to defend myself, I would like you to know that on the one hand, I haven't taken a bird's egg from anywhere other than a carton since I was about fourteen, nor have I once used a longbow or catapult in that time. On the other hand, when recently we had potentially one of our most magical family holidays ever, taking a campervan around Iceland's West Coast, I was able to feed my family on freshly caught trout and salmon and show them the nests, complete with eggs, of no fewer than eight different species of birds. It was an unprecedented bonding experience for the four of us and I don't think it was only me who considered it heaven.

So, what about this fishing lark then? It's impossible to convey how much joy and adventure this pastime brought to our lives. I remember vividly us both getting that first beginners' set from Bertie O'Neill's shop in Bridgend. A 4ft 6in green fibreglass rod with white rubber handle, eyes whipped in red and white, all complete with the most simple Daiwa spinning reel, a box of hooks, lead weights and a float. We were up and running. Naturally, we started off down at our shore on the Foyle. The river here is majestic, fast-flowing and tidal. It was home to mostly eels, flounder and mullet but it had a serious run of sea-trout and salmon and on one famous occasion, Russell's big brother Maurice landed, would you believe, a 10lb angler fish; supposedly a deep-sea fish. It scared the hell out of us and made the front page of the *Derry Journal*.

On one of those first visits, I brought a bucket so I could bring back my catch and put them in the garden pond where they would be nearer me and I could look after them. Sure enough, three or four small flounder, fluke as we called them, were slipped into the bucket, carried carefully all the way home and lovingly eased into the pond. It wasn't until after the operation had been carried out that I realised these are saltwater fish, now in a sweet water pond. I raced into the kitchen, frantically calling Mum.

"Mummy, where's the salt? I need salt right now, lots of it."

I took the large container of table salt and ran back outside, pouring every last drop into the little flounders' new home.

Phew, that should do it, I thought to myself, *just in time*.

I went off to bed, chuffed as could be. We now had fish in our pond, how cool was that?

Next morning, I was up with the lark and dashed out to see if I could spot my new friends. They weren't very difficult to see, as they were all belly-up on the surface. I was devastated, incredulous as to why the salt hadn't worked. The poor wee flatys were given a proper burial and we learnt our lesson; from then on, we got our pond fish (Russell had one too) from a freshwater source. Roach, even the odd trout were firm favourites; they thrived and gave us no end of entertainment over the years.

From worming on the Foyle, we quickly progressed to the piers and rocky Atlantic shores around Inishowen where we would mostly spin for pollack, coalfish, mackerel and any unsuspecting soul unlucky enough to come our way. Last but not least on our progression through the various fishing techniques came fly-fishing and more specifically dry-fly fishing for trout. This endeavour captured us above all others and was tailor-made for me in so many ways. There was a technique to be learnt in the form of casting the fly, knowledge to be gleaned in terms of the various flies, their state of development and also, how they behaved in these various stages. The equipment was more attractive too; cane rods and silk lines, on top of which you could make your own flies, an art in itself. But over and above all of this and particularly appealing, nothing had to die to produce the bait and because of the way trout take the fly, it always rests right there on the hard lip area from where it can be easily dislodged, the fish is soon free to swim away, carrying only a slight trauma which is almost immediately forgotten. The hours we spent trekking along remote river banks, circumnavigating hill loughs, fiercely determined to cover every inch of water before reluctantly having to head home, often in the pitch dark.

For me, this state of affairs was relatively short lived and came to an abrupt end when I left home aged sixteen. Russell's obsession with fishing however only grew and his desire to become more and more proficient intensified. He was always first out and last back, no one could possibly match his stamina and in the end, encyclopaedic knowledge of the art of fishing. He went on to become a much sought-after and inspirational ghillie, effortlessly making many people's day, not just in Eire but all over the world, by making fish appear where there seemed to be none and regaling his guests with an endless stream of fishy stories scoring '10' on anyone's scale.

5

Brendan

Now then, have I mentioned Brendan? How remiss of me. You see, there was a third musketeer involved in all this and his name was Brendan Begley. One of eight, Brendan was a bright lad with a great sense of humour and an infectious laugh; he had piercing blue eyes and a shock of light blond curls. His dad, Joe, was an architect. A Derry man, born and bred, he was strict but fair and was always up for a laugh. Brilliant at Art and Maths, he was also a stupendous billiards and snooker player and undoubtedly the catalyst for myself and Brendan taking up snooker in our early teens. Eileen, Brendan's mum, was a vivacious Liverpudlian, a fountain of knowledge and a bundle of laughs. She had an extraordinary voice and loved to sing as she tootled around the house preparing the next meal or clearing up the last. There is an uncanny coincidence thrown up here inasmuch as where Brendan's older sister Roisin was quite clearly the human guinea pig for the Disney character Snow White, Eileen was undoubtedly the voice. They lived on the edge of a place called Garden City about a fifteen-minute walk from my house towards town.

Do you remember those shoes called Commandos? They had animal footprints on the soles and a compass in the heel. At that moment in time they were the height of cool, so you can imagine the excitement when Brendan got a pair. Despite the name and the accessories, they were essentially urban footwear and we couldn't quite believe it when he wore them to go fishing down at the Shore on the very day he got them. Even in mid-summer it was a muddy place and certainly not best suited to such a stonking set of treads. Brendan, bless him, had spent the whole evening being super careful, dodging puddles and swampy bits, had even chosen an inferior rock to fish off, (the one that still housed one of the iron eyes, used to secure the boom erected by King James' men in 1698 to prevent King Billy's fleet gaining access to the besieged city of Derry) because it was dry and safe. But as the sun went down and we reluctantly pulled in our lines for the last time, Brendan, who'd been nursing an old bit of bubble gum, probably since the day before, finally decided that he'd had enough of this nasty substance which had given up its last atom of sugary taste many hours before. He spat the pink lump out into the open air and swung a right boot, or should I say Commando, at it. Not only did he miss the godforsaken chuddy, but the precious right shoe flew off and in an almost perfect recreation of that iconic scene from 2001, pirouetted more gracefully than you might imagine a Commando could, making a glorious arch before entering the water with an enormous splash! Time stood still. On that beautiful summer's evening, the surface of the Foyle was like a mirror and we stood there rooted to the spot watching the wavy circles emanate from the point of entry. All I could think was, boy am I glad I'm not in Brendan's shoes right now, neither the one nestling on the rocky, weedy bed of the Foyle nor the one still attached to his left foot. What was he going to tell his parents? I've never known him so quiet or look so worried. His trademark locks seemed to whiten and curl even more than usual. Between us we managed to give him a piggyback home through the fields of barley and left him to face the wrath of the parentals.

This event inadvertently led to one of the funniest school moments ever. That night, Brendan had somehow blagged his way past his parents and sneaked off to bed, his secret safe for the moment. Next morning proved to be more challenging however and as he inexplicably fished out his old shoes to go to school in, his mum confronted him in the hallway. Brendan waffled a bit, but it was a hopeless task and soon the truth was out. Listening incredulously to Brendan's pathetic explanation of events, Eileen could contain herself no longer. She grabbed one of his old shoes and ran after him down the hall, through the porch and out into the garden whereupon she let fly with the worn-out size 8. Brendan instinctively ducked as the incoming, mock leather missile whizzed past his head and continued its flight out into the adjoining field. Try though they might, their search for this spent shoe was futile. As luck would have it, Eileen had picked up the right shoe as opposed to the left, which now meant that Brendan was the proud owner of two very different left shoes. He was also increasingly late for school. A short time later, as Russell and I arrived customarily late for the dreaded school day we heard the unmistakable sound of Brendan's voice coming from behind us.

"Cass, Parsley… hang on a minute."

Turning around to acknowledge the friendly beckoning, our eyes fell upon a truly comical sight. There was Brendan, striding out towards us, unusually resplendent in full school uniform, the black blazer, grey V-neck, white shirt, even the school tie had put in an appearance. The only slight problem was that he had chosen to complete this vision of schoolboy perfection with the only footwear left available to him, a pair of slightly too big, bright green waders, extended fully so as to maximise the wonderful incongruity of it all. When we'd calmed down sufficiently to collectively advance the final few yards to the school entrance, we were, not for the first time, welcomed by the three people we hated probably more than any other human beings on the planet.

Bunkum, popping pills as quickly as he could release them from their foil encasements, clearly prescribed to him for reasons that, under normal circumstances, would prevent him from doing the job he was currently prevailed upon to carry out. Glondy, furtively hunting around deep within the folds of his shabby habit in search of God knows what, and Nipper, scurrying around like the little rat he was. (I'll introduce you to them properly a bit later.)

Though never anything other than cold, their reception on this fine morning was particularly frosty. Each of us was dispatched with twelve of the best, all three pillars of society palpably ecstatic and visibly aroused by the employment of their cherished leather strips of abuse. Russell and I were subsequently sent off to class while Brendan's very real excuse was completely ignored, and he was ordered to retrace his steps back to Garden City.

Twice, Brendan's family took me on holiday to an amazing little isolated house with its own beach, on Sheephaven Bay. Given that Brendan was one of eight, there must have been eleven of us sharing that tiny space; what hell for the poor parents, we didn't even notice. We were out from morning to night, fishing, preparing to go fishing, or dealing with what we'd just caught; only taking time to go up to the big nearby farmhouse where we were served up a hearty dinner every evening, presumably as part of the deal. The general idea there was to eat as much as you possibly could, a kind of a drinking game but with food. One evening, this culinary caper led to me eating sixteen spuds, big flowery ones too, helped down with generous portions of mutton stew. I remember being physically unable to retrace our steps back to the house because my tummy was hurting so much. Meanwhile, Brendan and co. remorselessly made me laugh till I had to lie down on the side of the lane, in fear that I might burst.

There were perilous excursions out into the North Atlantic in a miniscule, blow-up, yellow dinghy. Me, Brendan and Roisin, legs entwined, smoking, fishing heavy lures with industrial-size treble hooks, and armed with half a broken paddle; the mind boggles when I think back on it now, where we were on that insignificant craft. Imagine if we'd dropped a cigarette, lost control of one of those trebles or worse still, caught something!

An added bonus to these already adventurous summer sojourns was that a delightful French family came to stay nearby. They spoke very little English and Remy, the dad, loved to fish. Remy had no idea how to fish in these waters. Brendan and I could barely say 'bonjour'. We all learnt a lot.

That summer had been unusually warm and sunny, causing strange things to happen on the angling front. Gannets were dive-bombing right in by the shore, dolphin entertained us by jumping clean out of the surf, effortlessly head and tailing as they chased each other in between filling their bellies. One day, a shoal of mackerel came into the small bay affording us no end of fun and games; a bare hook will suffice when they're in the mood. I got the fright of my life when I was easing the latest bar of silver, black and green up onto the rock where I was standing when a huge blue shark exploded out of the deep; open mouthed, and crunching down on its prey, it ripped my catch in half. I was lucky it didn't get the whole fish because, had I hooked that thing, it would have smashed my rod and potentially pulled me in after it. Also, lucky that it didn't miss its prey and get my leg.

I have no doubt it was down to our inadequate schoolboy French, but Remy wouldn't listen to our advice and persisted in fishing off an admittedly well placed but way-too-high flat rock. Where we used spinners, Remy insisted on bait and where we used the more conventional open-faced reels and fibreglass rods, he employed a centrepin reel on a gigantic pole, more suited to coarse fishing. One day, as the natural display of craziness intensified, we heard a Gallic commotion coming from the direction of Remy's favoured perch.

"Aidez-moi. C'etait un monstre!!"

Next thing, a substantial Frenchman came over the hill as fast as his legs would transport his generous proportions. He was in a right state, sweating profusely and shouting random words.

"Paul, Brendan, come *avec moi*... hurry... he haseu *casse ma canne* à *pêche*... it was enorme... *vraiment, un* monster... *allez*... we must go!!!"

Intrigued, we ran over to the flat rock to find what was left of Remy's pole, the braided line dangling loose having been snapped like thread. He had been reeling in a sizeable fish when, sure enough, another shark decided to help himself to an easy meal, only this time, the monster had gulped the entire fish at once and gotten itself hooked. One thrash of that formidable tail and Remy's inadequate tackle was history, the story over in a terrifying instant of raw power. It was as we three stood there, awestruck, that we gradually became aware of a phenomenon I had never seen before and doubt I will ever see again. A huge dark shape gradually materialised, far out in the calm, azure ocean, indeed we only became aware of it because of the frenetic bird activity surrounding it. This enormous slick started coming towards us at a pace and in no time, the bay below us filled to overflowing with a frantic traffic-jam of creatures eating and being eaten. Pandemonium ensued, Brendan and I raced down the cliffs to get closer to this extraordinary spectacle. As we tripped and stumbled onto the beach, sand-eels and krill with nowhere left to go were literally throwing themselves out of the water onto the sand where a variety of seabirds were gorging themselves, oblivious to the presence of humans. Behind these small fish came the mackerel, pollock, coalfish etc., they in turn getting gobbled up by dolphin, shark and goodness knows what else. We tried throwing in our lines, but it seemed wrong somehow, criminal almost. Our spinners simply landed on a sea of shaped protein, foul-hooking whatever fish they landed on. Instead we just stood aghast and transfixed. The frenzy probably lasted about ten minutes before the madness dispersed again and vanished into the distant depths. I feel so privileged to have witnessed this snapshot, a brief glimpse of nature's might. I wonder if Remy's friends back home believed his tall, Irish story. I sometimes doubt its validity myself, and I was there.

Though I very much appreciated the game of snooker, I just couldn't deal with being cooped up indoors in dark, smoky rooms while life went on outside. Having taken up the game aged fourteen, I soon lost interest; Brendan on the other hand quickly became an expert, chalking up over 100 century breaks by the age of sixteen. He often played in exhibition games with all the big names of the day including Higgins, Reardon and Parrott, and often beat them. I think he unfortunately got put off when he entered the British Amateur Competition where he met a certain Jimmy White in the quarter finals. It's at moments like these you need enormous self-belief, an overwhelming desire to push further and, above all, expert guidance. With no one to turn to, Brendan sadly put away his cue.

Brendan was extremely gifted in many ways, but I guess where he really excelled was in art. Even the spidery old cynic who taught Art at the college, Fr McCarron, or 'Gunner' as he was known, once concurred that Brendan was probably the best student he'd had in forty years of teaching. Here again, lacking direction, Brendan let this talent slip away though it resurfaced later in life when he would design and make beautiful trout and salmon fly displays which would find their way into the White House no less. These displays have been bought by countless celebrities from Liam Neeson to Bill Clinton. Brendan also continues to tie flies to order, for the likes of Tiger Woods and other angling-mad members of the golfing fraternity. Like Russell you see, Brendan got seriously bitten by the fishing bug and though perhaps for very different reasons, also went on to pursue a career therein.

6

Pennyburn

St Patrick's Primary School in Pennyburn was a harmless enough sort of a place and my time there passed pretty much without incident. By my modest reckoning I was a model student and passed my Eleven-Plus routinely. Come on, there must have been some memories, some shenanigans… hmmm, let me see… Well, every day at 11am we got a third of a pint of creamy milk served up in the cutest little individual bottles. There was an adorable choirmaster called Freddie Campbell who could neither sing nor beat time but he did dress like Toad of Toad Hall, had a very impressive golden pocket watch and most crucially, a silver tuning device which he would proudly produce from his top pocket at various intervals in a vain attempt to keep our intervals from varying too much.

In terms of the other students, there was Dennis McKinney who never uttered a word yet somehow defied certain laws of nature by presenting two absolutely solid masses of bright green snot, one in each nostril, from one year to the next. William Brennan, who, when *we* began developing a taste for the damned Sir Walter Raleigh weed, *he* was already hooked. Problem was, he couldn't even afford the single Park Drives we would buy from the mobile van and so, would loiter thereabouts waiting for any spare butts that might come his way. All very normal perhaps but what was cool, actually not cool at all but extremely hot, was that he would take these tiny, still-lit offerings into his cupped hands and, making a gesture as though he was playing maracas, would inhale the smoke through a gap where his two thumbs met until there was literally nothing left.

What about Patrick Hargan who, for money, would let you hit him as hard as you liked. Fists, boots, whatever. No matter what, like a latter-day

Ali, he never flinched and having calmly collected your few coins, would matter-of-factly move on to his next victim.

As our carefree time there neared its end, a new buzz began to raise its head however. Whereas the craving for nicotine was very practical and could be soothed by simply dragging on a fag, this other desire, which was completely involuntary and totally intoxicating, proved to be somewhat more complex to deal with. Though ours was an all-boys school, the all-girls school actually adjoined it and our playgrounds merged. Gradually I found myself playing less football at break times; glorious games like Mugs, Boodlies and Scoots were replaced by merely hanging around the edges of the other playground praying for a stray netball to come my way. This would then be flamboyantly returned to the apple of your eye, whether she was engaged in the game of netball or not. It was a wholly frustrating business because even if you ever got anywhere near one of these goddesses you became a monosyllabic Neanderthal.

Derry in those days was home to no fewer than two Indian families. They ran shoe shops up in the centre of town but lived down our way. One of the daughters went to St Patrick's and it was she who at this time began to blur my mind. Jet black hair, dark eyes, gleaming smile, brown skin, the whole package was so different, altogether an irresistibly heady mix. I felt like Mowgli, bumping into trees and tripping over things that weren't even there. I would follow her home from school most days even though it was out of my way. I would get my mates to push me into her, I'd steal her bag and run off, then give it straight back when she'd caught up. She might reciprocate with a brief smile, lowering her eyes in that devastating way. This would keep me going till the next day. Curiously, we never said a word to one another, not then or at any other time, but a new aspect of life was opening its door to me, an aspect far removed from nests and dens and tight lines, it was uncharted territory, it was dangerous, exciting and impossibly attractive, I was powerless to resist.

I was twelve years old and still bumbling around trying to make sense of this new world when, inexplicably, a sixteen-year-old blonde bombshell appeared to me and, in no time at all, cleared things up. What possessed the very beautiful Mary Gill to single me out for special attention, I will never know; I was not aware of her before and never saw her again after our brief dalliance but her contribution to my young life was invaluable. As far as I remember, she had a friend who attached herself to Brendan and the four of us went off on a date. Totally clueless and out of our depth, we took these women on what must have been a thrilling tour of, you guessed it, the Shore! After a while, Mary would cleverly dilly-dally, allowing some distance between us and the other couple. She would brush up against me 'by mistake' or put an arm around me, bringing her fragrant face next to mine, as I pointed out a particularly enchanting goldcrest's nest. I knew I was supposed to be doing something but, my mind blank, found myself incapable of anything other than inane chit-chat. We must have stumbled around aimlessly for a good hour before our frustrated dames feigned tiredness and suggested calling it a night. We trudged up through the fields and said goodbye to Brendan before walking up the back lane to Kebroyde, which would then take them home. Once again, good old Mary managed to hang back, sniffing flowers or picking blackberries; her wily pal meanwhile upped her pace so that by the time we'd reached my back gate, Mary and I were alone.

"Ann seems to have gone on without you," I offered, now visibly shaking with the realisation that I had no cover.

"Och, she's probably just waiting round the corner. Sure it's only a wee dander back to the house anyway," said Mary confidently.

Bored and out of patience with the kid opposite her, who was clearly never going to make a move, she pinned me against the solid wooden gate and kissed me passionately, running her fingers through my hair, over my face and my entire body. I did my best to join in on what was my first kiss, but I'm pretty sure I just stood there involuntarily lapping it up, a tingling mass of boyhood. After five or ten minutes of this intense, heavenly experience, she unravelled herself from my limp frame, said bye, and headed off up the lane, leaving me punch drunk. My legs felt like they'd just done a marathon and could hardly be depended upon to carry me the few yards back home; my heart was busy trying to force its way up into my head, thereby blocking my ears and creating a cartoon grin which remained for days. Everyone I met asked if I was OK, but I was incapable of engaging in dialogue and would involuntarily nod in the affirmative whilst staring into the mid-distance. Though physically, I appeared to be inhabiting the same space, mentally, I was soaring at speed through uncharted dreamscapes.

I only saw Mary once more, this time there was no wandering around; we met at that same back gate and I wrapped myself round her like a leech, barely coming up for air. A couple of steamy hours later, my chest heaving and lips sore, Mary quietly explained that, though she liked me very much, she couldn't see me again. She was getting a lot of stick from her peers and being labelled a 'baby-snatcher'. I walked her as far as the top of Shantallow, where she lived, and grabbed a final embrace before she wafted off, out of my life, just as mysteriously as she had entered it.

7

First Notes

One day when I was eight years old, those of us who were around all filed out onto the forecourt of Kebroyde. A simple homemade banner reading 'Welcome Home' was pinned up across the front door and a general feeling of excitement began to build. I have no idea how we knew she was literally about to arrive, given that not only was this was way before mobile phones, it even predated the lowly house phone in our lives, but know we did. I remember it was a glorious spring day and I was busy annoying everyone by doing my Georgie Best impersonation, dribbling an old burst ball in and out through the gathered throng, accompanied by an incessant ongoing commentary. Perplexed as to what all this fuss was about, how was I to know the momentous influence this impending stranger would have on my life thereafter.

"Was that a car horn!?" I said.

"Oh, be quiet… I didn't hear anything," said some know-it-all big brother.

"It was, you know… I know my cars, so I do!" I bragged.

"Shut it, right, or I'll…"

"It's them! They're here!" shouted the detail who'd been sent down to the gate to forewarn of their arrival. Sure enough, the next thing I knew, a strange car pulled into the driveway, horn blaring, arms waving, screams and shouts… what a carry-on! Even I was interested now. Then, there she was. She emerged from the automobile like a movie star, '50s two-piece, scarf, shades, lipstick, stilettos… I'd never seen anyone so beautiful, elegant and glamorous, a picture of sophistication. I was bewitched! She had on her arm a tall, dark, handsome stranger who, despite his undeniably strong Derry accent, remains firmly a Yank in my mind to this day. This was my sister, Bridget. She and her husband Dell had gone to live in New York soon after I was born but after the birth of their second child (they would go on to have six) decided to return to their home soil to raise a family. We bonded immediately and it seemed like only a matter of minutes before she was asking me if I played any musical instruments. I said I had messed about on the piano a bit but that was it. Upon hearing this, she hunted out an old violin from under the piano in the music room and marched me upstairs to our parents' bedroom whereupon she showed me how to hold this awkward contraption and in a matter of minutes had me playing 'Annie Laurie'. Next thing I knew I was standing on the kitchen table before an audience, sawing my way through my solitary repertoire. Applause and whistles greeted that excruciating final note. Suddenly, thanks to Bridget, I played the violin.

I guess from this very moment, my whole life subtly changed. Strangely, I don't remember anything about learning to play or how I came to read music, perhaps that's because fifty years later I'm still learning this miraculous, endless process which is so life-affirming, at once overwhelmingly challenging and rewarding.

The all-important guilt trip, the self-flagellation, so vital for any classical musician was not something I had to learn, this was second nature to a good wee Catholic boy like myself. Not that this was much in evidence during these early days. The extent of my musical life was playing little parlour pieces on the rare occasion that was required, preparing for the next grade on the Trinity College path to greatness and, most important of all, limbering up for the rather terrifying Feis Season. Bridget was the luckless being charged with steering, or should I say dragging me along this path. Totally unpaid, she religiously persevered with my musical progress, forcing me into a room once a week and somehow gradually building my ability and awareness. She put up with my silly strops every time 'Salut d'Amour' was called for, my disdain for the Grade 6 scales and my complete indifference for the Feis repertoire until the day before the actual performance. Without ever complaining, she would carry my violin to school, thereby saving me that ultimate embarrassment and later still, send away for and pay for whatever piece I had fallen in love with next.

This Feis Season was an extraordinary business. They were like talent shows, little festivals of competitive song and dance and one prepared for them much in the way a golfer or tennis player prepared for their circuit…

well, sort of! Once they kicked in, they were relentless, so the real pros had
to know how to pace themselves, when to peak. It was no good winning
in Portrush or Moville if you failed in Belfast, Derry or Londonderry (yes,
Derry had two, divided through and through!). These were the Majors as
it were but the Masters (Augusta) or Wimbledon was undoubtedly the All-
Ireland. Come to think of it, though strawberries and cream might seem
a trifle out of place, wouldn't a green jacket be just the ticket for the lucky
victor of that most coveted prize.

Many of these competitions had bursaries attached to them, a fact
which had not escaped the notice of my dad. When these cash incentives
were up for grabs, he would miraculously appear from the side-lines and
chauffeur me to the venue. Once the loot was secured, he would instantly
relieve me of the still-sealed envelope, quietly consigning it to his inside
pocket for 'safe keeping'. I'd be lucky to get a pat on the head or, on a
good day, a '99'. I remember years later, on a visit home, ferreting around
in the music room cupboards and finding an old plastic bag containing
some of my medals and trophies from these years. I counted more than
ninety medals and a dozen cups, one of which was indeed the All-Ireland,
won in Limerick in the early '70s, but alas, no envelopes!

8

Coulterditz

The next step on the road to education for the likes of us Derry Boys was inevitably 'the college'. A bit like in footballing circles the world over, where United simply means the team in red from Manchester, so in Northern Ireland 'the college' was all the information a person needed to know you were talking about St Columb's College. From St Patrick's (the Patron Saint of Ireland) Pennyburn to St Columb's (Patron Saint of Derry) College in one easy step. Not *so* easy mind you, given that that one step was a thing called the Eleven-Plus and only the crème de la crème would be accepted into 'the college'.

Though these two guys weren't around on Earth at the same time, I am convinced they were big buddies on another spiritual plain. For example, that tall story about Patrick ridding Ireland of its indigenous snake population always seemed a bit far-fetched to me. I used to imagine this enormous, wriggling, coiling, twisting, angry reptilian mass, begrudgingly taking to the freezing waters of the North Atlantic, making their way to the balmy stretches of the Sargasso Sea only to return once a year with the sole purpose of snarling up kids' fishing lines in knots and slime, and scaring the be-Jaysus out of those small anglers when hauled into view. In truth what happened was he called his mate Columb and together, they rounded up this seething fur-ball of embittered life and housed them in a Gothic pile up in Derry's Bishop Street where they slithered around preparing themselves to gobble up the next influx of naive, unsuspecting boys.

Of course we'd heard the stories and were filled with trepidation as we arrived at those imposing gates on that first morning but nothing could have prepared us for the unspeakable behaviour we were to witness over the coming years. Yes, the older boys would duck us in the toilets, steal our lunches, trash our books, even strip us naked on occasion. But this, though humiliating, was standard practice, a form of induction that only lasted a week or two. Oh no, it was the behaviour of the teachers that was so shocking. The devils in God's clothing. These revered soldiers of the Lord, with two one-eyed snakes lurking in the billowing recesses of their filthy habits, both lead lined.

First thing that happened was on the preliminary day. Russell, Brendan and I were sitting together, joined at the hip but also clinging on to the limited security our closeness afforded us on such a challenging day. Almost immediately we were asked if we were friends.

"Oh yes," we replied in unison, grinning involuntarily. "We've been friends since—"

"OK, OK!" we were rudely interrupted, each assigned a letter there and then, A, B and C, and subsequently never shared the same class for the remaining years of our schooling. So what, I hear you say... actually not a bad idea in fact. True enough, I concur, clever move even. They had remembered the antics of some of our brothers five years earlier and decided to nip things in the bud. Nevertheless, I suggest it was an unnecessarily cynical move that foreshadowed the shocking level of distrust and aggression we were about to face in the years to come.

The very next day, lessons began in earnest and my first period was Geography. I was excited and feeling all grown-up sitting there in my fresh, new clothes, loving my crisp, unopened books, coloured pens, pencil, rubber, ruler. I hung on the teacher's every word. The little guy next to me didn't seem so eager, he hadn't quite gotten up to speed. About twenty minutes in, he was sitting there twiddling his thumbs and daydreaming when the hitherto bubbly bear of a teacher, whose question he had unwittingly ignored, picked up a chair and threw it at him. Before the kid had a chance to move, the chair had completed its flight, hitting him full-on and breaking his arm. Another boy was charged with escorting the screaming victim to the sick room and a fearful silence fell heavily upon those who remained. A sick feeling engulfed me, and those unopened books, just moments ago so full of hope and intrigue, now held only fear and revulsion.

No complaint was ever lodged regarding this incident. Both teacher, he was considered one of the nice ones, and class went about their business as though nothing had happened. This was a rude 'wake-up' call and we boys had to grow up fast in this shocking environment. None of the teachers could be trusted; all were armed and dangerous.

This archaic approach to learning, in which terror and violence reigned supreme over understanding and encouragement, did not have a good effect on me. As I saw it, we basically had two options going forward; forfeit one's character, become totally subservient to the powers that be and conduct one's school days in a meek little insular bubble or hold tight to one's character, rally against the barbarous bastards with every fibre of one's body and turn one's school days into a glorious piece of theatre, encompassing tragedy, humour but ultimately farce. One had to surrender or fight under these circumstances. I choose all-out war!

This unorthodox approach to schooling may well seem bizarre to you but I can assure you it was every bit as bizarre and unnatural to me. Unfortunately, education and I coincided at a pivotal moment historically. In previous decades this form of teaching was all too common and therefore accepted by parents and pupils alike. By the time I'd left school, these archaic practices were generally outlawed with neither parents nor pupils prepared to put up with them anymore; we therefore found ourselves pioneers, unwittingly at the forefront of a seismic shift in attitudes.

Getting earmarked as troublemakers before school had even got started, all based on some shenanigans our brothers had previously gotten up to, was clearly not only grossly unfair but tragically misguided. I actually enjoyed school, was eager to learn and was suitably impressed and excited by the challenges that lay ahead but those responsible for my education had already decided otherwise.

This endemic approach of distrust and suspicion was instilled with alacrity by the three stooges in charge, who accompanied our stay;

Monsignor Coulter, better known as Bunkum. He was the president of this glorious institution whose only positive contribution to proceedings was providing us with a suitable name for the place, 'Coulterditz'.

Fr Clerkin was the delightful Dean. Affectionately known as Glondy, a nickname that remains completely meaningless to me, though somehow perfectly suits such a brutal, pasty, nothing sort of a character.

Last but not least was Nipper, Mr McGonagle, the Vice President and ironically, Brendan's uncle. Lacking the clerical weight of the other two, he cut the stunted figure of a bumbling twit in his little tweed suits. He was potentially more comedic than the other two demons, but one had to remember the power he wielded, not only in his rank but on the end of that metre-long, lead-lined, leather strap that he was particularly fond of exercising.

Their relentless aggression set me off on a false path of confrontation. Injustice sparks a reaction within me that knows no bounds. I have little control over it and even I am scared of it. It propels me on a single track with a short fuse, no regard for self-preservation or consequence; I'm on a mission. These people had lit the match.

News quickly filtered down through the ranks and the bloodthirsty foot soldiers were put on high alert. These, I must point out, were not merely people obeying orders, on the contrary, these were twisted, sadistic people whose lives had been cunningly stolen from them by a society which in turn had been brainwashed and hoodwinked into following the doctrine of some geezer, the star of the tallest of tall stories, with an ending which far outdoes anything Hollywood could possibly dream up. In fact, when I look back on it, the college had done little more than reflect the society as a whole; in school, as in life, I was a no-good, lowly sinner upon arrival and would continue as such to the bitter end.

And so here we were, a sorry bunch indeed. The folks entrusted with that most delicate of matters, our education, folk who were supposed to enlighten us and show us the joy of knowledge, the beauty and excitement of information were instead nothing more than a seething sore of cynicism, often teaching subjects they had no love for and little knowledge of, frustrated beyond belief on so many levels, confronted by young, happy-go-lucky boys with their lives stretching out before them. What a caustic cauldron of venom. Welcome to St Columb's!

The building itself is a proper affair in the Gothic style with sweeping lawns to the front, tree-lined paths, gate house, granite walls, fearsome railings, the lot. To the back, it commands an impressive view west across the Bogside, Brandywell and Creggan areas towards Donegal. On approaching the place, you have on the right two football pitches and on the left, a splendid double-sided handball alley. The interior had all the ingredients for a magical education experience. Everywhere was mahogany, York stone and Carrera marble, all polished to within an inch of its life. The Junior and Senior houses were linked by a grand corridor, flanked with hanging portraits of past presidents and other luminaries. Off this corridor was the gorgeous little chapel, the Dean's room, the President's Room, even the Study seemed just right, with its long line of stained-glass windows and rows of old-style desks, the ones which opened up and had a built-in inkwell. All was as it should be.

The reality however could not have been more different. The school had long since outgrown this imposing building and was now surrounded on three sides by a small town of prefab units. This was to be our school for the next two years. I say two because this house of torture had perversely become so popular that they had to build a whole new school in a completely different part of town. The plan was that pupils would now spend the first two years up at the Old College and move down to the new building in their third year; we just happened to be the first intake so to do. This new campus was a state-of-the-art, purpose-built job; though superior in every way to the hopelessly outdated Victorian place, it could never exude the magic or gravitas of such an image. This was a vision of the future, creating an environment where children's dreams and ideals could be nurtured and realised; someone should have informed the old guard!

My school life quickly crumbled into a sorry state from which it would never recover. I found myself cornered, back against the wall, facing hostility and oppression at every juncture, with no one to turn to. The outrage was universally greeted with nervous laughter, one big joke. Parents saw it as character building, friends as a rite of passage… I saw red.

Throughout my six years in this hell hole I encountered only one teacher who didn't beat me. His name was Mr North. He had just arrived from England and managed in the space of one year to get me from nowhere in Maths, up to a B in my O level without ever once resorting to violence of any kind.

I had started that year quite upbeat about Maths because I had been put in Fr Keaveny's class. He was vaguely related to me in that one of my sisters had married one of his brothers, so I naively imagined we might have a bit of a rapport. About fifteen minutes into my very first class with him I was, along with everyone else, copying down some work that he had chalked up on the blackboard for us to do. The room was quiet, and he was gently pacing up and down between the lines of desks when suddenly, out of nowhere, he hit me very hard on the back of my head with the middle knuckle of his middle finger. Quite apart from the shock of this outburst, it was an extremely dangerous thing to do and was horribly painful. Evidently, he had spotted a cigarette in the top pocket of my blazer. The force of the blow brought tears to my eyes and I found the whole incident deeply upsetting. I take some solace and comfort from the fact that I never entered his class again. I point blank refused and eventually was transferred to the relative sanity of the lovely Mr North.

Some of these people had really lost their marbles and we as kids were having to deal with the remains. Take Fr Tiernan for example; he would famously ask questions of random pupils at random moments and for no good reason, like; "What's my nickname boy?"

If you lied and answered, "I don't know Father," you got six slaps. Alternatively, if you told the truth and answered, "The Bird, Father," you got six slaps.

In an effort not to be too predictable he would spice things up by asking, "See that hill over there boy, what's over that hill?"

If you said, "Co. Donegal Father," you got six slaps and were told, "The land of milk and honey son."

Once again, the inverse response resulted in the same punishment... Bonkers!

Or, how's about the charming Fr Rainey who, if he got fed up hitting you, would make you stand outside his class, in all weathers, having first taken off your shoes, socks and top, only trousers were left. Once, having been standing there for a good twenty minutes, Nipper came along and gave me six of the best as punishment for whatever I had done to upset Fr Rainey. These slaps were always doubly painful with cold hands, especially as the perpetrator purposefully aimed for the very tips of your fingers, and had a particular technique whereby he hit you on the way down and on the way up again, a double whammy... nice!

Moving swiftly on through our pick of the bunch; what about the grotesque buffoon who went by the name of Mr McKeown, affectionately entitled 'Big Hughie'. Here was a truly grotesque example of humanity. Borderline obese, alcohol was one of the more pleasing odours he exuded. He had his very own little bag of tricks up his sleeve, which he happily paraded on a daily basis. When he moved towards the radiator or 'accidentally' collided with your desk, you knew there was more than the North East wind blowing. He would literally stand there next to you and skilfully back-heel the radiator to create a diversion as he let fly. Another endearing habit of his was to empty his nasal passages in full view of the class then choosing some sitting duck, would lift him to his feet saying, "Define the verb 'to be'," deftly depositing the gross, globular mass under his victim's lapel.

These however are only some of his more affable attributes. He too, was a violent bugger. He enjoyed lifting students off the ground by their sideburns and could perform this trick with just one hand. Arguably, his *pièce de résistance* was when he got out his strap (which would happen every class), he would make you take off your blazer and roll up your sleeves; you would then have to place one arm on top of the other and stretch them out, chest high, towards him. On occasion, he would also remove his jacket before literally taking a run up, like a fast bowler, and delivering a series of almighty thwacks, would leave you with marks right up your arm.

Of all the opponents I had to face back then, top of the bill was undoubtedly, Fr O'Flaherty, (Flah). Going toe-to-toe with him for a thirty-minute Irish class, you knew you were in a fight. Standing 6'2" in his stocking feet and built like a house, he was a fine figure of a man, an ex-prize fighter in fact, who had exchanged the canvas for a more celestial path. The leather he did not relinquish however, simply cashed in the gloves for a 'Hardcore 5 Series', hand-stitched, super tanner deluxe model, which he kept up his left sleeve for swift employment.

Who made these things by the way!? Canes and rulers didn't cut it for these guys. They all seemed to have variations of this two-sided leather strap, with or without the internal lead strip, all nicely sewn up, polished and ready to go. Someone, somewhere must have produced them, even had a little premises complete with display cabinet. Would they offer themselves up as a guinea pig for their customers?

"Oh, why not try this latest design? I call it The Tearjerker. It has a double lead strip and I've used a particularly coarse stitch which I've left proud, the more injury to inflict. Hit me, hit me. Harder, harder!!"

I studied the Irish language for five years and throughout that period, Flah was my teacher. I was good at Irish and enjoyed the subject, but this held no sway in how Flah would treat you. We were being beaten left, right and centre but there was something in the way Flah meted out his punishments that was slightly different. There didn't seem to be any malice, no warped, twisted mind. To him, thumping someone was like second nature and for that reason, curiously refreshing. Our bouts were too numerous to mention though I believe two are worthy of report. Interestingly both incidents, though years apart, were as a result of the same misdemeanours on my part; I had turned up late to class and was subsequently found to have not done my homework. On the first occasion, he snapped, he completely lost it, sprung up from his chair and lunged in my direction. Then, picking me up off the floor by my hair, literally threw me through the concertina-style partition wall that separated the classrooms in those prefab huts, thereby completely destroying it. As luck would have it, I did not smack my head on the corner of a desk, or collide with some unsuspecting student in the other class but instead, came to rest on the floor next to none other than Brendan. Upon seeing his mop of curls and beady eyes, and he my no doubt bemused expression, the two of us burst out laughing, more from shock than anything malicious. For this show of impertinence, his teacher, Nipper, gave us both six of the best and ordered me back through the crumpled wall to the relative safety of the manic cleric.

On the second occasion, I again arrived late for class. Though I had a good excuse for this, he wouldn't listen – he simply ignored my efforts to explain and administered twelve lashes.

"Where's your school tie, Cassidy?"

"I'm sorry sir, I forgot it."

… Twelve more.

"Leave your homework on my desk."

"Ah sir, I'm afraid I didn't get it completed, sorry."

… Another twelve.

By this stage my hands were bright red, severely swollen, pulsating and totally numb. Even by St Columb's standards this was pretty far-out, and my classmates were either dumbstruck or employing a kind of nervous giggle. Upon finally taking my seat, I foolishly made a face at one of them, feigning tears whereupon another twelve were duly dispatched. I broke every record that day by amassing the grand total of seventy-two slaps in one half-hour class, for which I had been ten minutes late. Not for the first time, the teaching of Irish had taken a back seat.

Bizarrely, though this archaic, heavy-handed treatment was commonplace within the school and some of the incidents I've highlighted, rather extreme, probably my most poignant encounter occurred, not with Flah, Big Hughie or even Glondy but with a vastly inferior, mousey little runt of a being. He spent his days holed up in the deep recesses of the library, so insignificant barely anyone knew his name or purpose. I would get to know his name. This little shit was about to sneak up on me like a bad smell.

It was a day like so many others; a few of us were in the library working, it was last period before lunch. Someone at our table started making farting noises.

"Shhh. Quiet in the library," said Mole, whose name turned out to be Gallagher.

Another windy exchange.

"Quiet."

Yet more noises; you get the picture.

Eventually he approached our table of eight or ten boys.

"OK, who's making that noise?"

This was inevitably met with a stony silence. After a couple of vain attempts to identify the culprit he decided to choose and make an example of, me. At this moment the bell went for lunch and the occupants of the library jumped up to make their way to lunch. But something sinister had twitched into action in the book-tender's little brain. He locked the door and made everyone retake their seats. In true Big Hughie style, I was ordered to remove my blazer, roll up my sleeves and lay my arms one on top of the other upon his desk, pointing at him. He then removed his jacket and produced from behind a bookshelf quite the most fearsome weapon one could imagine in the mitts of such a punitive figure. He proceeded to silently and remorselessly quite literally leather me. Each of the six excruciating blows, all to the same arm, were preceded by a lengthy run-up and expertly administered with the kind of pent-up, bile-infused rage that must surely come from having to live with rodent features and a pin-sized prick. Upon completion of his task, Mole quietly and calmly replaced the strap, donned his jacket, opened the door and taking a foil-wrapped, fish-paste sandwich from his ample briefcase settled down to lunch. Not a word was uttered in my direction. I was roundly ignored, left to gather my things and leave the scene. Luckily Brendan had stuck around because on this occasion my injuries were such that I could not carry my schoolbag. A substantial portion of my left arm, from the fingers on my hand to the elbow was already very swollen and showing signs of severe bruising. It was throbbing unmercifully and alongside the nasty white welts on my hand and wrist you could plainly see the outline of the strap on my arm. Even for a seasoned pro like myself, this guy had overstepped the mark. But what to do!?

As luck would have it, I had my Grade 7 violin exam that very weekend, and my crucial last-minute preparations had just been scuppered. This particular scenario paved the way to the unthinkable, a course of action hitherto unimaginable, it was the big one… I was going to tell my parents. This was unprecedented behaviour on my part, but I reckoned that, given the facts of the situation, my innocence coupled with the state of my arm and the upcoming exam, this was surely the time to play my ace.

I escaped the building and headed for home. My mum's reaction was predictable. She was moderately upset and concerned for me but merely pointed me in dad's direction. He was out in the back garden putting the final touches to a horse jump. My approach gave him a start. His initial reaction was no less predictable. Upon seeing my injury his first words were; "What did you do?"

However, once I'd related the story, and after gaining my absolute assertion of my innocence, to my amazement, he told me to get in the car and together we set off for the school.

This was unchartered territory, but it felt good to have his support. It was odd approaching the place via the main driveway and parking where all the teachers parked. It must have been vaguely interesting for my dad too as we entered the building, this being his one and only visit to the great halls of learning. He didn't get to see very much of the place as the President's office was situated just off the foyer to the right and we were shown straight in. The dynamics of the situation were instantly and sickeningly dictated by that society's hierarchy. In Ireland these guys were top dog. They invariably had the best houses complete with housekeeper and swanned around in fancy cars, smoking cigars, giving the Royal Wave to those chosen few deemed worthy of their acknowledgment. Next in line were probably teachers, then doctors and so on down the line. In the Monsignor, we faced a formidable character in Irish society. My dad, normally a fearsome individual with quite some considerable charm, became a gibbering wreck in the presence of the Monsignor who, though gracious enough towards him, had completely ignored me and employed a clear physical distance by remaining firmly behind his oversized leather desk.

"What can I do for you, Mr Cassidy?"

"Obviously Monsignor, I wouldn't normally take up your time on such a matter but... Paul, show Monsignor Coulter your arm."

I duly displayed the evidence with an unhealthy degree of satisfaction.

"How did you do this?" asked the Monsignor without a moment's thought.

"Mr Gallagher, the librarian, strapped me Father. He gave me six for something I didn't—"

"I beg your pardon?" he interrupted. "Mr Cassidy, this school does not employ corporal punishment of any kind. I have no idea how your son has sustained these injuries, but they certainly didn't come from any teacher in my school. Now, I strongly suggest you get him out of my office and back to class before he lands himself in even more trouble than he's already in."

The bewildering blatancy of the blasphemous lies I had just witnessed pouring forth from the blessed lips of this most holy personage was incomprehensible. It was common knowledge that St Columb's was run by the whip and yet the man in charge, a very high-ranking official within the Catholic Church, could stand there, with a strap, if not in his pocket, then certainly hidden somewhere within the walls of that very office, and lie to my father, thereby making me out to be not only a liar, but presumably someone prepared and capable of a high degree of self-harm. My dad humbly thanked the Monsignor and apologised for the intrusion. We scurried out into the foyer, barely a word between us; he exited the building at a pace, leaving me to return to class.

I wandered off in a daze, trying to make some sense of what had just happened. I felt shell-shocked and trapped in a society that seemed to blindly follow a religion in which the vast majority of cardinal rules were routinely broken by the gangsters who ran this particular mafia. Give me a quaint little Norman church at the end of a leafy lane any day to one of those grotesque statements of power which all too often stand on the high ground, whose tolling bells and stone crosses weigh heavily on the already distorted backs of people whose horizons are horribly hazy. Mass chanting in a language no one understands (my dad would pride himself in bellowing out the responses before the priest had even finished his bit), interspersed with sections of extremely plain English during which the names of donors and the amount of their donation to what was known as the silent collection would be slowly and callously called out over the microphone. Pose the question, who's the mysterious woman in Da Vinci's depiction of *The Last Supper* and I'm all ears, talk to me of Immaculate Conceptions and I'm gone.

I hadn't even left the foyer, my dad would not have reached the car when round the corner buzzed the Nip. His eyes lit up when he saw me, a bit of guaranteed entertainment. He pushed me into his office and went off on one. I don't even know what he was rabbiting on about but on this occasion his whining, rapid-fire monologue coupled with his distasteful physical closeness, all fingers and verbal was just too much for my already over-sensitive disposition. Before I knew what was happening, I had lifted him off the ground by his tweedy lapels and pinned him against his wall. Time stood still and for a brief glorious moment I luxuriated in the look of fear in his eyes and the sight of him dangling there helplessly, looking for all the world like a deflated Humpty Dumpty. Silently, gently, I eased his cheap little brogues back to terra firma. I allowed him his whispered "Get out of my office," in the sure knowledge that our secret was safe. Our Vice President had been spooked. Our relationship was now on a different footing and I realised that in that moment of release from the chains of conscience, my tentative grip on reality, my blurred vision of my own self had begun to clear. St Columb's and I had been at loggerheads from the start. This farcical situation whereby my education was being totally side-lined and replaced by some kind of pantomime had to stop. I had things to do. I was not a no-good troublemaker; I was in fact, a force for good. I was an artistic soul itching to interact with hard-working, open-minded people whose lives were driven by positivity, fuelled by a burning desire to create. I had to escape!

They gaily say, 'education is wasted on the young'. I've always found this an absolutely ludicrous statement. Surely education shouldn't be something that starts at one point and finishes at another. Isn't a healthier outlook one that embraces each new day as an opportunity to expand your appreciation of the world? 'Well, you learn something new every day' should never be a statement of surprise. If only we could encourage more of a community spirit to our existence, even within our cities where clearly, it's more of a challenge. If the feel of education could be much more nurturing and inclusive rather than a shoddily designed child-care scheme in which kids are snatched from their much-needed sleep, often still in the hours of darkness and shipped off to a regime of nonsense, a lot of which has no relevance to their lives. All too often I hear children say, "I hate Maths – what's even the point of it?"

This is a result of bad teaching, this is a result of kids being told they have to do x, y, z in a totally abstract fashion. If they could be shown, in a more colourful way, how Maths enters their everyday lives, this question would never arise. Instead they would see how invaluable it is in almost every walk of life, from music to design, art to construction. All subjects have their potential to fascinate and bore; the trick is teasing the fascination whilst secretly tending to the boredom. Imagine a world where we could rub shoulders with the very best people from the earliest stages of development. All too often, teaching is seen very much as a secondary occupation for people at the top of their field, a bit of a scary commitment for little remuneration. This is all wrong. How often have you heard, "it wasn't until I heard Perlman play" or "it wasn't until I saw Bernstein conduct that I knew I wanted to be a violinist/conductor"? We should grab inspiration and feed it into the very roots of the next generation, not apply it later to the walking wounded as a kind of Band-Aid. I'm well aware that this is a dreamland given the world we live in but why not aim high; one should not be ridiculed for imagining there might be something available between dreams and nightmares. So much of the time I felt like the proverbial fish out of water, flapping around in a hostile environment unable to breathe. It's in these choppy waters where particularly young disillusioned minds can be lost; unfortunately, sometimes quite literally. We're all well aware of how vulnerable a teenage mind can be, I find it extraordinary therefore that it's only very recently 'teenage' was recognised as a specific life stage with its own particular set of problems and remedies. Before, they'd just been lumped in with 'children' going through an annoyingly difficult stage before becoming adults. None of this information would have had the slightest effect on the adults I was coming up against, but hopefully, as we slowly become more enlightened, maybe some of these hormonally afflicted youngsters will receive a bit more understanding.

Teenage life was a pricey business; fags, booze, dances, clothes… underarm. Basically, girls came at a price! Money, as always, was elusive, and free time, something of a premium. Imagine my excitement therefore at discovering that the school Art Department housed within the deep recesses of its cupboard space the very same card, in the very same colours, as the school dinner tickets. As one approached the dining hall each day, there stood a teacher holding a simple cardboard box into which we would each throw our daily ticket. Suddenly, gone were the days when you would get a friend to push you as you deposited your ticket, thereby opening up the possibility of either grabbing a handful of tickets rather than leaving one, or knocking the whole shebang to the floor whereupon a gaggle of usually morose and disaffected teenagers would suddenly become enthused and eager to tidy up the mess. Not all the tickets would necessarily find their way back into the box. Instead, the discovery in the Art room opened up a whole new approach to the dining experience and fanned a dormant business flame I didn't know I had. I invested much time and effort into recreating these dinner tickets in meticulous detail; yellow, green, red and blue, all faithfully reproduced, complete with weekdays and serial numbers. The perforated edges were the most challenging but even these were eventually mastered. All that remained to do was to make the appropriate people aware of their existence and to decide on a price. This little side-line actually did very well. Kids were lining up to get their mitts on them and I had to exercise extreme caution so as not to flood the market. The revenue proved to be an invaluable asset to me given what was about to happen in my life. Sorry to disappoint but despite the popularity of this endeavour, this was pretty much the extent of my gansta activities.

In an effort to close this tiresome chapter, much of the five and a half years I passed enrolled in St Columb's, was spent 'dobbing'. That's what we called it, at any rate. In other words, not going to school. Ducking and diving by whatever means necessary. Endless days were spent fishing down at the river, our rods hidden in the bushes by the front gate. I would wave goodbye to my poor mum, who had risen early to see to my breakfast, ditch my schoolbag, grab the fibreglass wand and bound off in the opposite direction of school. Russell and Brendan would arrive in their own times. I appreciate you're probably thinking 'bunch of wasters', but I can assure you, in all honesty, these days never felt good, rarely fulfilling in any way. They were nothing more than time wasted in avoidance of a greater evil. The granules of sand dropped slowly. It was often cold and wet, and we rarely had any sustenance, the highlight, maybe a shared cancer stick. Things would pick up in later years when girls began to enter the equation. We found that they were drawn to the makeshift stables down at McDevitt's old ruin where a local farmer by the name of McCloskey would house his horses. This was an absolute godsend. Mr McCloskey would spend his days down there and for a bit of help around the place would provide us with shelter, an open fire, even tea and the odd fag; but inadvertently and best of all, these perfumed angels who would make the sands of time drain away in an infuriating rush, and cause our blood flow to change course. Overnight our fibreglass wands were replaced by a more natural variety. Even though they too were absconding, often these same girls would get babysitting opportunities during the school hours. This was the optimum scenario. To have all one's home comforts at hand, coupled with the very real possibility of a bit of female interaction... school had no chance!

How did we get away with it?

We would intercept the mail, writing wholly implausible sick notes in reply to enquiries from the school as to our whereabouts, but given the frequency of our absences, it is more than a trifle puzzling that I was only ever caught dobbing once in all my time there. But then this is nothing compared to the fact that in a school where everyone did eleven O levels, I did eight! This is a reality that I find unfathomable to this day. I doubt I will ever quite believe it except that I actually lived it.

You remember how, after two years of big school, the time came when you had to choose your subjects for O level? Well at that moment I was all set with my list, only to find, in a typical example of school bureaucracy, that most of my choices would not be possible.

Oh no, you can't do both Art *and* Music; it has to be Irish *or* German, French *or* Spanish. Oh but you're welcome to do Physics, Chemistry and Biology...

I wonder who dreamt up these rules? Who wheeled in these unforeseen obstacles to further frustrate students, maximising some kids' potential and minimising others? The thought that someone in my position wouldn't do Music was so ridiculous yet I chose to do Art. I enjoyed Art and wanted to take it to at least O level standard hoping that my involvement in Music would somehow cover missing out on a certain A*. I was good at Irish and French, so naturally, was excited to extend my grasp of language. It was not to be, however. I still recall that dark, rainy Monday as I sat in my first double period of Economics, probably chosen blindfolded with a pin. The very sight of a GDP growth chart sent me into an immediate shutdown, my brain instantly entering a black hole of reverse energy. Later that day, a feeling of desperation led to my employment of some economics of my own. If seven or eight O levels were all you needed to progress, why would anyone do eleven when some were not even of your own choice? I immediately set about implementing this plan. I chose the three subjects to be discarded and made myself forty-five timetables, each one displaying a free period in place of the offending subject I should have had at that time. This meant that, should I get stopped and asked why I wasn't in class, providing I produced the correct timetable for that particular period, I would be seen to have a free. Cute enough I suppose but to have escaped three years of this, exams and all, is simply mind-boggling. In the end, I managed to secure good grades in seven of my eight chosen subjects, having employed a bit of a kamikaze approach to my RE exam, speaking my mind instead of quoting the book, something for which I was hauled up in front of the school board, glowered at as a lost soul and given a jolly good talking-to.

One final curiosity. I guess overall, my nemesis was probably Flah; in Brendan's case I would suggest it was Nipper whilst Russell would undoubtedly cite Ramey as his most hated tormentor. Ramey, or Mr Raymond Gallagher, was well known as a right tough cookie who could dish out abuse with the best of them. The flip side of this dodgy character was that he was mad keen on music and indeed taught the subject along with Irish and RE. My prowess in this area endeared me to him and after one particular occasion when, during a school's concert in which he was conducting the orchestra, the lights fused, everyone fell silent except yours truly who continued the piece, solo, to the end. By the time the lights came back on, my instinctive yet seemingly heroic act had stirred the packed hall to a standing ovation and propelled me straight to the number one spot in Mr Gallagher's good books. From that moment on I could do no wrong and much of my ill-gotten 'free-time' would be spent in the anteroom next to his class, a tiny space which housed a record player and four classical LPs. This cramped, dark place saved my life. It was sound-proofed and had a smoked-glass window onto the main classroom so I could see what was going on without being seen. I would sit there hour after hour wearing grooves in the grooves of these vinyl bibles: Beethoven's Violin Concerto, the Spring and Kreutzer Sonatas with Menuhin, Shostakovich's 5th Symphony, Stravinsky's 'Firebird': who were these people? Who could write and perform this music? Indeed, what was this music? An extraordinary mix of sounds that could not only make one laugh and cry in a moment but excite all kinds of emotions, unnamed primal impulses which were irresistible. Never once did Ramey ask me how I'd come to have so many free periods, never did he suggest I should perhaps be elsewhere, he persistently ignored the smoke that would sometimes have been filling his listening room after I'd left. I could do no wrong. Russell's devil had become my saviour.

9

The Church

Speaking of saviours, there was another charming side to life in Ireland which one had to negotiate; the Roman Catholic Church.

Like most things one encountered growing up, nothing of any import was ever explained:

Father and young son doing the milk run;

Dad; "Are ye hungry son?"

Son; "Aye, I'm starved so I am."

Dad; "Have a look in that wee bag. Got ye a doughnut, so I did. Ye can wash it down wi' one o' them wee bottles there."

Son; "Aw, this is brilliant da."

Pause

Son; "Hi, Da."

Dad; "What son?"

Son; "Where does milk come from?"

Dad; "From a cow, son. From a cow."

Pause

Son; "Hi Da."

Dad; "What son?"

Son; "What's in a doughnut?"

Dad; "Flour 'n' water, son. Flour 'n' water."

Pause

Son; "Hi Da."

Dad; "What son?"

Son; "What makes this van work?"

Dad; "Alectricity, son. Alectricity."

Son; "Hi Da. What's alectricity?"

Sudden anger…
Dad; "Sit quiet 'n' eat yer bun!!"

No questions got asked. Well, plenty of questions got asked, but, as in the tale above, you soon learnt to duck the answer, literally.

Q. "How did my brother die?"
A. "Would you shut up about that. You'll upset yer ma."
Q. "Why is my sister not allowed in the house?"
A. "Never you mind."
Q. "How come we're not going to my brother's wedding?"
A. "What's it to you."
Q. "Why are we at war?"
A. "Just!!"

So, hang on a minute here, what exactly are you telling me? There was this guy, 2,000 years ago, appeared outta nowhere, was a good egg who could spin a yarn, and was a dab hand at magic. Had a wonderful dad who wasn't really his dad (stepdad I think), an angelic mum who wasn't really his mum, and a stonking girlfriend who wasn't really his girlfriend. (I owe that Mary M one actually. I've employed that 'anointing the feet' routine once or twice over the years, works a treat.) People liked him alright but, being a bit of a smart alec, he notched up a few enemies too, on account of which, he got nailed early doors. Being a feisty sort, he managed to survive this ordeal, but soon threw in the towel, choosing a future up in heaven with his biological dad (I think), or did he merely retire to India, whatever!

Anyway, most of what he went around preaching just seems like common sense to me, me being a nice guy; and I can understand why he decided to leave us a load of guilt trips and stuff after the way they treated him, but in fairness, you don't have to threaten me and make me feel like a perpetual rotter to get me to act humanely, I'd do that naturally. In fact, if you ask me, I reckon it got to him in the end, 'cause only an angry narcissist would crave the result he's achieved. By his rules, you enter the world already a sinner and spend the rest of your life beating yourself up about one thing or another, heck, even your strongest and most basic natural instinct, courtesy of him, turns out to be a filthy endeavour, nay, entertaining the very thought of it just shows you up for what you are, a depraved piece of dirt. Then, not content with controlling all subconscious thought, he makes a darn good play for much of your conscious thought too. Even though *we* didn't get to celebrate *our* strategic events, like birthdays, deaths, marriages and so on, we sure as hell had to acknowledge all his, again and again. Just because he decided to piss off for a while to try to clear his mind, we have to follow suit. It was this carry-on that eventually caused my brother Joe, whose every move I copied, to stop having sugar in his tea, saddling me with the same horrid outcome at a tender age.

You had to go to Mass every Sunday but were considered a bit of a lightweight if you left it at that. Some of the charlatans I watched going to Mass daily didn't half turn my stomach, my dad being one of them. Why didn't he face his demons and sort out his real problems instead of buying false credit down the Bible hut?

I'd say that by the age of nine, I was already asking way too many questions and feeling thoroughly disenchanted with this game of 'follow thy leader'. It was around about then that a white rose, in the unlikely form of Russell's old man, came along to help deal with this thorn in my side. Uniquely, in my experience hitherto, this gentleman didn't go along with this story either and so his gaffe became the destination of choice come Sunday morning. Strategically it was heaven sent, nestling as it did, directly opposite the church itself. I would arrive in good time for Mass, call for my best friend, then invariably get caught up in some riveting debate about the merits of bamboo versus yew for a longbow stick, emerging just in time to ask the flock, who had said Mass, whether anything untoward had taken place during the service and pick up the all-important leaflet, an A4 sheet packed full of the latest, wildly exciting parish news, for delivery back at HQ.

The only bearable alternative to this routine was to find out in advance which Mass Fr Gildea was officiating. Though you still had to wade through the same mind-numbing script, old Fr G mercifully did this at a pace. He'd be halfway down the first page by the time he'd exited the sacristy and would never wait for the sheep to reply, choosing instead to forge ahead with what he clearly saw as his very own soliloquy. Even the most heavenly sacrament was dispatched with gusto. Hey, by the way Fr, it says here, body AND blood. How come only you ever get the blood bit of this deal, and quite a generous vial of it too, if you don't mind me saying.

Instead, we kneel in hope that your generous glug will have already kicked in, making you a tad less dexterous than usual, resulting in us receiving more than one of those wee wafers. This seemingly inconsequential detail gains significance if you've just been fasting for twenty-four hours. The amount of people I've seen falling over in these circumstances, especially if the padre starts swinging the old thurible.

My dad once took me aside and, for maybe the only time in my life, looked into my eyes and communicated something he obviously felt was hugely meaningful.

"Paul, you know you're the seventh son of a seventh son."

I had no idea what he was talking about, but I could sense the gravity in his voice.

"Am I? What does that mean?" I asked, falteringly.

"The seventh son of a seventh son has special powers, Paul. You're blessed."

In the pregnant pause that followed, I didn't need a pen and paper to figure out that my dad had unfortunately got it wrong.

"But dad, I'm the eighth son, aren't I?"

"Ah, but you're not you see. Whereas William was baptised, Andrew never was. That makes you the seventh!" he proudly announced.

I never had the heart to tell him that, strictly speaking, the seven sons can't have any annoying girls in between them, which is probably why I've never felt particularly blessed and certainly don't appear to have any special powers if those lottery tickets are anything to go by. The shocking reality however is that, in my dad's eyes at least, my brother never properly existed because he had not been baptised.

Which brings me back to JC for a minute (that's Jesus Christ btw, not Joseph Cassidy), unless he himself had had a swig too many of the Vin Santo, this is surely a decidedly dodgy decision, isn't it? People don't actually exist in My world unless they are formally handed over to Me without their consent, is not a dogma I would sign up for. Equally, dressing up your virgin daughters as brides, at a tender age, and marrying them off to this same guy does not have a good ring to it, not to my ears at least.

Having miraculously rid you of the stain you were born with, with the sacrament of baptism, they cut you some slack, till you reach an age when you really want to start doing some full-on sinning, before introducing you to the romance of the confessional box. This is a particularly intimate space where you whisper in the cleric's ear your private thoughts and transgressions so he can judge your hopeless character and pass sentence accordingly. How many times did I sit in the queue outside, yes, they queue up for this degrading exercise, looking on in horror as the spiritual guide started screaming abuse at the penitent, often bursting out of the box, ordering the confessor out of theirs and on many occasions, depending on their physique, lashing out at them.

Such was their arrogance and self-righteous assurance, their almost God-like status in that society, that they could get away with this sort of appalling behaviour.

I'm just wired all wrong for this kinda shit. I crave individuality over all that copycat, fitting-in mindset. I'm much more suited to the 'rules are there to be broken' school of thought.

I think fear is the overwhelming emotion I feel when I see brainwashing at work, the extent to which people are prepared to do what they're told without question. In the music world we have a wonderful saying; 'Just play well.' Translated it means; 'Just behave properly.' It makes me so angry when I see my lot, clearing their consciences by all herding together at a preordained time to mumble gibberish. Regardless of what they've been up to during the week, they've been to Mass, ticked that one off the list. How many of these devout beings actually know what they're saying, how many have analysed the words they chant daily. For the majority, it's really nothing but a collection of phrases learnt by rote when too young to know or care;

"HOLY MAry motheragod rhubarblaherrrrr…"

For most, it's little more than peer pressure, being seen to do the right thing. Scared half to death, they'll do whatever it takes to fit into their society which has embraced this nonsense.

How many fun evenings were ruined by the call to prayer in our house. Just as the light would fade and we'd have gotten out the magical, white cricket ball to continue our assault on the wicket, Bonzo (Paul's best friend and the most heavenly dog in Christendom) at the ready for any sixes over the boundary wall, the dreaded sound of my dad's voice would emanate from the relative safety of the porch door;

"Time for the Rosary, boys."

OMG, how the gloom descended at that moment, it was like all your darkest Good Friday afternoons rolled into one. We would begrudgingly and silently file into the unlit kitchen, find a place to kneel on the tiled floor and the torture would begin. The deal was, we would each have to lead a decade, everyone kicking in for the grand finale. You therefore had to pay attention; if you inadvertently dozed off and missed your cue, there was all hell to pay.

"HAIL HOly quen, motheramery… halorliufeorrrressww…

TO THee dowekripobanch…"

I feel lucky that I have almost entirely escaped this indoctrination though it took bravery and determination to accomplish. I take responsibility for my actions, think for myself and do not try to convert. Unfortunately, they have successfully instilled a high level of guilt and self-doubt, emotions I struggle with daily, but while they may still have the upper hand in that particular battle, I feel I have won the war and though I glean a certain amount of satisfaction and vindication from witnessing the current, glorious unravelling of this fearsome beast, these feelings are superseded by ones of horror and disgust. I am so proud and happy at the way Ireland is beginning to fight back on issues like abortion and gay equality, hopefully ditching this degrading label of being a God-fearing, Catholic country and instead embracing a new advertising campaign;

'Come to Ireland, a liberal, highly educated, multicultural society noted for its music, art, literature, hospitality, scenery and of course, the craic.'

10

War

I like to imagine the '60s as the perfect example of Communism.

"Hey man, did you say you've got nowhere to sleep… cool, come and hang out at our place."

"What, you've run out of drugs… don't worry, I've got some you can have."

"My girl's prettier than yours… no problem man, we're happy to share." … Groovy!

Interestingly though, this experimental, more liberal attitude did have powerful, far-reaching consequences. Throughout the Western world, people were beginning to stand up for themselves and make demands. Whether it was Martin Luther King and his Black Panthers in America seeking equal rights, the students in France wishing to change university laws or the people of Central and Eastern Europe looking for freedom of speech, among other things. A fever had gripped these people and they grasped the possibility of enforcing change with heartfelt alacrity. These movements did not go unnoticed in NI

The people of Ireland had been persecuted by the British for over 700 years. The island itself, though never formally conquered, was perpetually invaded, huge swathes of it annexed and handed out among deserving subjects of the Realm, the indigenous people increasingly downtrodden and corralled 'beyond the pale'. Unfathomable, how this once great empire could seemingly waltz in and take over vast countries on the other side of the world yet never successfully deal with the relatively minor irritant just a hop, skip and a jump to the west of it. The Irish simply wouldn't lie down and so the itch continued to avoid the nail until finally, in a moment of great enlightenment, the Brits decided to settle for just a bit of it. Let's draw a line say, here; we'll have this bit and you have that bit... genius. Those Irish Catholic people in the northwest portion of the island are living proof of that old adage; the pen is mightier than the sword. After all those hundreds of years of strife, a simple swish of ink sentenced 500,000 unwilling citizens to a new life of apartheid. Having said that, that primitive and ill-conceived drawing of a line only served to divide yet further, those who had to live within it. The anger and hatred just became more complicated and even closer to home.

It frustrates me no end. Why on earth didn't the Orangemen throw us even a few crumbs? Things just might have been very different. It's not like they had an overwhelming majority, and now, with the help of Mr and Mrs Cassidy and a few others, we're fast catching them up. Both Derry and Belfast are now predominantly Catholic. It's only a matter of time folks. What then? Gerrymander I hear you cry! Well, it's true that this decidedly underhand tactic was one of the many injustices that led to the formation of the Civil Rights Movement in NI in 1967. A one-sided government, council, police force; no jobs, no housing and poor education had brought the Nationalists to the end of their collective tether.

These early Civil Rights demonstrations were peaceful events until a misguided, heavy-handed approach from the police sent them quickly spiralling towards violent reactions. One such incident in Derry saw 400 peaceful demonstrators, in their Sunday-best and armed with nothing more than placards and the words to 'We Shall Overcome', confronted and brutally beaten. There were more people in The Brandywell for the football that day, yet as a result of that unprovoked brutality, at the rescheduled march six weeks later, 20,000 turned up. While marches such as these were being suppressed with horrendous barbarity, other annual marches were allowed to continue unperturbed. The 12th of July march every year commemorates some poxy battle fought over 400 years ago between a father, James II, and his son-in-law, William II, Prince of Orange. Both after the British throne, they chose to have the skirmish on Irish soil so as not to make a mess of the lovely Cotswolds. James II was backed by the most powerful man in Europe at the time, Louis XIV (Billy's arch enemy), and wait for it, Queen Billy resplendent on his big, white charger darling, was backed by none other than... Pope Alexander VIII. How's that for irony!

Then, every 12th of August, another bunch of halfwits get all dolled up to keep alive the memory of some siege or other, dating from the same savage period. It was this very show of ignorance on 12th August 1969 that degenerated into seventy-two hours of carnage, a debauched scene that became known as the Battle of the Bogside and heralded the arrival of the British Army.

They arrived under the title of Operation Banner. Whether this was someone's idea of a sick joke aimed at the clash of the marchers, I don't know, but what I do know is that their little summer training camp, where they would rap a few knuckles and put out a few fires, resulted in the longest continuous deployment of the British Army in its history. What shall we call this forty-year war then... oh I know, The Troubles!!

There had been much unrest since Partition on 3rd May 1921, but it was always quietly and efficiently quashed. The difference this time was that the relatively newfound world media was focusing on it, just as it had in Philadelphia, Paris and Prague. The RUC and their merry men, the B-Specials, could no longer get away with killing innocent people or burning them out of their homes. The eyes of the world were suddenly upon them and even Westminster had to admit embarrassment and deal with the situation.

Of course there was talk of all this at home. Both my parents had been born in a United Ireland; my uncle was shot dead by the Black and Tans;

"Shot in the back on a Sunday morning as he turned the key in his door," Dad used to always say.

I could already sense the fear in my elders as we watched the grainy, black-and-white images of violence on our own back door. Many of my brothers and sisters were out taking part in these initial marches. Soon, there was talk of little else. It was however mostly gobbledygook to a nine-year-old boy interested only in nature and football.

This all changed on the evening of 12th August 1969. The unrest had been building for nearly a year, reaching fever-pitch during the Apprentice Boys' March in Derry on that day.

As my dad bundled me into the car, my mind was firmly fixed on my first pair of Beatle Boots, which I had got that day. The raised heel, the zip up the side, the red satin lining... how I loved them. It was only when we had parked and scrambled over to the vantage point in the grounds of the cathedral that my mind was unmercifully wrenched from my footwear and the second verse of 'Help'. The sight before me would become emblazoned on my mind for evermore. Derry was alight. Huge tongues of fire licked the black night sky, windows exploded with the heat and crackling timbers spat volleys of sparks high into the air. Everywhere there was madness and pandemonium. People seemed to be running randomly in every direction, screaming and shouting, while families like ours stood looking on in disbelief. Sticks, stones, bottles, petrol bombs, water cannon, tear gas and more filled the air. As the police wantonly drove armoured vehicles into the crowds, cars and buses were hijacked, set on fire and used as barricades for a bit of protection. Though I would come to live through many such scenes in the next six or seven years, none would leave such an impression as this night. Even with my tender years, I knew that what I was witnessing was not about to go away. This intense wave of feeling was coming my way, it would soon engulf me and I needed to learn how to ride it, fast.

And so it was that these little green men arrived in our midst. They weren't exactly Martians, but they didn't 'alf speak funny. When they first landed, we greeted them with open arms, they were treated to the infamous Irish hospitality. They were our saviours after all, intervening to save us from a situation that was getting increasingly out of control. Sadly, this was short-sighted. Imagine these kids suddenly finding themselves in Derry, they didn't even know where the place was on the map, much less why they were there in the first place. Given their complete ignorance of the situation, who do you think they would turn to for intelligence? Why, the local police force of course. Bad idea! This had a devastating effect on their blossoming relationship with the Nationalist community. Within a matter of weeks, they had simply taken over where the police had left off, not yet shooting innocent people and burning them out of their homes but certainly focusing their undivided attention on us, the perceived troublemakers.

Life quite quickly dissolved into a full-scale military operation. One rarely felt safe. People were randomly picked up and thrown in jail, homes were raided at all hours of the day and night, low-flying helicopters would keep us from sleep well into the night and wake us in the early morning. We would often be stopped and searched two or three times on the way to school and the same again on the way home. Riots were a daily occurrence and bombings and shootings were becoming increasingly commonplace. In many ways we were as clueless as our new camouflaged friends. At school, we were taught British history, which conveniently left out the bits to do with Ireland. At home, my parents, or rather my dad, spoke of the whole thing from the gut. His, like so many, was an emotional response. It was our land, our home, our family that was being fucked with here. My mum politely ignored the whole carry-on apart from expressing concern, outrage or regret at the latest atrocity to be reported. One felt powerless and trapped.

"Oi, Cass, y'wanna Vienna?"

Hang on, did I just hear Bronco right? Our route home from school took us straight through the middle of the most riotous area in NI, a sprawling council estate by the name of Shantallow. This was a day much like any other, a few of us were dandering vaguely homeward and as we took the alleyway by the side of Owens' shop, Bronco and a couple of his mates stopped us and took me aside. Bronco, who looked for all the world like a rough Charles Bronson, was a couple of years older than me and came with a scary reputation.

"Well, y'wanna Vienna or don't ye?" he growled conspiratorially in my face as he pushed into me, forcing me against the wall. I could smell the last fag on his breath; his face was contorted in a disgusted grimace at having to deal with a lowlife wimp like me. Shoulders hunched, both hands stuffed in the pockets of his black bomber jacket, cut-off Wranglers, tailored to the top of his polished DMs. I was dumbstruck. Bronco had never so much as thrown me a sideways glance, had certainly never taken the time to waste a word on me, now here he was, offering me a biscuit.

It has to be said, we Cassidys have a reputation for having a bit of a sweet tooth, so when someone, even Bronco, offers you one of your absolute favourite sources of sugar, that divine, triangular, thicker than usual wafer coated in heavenly dark chocolate, there really isn't any decision to be made, you just jump all over it.

"Aye surely. 'At'd be brilliant, so it would. Thanks Bronco," said I, trying to pitch my response somewhere between enthusiastic and cool.

"Right, OK then. I'll meet you here at six in the evenin' on Saturday. Don't be late!"

What on earth is going on here, I thought to myself. *Does he seriously expect me to come back here on Saturday evening for a lousy biscuit?*

"Fuckin'ell Cass, you're in so ye are!" said one of my pals who had overheard the exchange.

"You what, Marty. What are ye talkin' about. In what??" said I.

"The Fianna, you eejit. You're in the Fianna!"

This was a fairly monumental error of judgment, but I've often thought since, had I heard Bronco correctly, would I have had the nerve to say no anyway? I would have been immediately blacklisted and Shantallow, my stomping ground, would have become off limits had I declined the offer.

I was in quite a state for the next couple of days and by 6pm on the Saturday, as I arrived at the appointed rendezvous, I was downright shaking. Bronco and a couple of other guys arrived on time and escorted me to a house in the middle of the estate. We were let in, ushered upstairs and shown into the room at the front of the house. There were several young men in there dressed in black, wearing balaclavas and one middle-aged man looking for all the world like a bog-standard teacher in his cheap suit, shirt and tie. His face was uncovered and plain to see. In front of him was a table on which there was a large tricolour flag and a Bible. He welcomed me and as the men in black stood to attention, approached me. Taking the book and flag, he put the book in my hands and draped the flag over it. He proceeded to intone some bullshit, which I then had to endorse. He shook my hand before showing me the door and as I turned to leave, the foot soldiers clicked their heels and saluted the open air. I had just been sworn in to the Fianna, the youth section of the IRA. I was twelve.

Before leaving that house, I was issued with a black whistle and told to report for duty the following Monday. In fact, we had to report for duty at 6pm every day from then on unless instructed otherwise. In truth, not a hell of a lot happened; the girls were mainly used to transport weapons and the boys, to keep an eye out for army patrols who may have gotten wind of higher-level activities taking place within the estate. If and when the army arrived, it was our job to raise the alarm and waylay them, giving the bigwigs enough time to disperse. We only found out later that if we were caught in possession of one of those pathetic little black whistles with which we would raise the alarm, we would get seven years in jail, no questions asked.

This whole Fianna business was a real drag and a frightful waste of precious time. It felt like make-believe but in reality, it was not something you could easily walk away from. Since the days following the Battle of the Bogside, and in an effort to protect ourselves from the increasingly aggressive tactics of the RUC's new best friends, the Nationalist community erected colossal barricades around the main Nationalist enclaves and the IRA were called upon to police these no-go areas. Permanent checkpoints were set up and all traffic in and out thoroughly searched and monitored. Behind the barricades, life went on pretty much as normal but life, both here and in general, had become totally fixated on the struggle. A high level of violence became normal and one lived in a permanent state of fear.

For the most part, the IRA just left you alone and got on with their business, but misdemeanours of any kind were punished in a most brutal fashion. Men deemed to have stepped out of line sufficiently were kneecapped, women, tied to a prominent lamppost, tarred and feathered, and left for twenty-four hours for all to witness. Very often, at the hop on a Saturday night, as we danced to Slade, the status quo would be rudely interrupted by hooded, armed men. They would smash open the double doors, two would stand guard at the only exit while two more would scour the dancefloor for their quarry. Often, shots were fired, young girls would scream and faint, we boys would hope that the stain on our pants wasn't too visible, as these marauders went calmly about their task. Once discovered, whoever it was would be dragged outside and promptly dealt with. One could often hear the sickening sound of a young arm being broken. That'll teach him for stealing from the local shop, or worse still, young knees being blown off, what transgression could honestly deserve such a punishment?

Though things had already become very serious, it was on the 30th of January 1972 that all hell broke loose. That Bloody Sunday in Derry, a folly-up to the horrendous 'Massacre at Ballymurphy' a few months earlier, signalled all-out war. In a repeat performance of October '68; the IRA was not exactly inundated with volunteers up until this moment but by Monday morning they couldn't cope with the numbers of people, young, old, male, female, who wanted to join their ranks. It is not my place to comment on the harrowing and regrettable events of that day, but I do feel compelled to share one horrific, oft-forgotten incident. One of my best friends' beautiful, sixteen-year-old sister was doing her best to escape the madness but found she could not outrun these licensed killers. Out of breath and out of luck, she decided to stand still, up against the outside walls of the Rossville Street Flats. As the lines of armoured personnel carriers thundered past on their murderous journey, poor Marcella thought her plan had worked. Just then, the 'pig' closest to her slammed on the brakes, reversed and turning to face her, rammed her up against the pebble-dashed wall, smashing both her legs before continuing on its way.

On the 31st of July that same year, the Brits flexed their muscle again in an attempt to drive home what was obviously their new hard-line initiative aimed at bringing this annoying unrest to an end. Operation Motorman saw 22,000 troops, (the biggest British Army deployment since the Suez Crisis of '56) smash their way into the no-go areas of NI. This clearing of the barricades signalled a new phase in the conflict.

By now there were riots, shootings and bombings every day and most Saturday afternoons, a bunch of mad Tadhgs and Orangemen would face-off in Derry's central square. A mass brawl would ensue, mostly ignored by the police and army. Nowhere was safe. For example, one day Brendan and I were crossing the old Craigavon Bridge on a rare excursion to the predominantly Protestant Waterside area of Derry when a carload of them mounted the pavement in an effort to score maximum points. By some miracle, we managed to leap up onto the protective railing thereby narrowly avoiding the speeding vehicle. Had we mistimed that leap or lost our footing, we would have plunged all of sixty feet into the icy waters of the mighty Foyle and been swept away to a certain death. On another occasion, I braved the Waterside to visit my girlfriend Deirdre, who had just had a minor operation in the hospital there. In the short time I was there, word got out that an alien was in town. A gang of young men actually stormed the hospital in an effort to get me. Not knowing the layout of the place, I somehow managed to find a back fire escape and leaving the grounds, raced for my life down the middle of the road. I caught up with a bus at the lights and when the driver saw the terror on my face and the lynch mob on my tail, he opened the doors to let me on, then sped off as best he could, ignoring red lights as he crossed the bridge to relative safety.

One day on our way home from school we were forced to stop in the Diamond, Derry's main square, as there was a bomb scare in nearby

Ferryquay Street and the army had chosen to close all the neighbouring streets. The square was packed with folk, young and old, nonchalant about the idea of yet another bomb but frustrated at having yet another day disrupted in this way. As we stood there waiting for something to happen, an enormous explosion rocked the whole place. Instead of the device being planted in one of the shops as had been previously thought, we had witnessed Derry's first car bomb. The huge blast had virtually destroyed the entire street and quite large bits of the car had flown right over our heads, landing as far away as Magazine Street on the opposite side of the square.

On the subject of cars, my dad's old maroon Ford Zodiac, license plate, 471 UI, formed part of the first barricade in Derry, at the top of William Street. Though it was no longer his at the time, it was curious to see it had become a city landmark.

My dad was very keen on cars and horses and we kids always dreaded having the bad luck to be in the car with him before race time. One may have been out getting petrol or a loaf of bread when suddenly he would take a silent turn, off track. At that moment your heart sank, and your gut told you that you were trapped and about to have to spend a cold, lonely hour sitting quietly in a locked car while he perused the runners and riders in the bookies.

One such day, he and I had been up town on some errand or other and he elected to visit a betting shop on William Street. He was driving his latest purchase, a rarity in Derry in those days, a white Saab 99. He decided to park in one of those little terraced streets that run from Waterloo Street down towards the Bogside. As he turned off the engine and opened his door, two masked men appeared out of nowhere. One covered my side of the car, pointing his gun at me, while the other held his gun against my dad's head.

"Get out. We're taking your car," scowled the hooded outlaw. I was shaking in my seat.

Almost nonchalantly, my dad replied, "Now you listen to me sonny. I only just got this car myself, so there's no way I'm giving it over to you. Get that gun out of my face before I close the door on you."

My dad's voice was so matter-of-fact and authoritative that the gunman, bewildered, just did as he said. Clearly frustrated at having to find an alternative establishment in which to throw away his pennies, dad calmly closed the door, started the car and drove off, brushing against the other guy who was still standing, brandishing his weapon, in the middle of the road. I was terrified and silent, my dad simply huffed and puffed and rabbited on about how he'd worked all his life so he could get a car like this while those guttersnipes never worked a day in their crummy lives. He figured that from then on, he'd get to the bookies earlier before these layabouts had gotten out of the scratcher.

This ploy of taking people's cars to carry out missions became a real feature in the late '70s early '80s. Both my parents and my sister Joan fell foul of this strategy. In Joan's case, she had gone with one daughter to pick up the other daughter from a kid's birthday party when armed men stormed the house, holding them all hostage till the guys who had subsequently taken the homeowner's car, had done what they had to do. Though thankfully no one was hurt, this extremely frightening, long drawn-out incident had a lasting effect on the hostages, both young and old.

In my parents' case, the gang came to the back door of the house. This was a solid door so my mum couldn't see who was there. As she opened the door she was overwhelmed by youths in balaclavas and both she and my dad were held at gunpoint for many hours while my dad's fancy BMW was put through its paces in a drive-by shooting over in Shantallow. This must have been horribly unnerving for my aging parents, all alone in that big, empty, secluded house, surrounded by a bunch of trigger-happy teenagers. The car was written off. No one died.

It was a fine spring day in 1973 as we boarded the school bus home. Upon taking our seats, the driver explained that the town centre and certain other areas had been brought to a standstill by a series of bomb scares. This meant that the normal route home was disrupted but we were assured that the traffic wasn't too bad and that the journey wouldn't take much longer than usual. I remember so clearly, as we came down the Strand Road and followed the diversion, up Lawrence Hill, across the Northland Road and down Duncreggan Road thinking that this somehow felt like a big day. Even by Derry standards, this felt major. Huge areas were completely deserted, cordoned off with tape and heavy army vehicles. Crowds of workers gathered on street corners waiting for the all-clear. Ambulances and fire engines stood poised and ready for action. The helicopters were out in force, hanging motionless like giant bees in the clear sky. Army and police Land Rovers sped left and right; the constant wail of sirens filled the thin air. On that short journey home, four massive car bombs rocked the city, each one greeted by a half-hearted, involuntary cheer from the packed bus. As I got off the bus at the foot of Shantallow a young lad shouted over to me,

"Hey Cass, I hear your dad's place got it the day!!"

Though this flippant remark went in one ear and out the other, it was typical of guys like that to take cheap shots, something about it unnerved me. I quickened my step, on the one hand in the hope that I might avoid any more smart alecs, but on the other, that I might get home the sooner, in order to dispel this horrid myth.

I arrived to an empty house. The key was in the usual place but there was no one home. Something wasn't right and I got a hollow, nervous feeling in the pit of my stomach. My heart began to race, and I got that rush of adrenaline, flooding my mind with a zillion random thoughts. In this confused state, all I could think to do was to get myself to the bar as quickly as possible. I ran that mile without stopping.

The Strand Road is a straight thoroughfare and I could tell from afar that my worst suspicions were about to be realised, the lad by the bus stop had been well informed. A large crowd surveyed the chaotic scene from behind the ring fence, a full 200 yards away. In the midst of that crowd of strangers I found my mum and dad quietly observing. Only now, as I close in on the age he would have been on that day, can I begin to grasp the enormity of the moment. In their own very different ways, these two people had devoted the last forty years of their lives to the building that lay crumpled before them. They had built it, designed it, furnished it, every coloured glass in the renowned display behind the oval bar, individually chosen with care and love. They had even lived in it as a young family and now it lay strewn across the road like a deck of cards shaken from its carefully balanced tower.

Luckily it was one of my brothers who had been serving in the bar at the time the men sauntered in with their box of tricks. Had my dad been there, he would undoubtedly have confronted them and tried to stop them; not a good idea. Instead they placed their surprise package expertly and told the customers they had fifteen minutes before the device would go off but that they mustn't leave the premises for at least five minutes, to allow for their safe getaway. Anyone disobeying this order would be shot. And so, the warning was phoned through to the security forces in the usual way, the area was evacuated, and the colossal bomb went off as planned. Half a pound of gelignite, in the right hands, can obliterate a family saloon, so you can imagine what 150 pounds of the stuff can do. The impressive, three-storey edifice imploded, a lifetime's attentive care sucked in and blown away in an instant, like a casual drag on a cigarette.

We knew the individuals who did it. They were 'one of us'. One of us indeed. Not by any stretch of the imagination could these people be considered one of us. How on earth could an act of such callous cruelty be seen as camaraderie??

Two stories were bandied about as to why we were singled out for punishment. One was that apparently a short time before, one of my brothers had somewhat forcefully insisted that a particular gentleman should vacate the premises since he would insist on insulting my dad. How was my dear bro to know that that well-crafted right cross would cause our belligerent friend to lose his footing, career down the heavily polished staircase and conveniently tumble out onto the pavement? We would later learn that this customer was a prominent member of the Provisional IRA.

Despite the indisputable seriousness of this unfortunate incident, I imagine the real reason for the bombing was that, in times when these paramilitary organisations were all engaged in drug running and protection rackets, my dad would never have countenanced the handing over of money in return for protection. He was a tremendously proud Irish man and a fine ambassador for the country he loved but he had no time for gangsters who dressed up criminal activity in a green jacket and black beret.

My dad's love of the Railway Bar ended that day. His heart was broken by the sight of it, collapsed on the pavement like so many drunks. As we walked silently away from the scene, he had already taken the decision to sell the site and not, as so many others would have done, get compensation and rebuild. He was a stubborn son of a gun and, rightly or wrongly, that hasty resolve was final.

On a more mundane note, what little was left of the bar stock was transported out to Kebroyde and stored in the back rooms. Dad would have cornered any of the spirits for his own furtive snifters, but cases of beer were suddenly right there under the nose of a curious teenager.

Guzzling that first bottle of Tuborg Gold, sneaked from the depths of one of the hidden cases, on my way to the Saturday hop, and feeling that all-over fuzzy feeling, hugely enjoying it but equally, hoping it levels out soon before I fall over, was a landmark moment in my young life and certainly made chatting and dancing with the local talent considerably easier. Those cases steadily got depleted from the bottom up and yet my dad never did seem to notice. At least he never pulled me up about it. He was either getting soft or more likely, had lost the will.

11

First Night

By 1973 I was surrounded by fear and violence. Fear and violence surrounded me. The streets were a war zone, the TV and local papers spoke of little other than the latest atrocities. School was a survival course and home a dreadfully dreary place, again, run on fear. Aged fourteen, culture was a side of life I had not yet encountered. One could sense what life might be like, but it was an unattainable dream. Fags, booze and girls were my oases in this desert. Then, one day, Bridget mentioned that she'd been contacted by a youth orchestra in search of players.

"They meet every Friday night in Omagh," she said. "Why don't you go?"

"Orchestra, what even is that? Friday nights. Omagh. You've got to be joking. There's no way I'm doing that."

Came the predictable, teenage response to such a ridiculous suggestion. My dad, who'd been engaged in his usual 'pretending to sleep' routine over in his grossly misshapen leather outpost suddenly piped up.

"Did you say, orchestra? That'd be good for you, Paul. I'll drop you up at the bus on Friday."

This decision taken, the old man calmly placed his shovel-like hands back on his portly tummy and eased back into his somnolent state that, for the most part, saved him from having to deal with reality.

Getting on a stinky, dilapidated bus for a lengthy, rickety drive to stinky, dilapidated Omagh, was not what Friday evenings were designed for. Nevertheless, despite my constant protestations, even from the steps of the vehicle itself, Joseph saw to it that I took the bus.

The bus was undeniably awful, and the journey seemed endless as we meandered through villages and made random stops to pick up other strays along the way, but there were already encouraging signs. I found a pal on the back seat, another fiddle player from Derry by the name of Brian Bergin. He was a lovely chap and always seemed to have a full pack of Embassy Regals. Also, it hadn't escaped my notice that many of these waifs we picked up along the roadside were girls, so, a can of beer and this new-fangled orchestra carry-on wasn't looking so bad after all.

Ninety minutes later, our smoke-belching bone-shaker pulled into the forecourt of a school and we gratefully jumped off and filed into the strip-lit assembly hall which had already been laid out with enough chairs and stands to accommodate the eighty or so young musicians who had filled the room and were noisily catching up and tuning up. I, feeling thoroughly out of my depth, hung onto Brian Bergin, already a veteran of three or four such occasions. Soon though, a nice lady-helper hounded me out and showed me to my preordained seat, inside, third desk of first violins. It was strangely disorientating to feel so at sea whilst doing something so familiar. Getting out my instrument, tuning up and preparing to play, I was very comfortable with, but being seated in this sea of eager, like-minded colleagues, I certainly was not. The cacophony of sound fell away to silence upon the arrival of our maestro. With the benefit of hindsight, I realise now that Alfie Bell had fashioned himself on someone I hadn't even heard of yet, but someone who would become one of my musical heroes, Leonard Bernstein. The sweater draped over the shoulders, the tousled wave of grey hair, the almost constant cigarette and the not-so-faint aroma of hard liquor, all lent him a studied air of authority. It may as well have been Lenny who took to the podium that night considering the terror he instilled in my scrambled mind.

"Rossini," he bellowed.

This one, for me indistinguishable command, set off a flurry of activity all around me and within seconds, this random gathering of unruly teenagers had organised the music on their stands and had 'struck the pose' in readiness to begin playing. Before I knew what was happening, Lenny started waving about and they were off. 'The Thieving Magpie' took off at such a rate that, though I tried to feign some attempt at playing something, I found myself rooted to the spot, frozen, unable to move. Apart from anything else, the hieroglyphics before me on the page were indecipherable. This wasn't sheet music as I knew it. This wasn't some little Grade 6-level set work for the local Feis; this was full-on orchestral music. It was like someone had closed the book on a swarm of mosquitos, trapping and squashing them mid-flight. There were endless directions written on the pages, the majority of which meant absolutely nothing to me whatsoever; tremolo, sul ponticello, pizzicato, con sordino, and so on. What, oh what did this all mean!? The playthrough and subsequent rehearsal of that overture went by in a blur, I was in shock, everything happened so quickly. As the conductor and leader gave out instructions like; "Let's go from B; Upbow, seven after G; Too loud at the change of key; Remember it's senza sordini at J..." I could hear them, but being numb, was too slow to react.

'The Thieving Magpie' flew out of my life just as suddenly as it had entered it. My trusty desk partner, reacting to yet another command I had completely missed, closed this book of tricks, consigning those busy mozzies back to their dark, silent and rather flat world.

A bit of a commotion accompanied the unearthing of the next magic book on our stands. As its cover was lifted and the first of its many secrets lay exposed before us, a grand piano was wheeled into position next to the conductor, just a few feet from my chair. This fairy-tale scenario continued as a little leprechaun of a man appeared from nowhere and approached the keyboard. He embraced the conductor, shook hands with our concertmistress, and with a short bow to us all, took his place. Our conductor introduced him.

"Ladies and gentlemen of the orchestra, please welcome our soloist, Mr Derek Bell."

I thought Derek Bell was the world-famous harp player in the mighty Chieftains, yet here he was, nonchalantly turning up to play a piano concerto with an orchestra.

I couldn't help noticing that our soloist could only really perch on his stool if he were to reach the pedals, but this was no impediment to his brilliance, indeed if anything it enhanced the whole spectacle. From that magnificent opening exclamation, that 'call to arms' of Grieg's masterpiece, I was once again sent into shock. Released from mere reality, I was transported to a dreamworld, luxuriating in a warm, emotional bath. I'm not sure I even pretended to play my violin this time. I was oblivious to my surroundings, high as a kite, not a drug in sight. It was when we entered the intensely intoxicating world of the slow movement however that our elfin musician really started to weave his magic. I think maybe the beauty lies in the conversational aspect of the music, this idea of a universal language with which we can somehow all communicate. Already, from the first utterances of the muted strings (it mattered not that I didn't even have a mute, I was in no fit state to take part) then the horn, the solo cello, and finally the entrance of the piano, those oh-so intimate, transcendental phrases cast a spell on me that would not only change my life from that moment, but remain equally powerful for a whole lifetime. I seemed to be absorbing this heady potion through my entire body because my ears were blocked and my throat dry; my chest ached and my head felt as though it might explode, which, I suppose, it did in a way, causing a flood of hot, salty tears to flow freely from my red eyes. They cascaded down my cheeks, falling onto my violin, leaving stains that would prove difficult to erase.

I feel blessed that my entire world was brought sharply into focus in those few short moments. It wasn't a decision I made really; it was a calling I was powerless to resist. The Pied Piper had come to Omagh and I, hypnotised, was now following his tune.

12

Late Nights

Returning to the subject of the bar for a moment, there was an extraordinary sequence of events in 1971, which could arguably offer a third explanation for the eventual bombing of the place.

We experienced two break-ins in quick succession. Not a tremendous amount was taken but it was nonetheless an unnerving and unsavoury situation made all the more perplexing by the fact that we couldn't figure out how the burglar was getting in. We guessed it had been the same person because the two incidents were so close together and the same sort of merchandise stolen but there were no forced doors, no broken windows… nothing. We came to the conclusion that the only possible way for this to happen was that the culprit was somehow hiding himself away before closing time and reappearing in the dark, vacated premises to help himself at his leisure. We went on high alert and sure enough, it didn't take long till our new friend decided his cocktail cabinet needed refilling. One night, as last orders were called, we noticed a man sneaking into the ladies' toilet and not returning. It had been that simple. He was canny enough to use the ladies' because there were more cubicles in there and we, who would have been checking such places before closing, were likely to be less thorough with our security detail in that particular area; maybe even just calling in from the door before turning off the light for the night. So, that night, not only did we foil his third attempt at filling his bags with our goods, we had found our man. Nothing was said. By expertly acting the drunk, he was able to deftly sidestep the embarrassing situation of being caught alone in the ladies' after lights-out. We played him at his own game. When our calls were met with silence, we killed the lights only to return a short time later just to double-check. We, for our part, feigned shock at finding him there and ushered him out the main door, into the street and pointed him in the direction of his nearby home.

Uncovering Dick's dastardly plot brought a huge sense of relief upon our house. We swallowed our losses, as he no doubt swallowed his gains, and moved on, safe in the knowledge that with our extra vigilant security checks, this incident was behind us. Our respite was to be short-lived however and it was with mounting dread and frustration that, only a matter of months later, the pub was burgled again. This time the means of entry was more obvious; a tiny horizontal window giving onto a flat roof at the back of the building had been smashed and this time, considerably more stock had disappeared. My dad was fuming. His initial, laissez-faire attitude to the first two break-ins was replaced with a palpable fury. It was too much of a coincidence to imagine that this latest breach was the work of anyone other than the guy from the ladies'. He'd unwittingly broken the unspoken rules of my dad's little game and Daddy was out to get this son-of-a-gun.

Which brings me nicely to the next chapter of this beer-room farce.

In the twinkling of an eye it was as though you had stepped from the set of *Coronation Street* onto the set of *The Untouchables*. Rather than report these incidents to the cops, my dad set about taking the law into his own hands. All fine and dandy but for the fact that he also decided, for reasons best known to his good self, that he needed a sidekick in order to fully carry out his plan. And so it was, that for the next couple of weeks, each night at around midnight, he and I would steal away from Kebroyde in the car. Not a word was uttered as he prematurely turned off the headlights and idled into a quiet cul-de-sac a short walk shy of the Railway Bar. We would silently vacate the vehicle and Dad, who always bore a striking resemblance to one of Al Capone's henchmen, carried the image one stage further by taking his double-barrelled Webley and Scott from the boot and concealing it most professionally along his side. This unlikely pair would then purposefully make their way through the shadows to the side door of the pub. My dad had left this door unlocked during the hour or so since closing time to facilitate our fleeting re-entry and in no time, we were in and taking up our positions. Our subject's point of entry, that little window, was at the top of the stairs to the lounge, a long, carpeted space on two levels, filled with low mahogany tables and plush sofas and chairs. About halfway down the substantial space, just where the floor sloped down to the lower level, we dragged out one of these sofas placing it across the room. It was here we bedded in and lay in wait for our unsuspecting pilferer to make his second mistake.

I have to tell you that, for a boy of eleven or twelve years of age, this was a scary scene. As soon as we snuggled into the luxurious velour fabric of that Chesterfield, my dad would be fast asleep, his thunderous snores making a mockery of our previous stealth. I, on the other hand, would be left wide awake and surrounded by the very sobering reality that here I was, in the middle of a war-torn town, next to an armed man, waiting for a burglar to materialise in the very same room. If this man was prepared to break into a place, who's to say he wouldn't be armed too; what then!? From time to time a helicopter spotlight or the flashing lights of a passing police patrol or army convoy would briefly enlighten the eerie darkness of my new bedroom. We would remain there doggedly till 3am, my dad snoozing and blissfully nonchalant, me, very much awake and manic. At the very least, one would imagine that such shenanigans would result in some time off school, but not a bit of it. I was ripped from my slumbers and booted out the door as per normal.

Every night for a month we played out this scene till, in truth, my charismatic co-star began to appear less like Elliot Ness and more like Ken Barlow. Having said that, I'm amazed that we never once encountered the security forces. Yes, my dad had a license for that gun but to be walking around the streets of Derry, late at night, with a loaded shotgun; only takes one itchy trigger! I had already lived through three years of this war and witnessed some disturbing images but truthfully, to me at that tender age, it was still some elaborate game in which I was an unwilling participant.

It was just another night. By now I found myself able to join my dad in la-la-land but on this occasion our dreams were rudely interrupted by the unmistakable sound of breaking glass. Maybe the pitter-patter of the steady rain on the corrugated tin roof was enough to block out the farmyard noises coming from within or maybe our burglar had just gotten too cocky, thinking he could waltz in and out of this place as and when the fancy took him. Either way, he blatantly used the same tried and tested way in, smashed the recently replaced pane, it's putty still soft, and forced his bulky frame through that tiny opening allowing himself to fall the short distance down onto the red carpet of the lounge. How I wished I was still dreaming. The events however were horribly real. Though I had played out this scene a thousand times, I had never once imagined how it might end. As the burly figure got to his feet and made his way behind the counter, to my absolute surprise and horror, my dad let him have it with both barrels. The noise, as those explosions ripped through the silence, was ear splitting. If this was some sort of game, my dad had surely just ditched the rulebook. Not only had he just shot at another human being from quite close range, he had emptied two No.8s straight at his beloved lounge bar with all its mahogany, crystal, hand-engraved mirrors etc. Somehow, the gods were with us that night. My dad could take down a snipe at forty paces, nine times out of ten, yet though we'll never know for sure, he managed to miss this brute from only ten. We'll never know for sure because before you could say Jack Daniels, our intruder had vaulted back out that impossibly small gap and was making his way down to the alleyway that ran behind the pub.

"Come on!" my dad shouted.

We hared down the stairs and out the door onto the Strand Road. We could hear a motorbike starting up and Dad sent me up the alley after our friend, forcing him to take the other exit where he would be waiting. By the time I got into position, the man had already built up a head of steam and despite my wild gesticulations roared past me, out onto the main drag and away. He never darkened our door or window again.

What just happened was yet another totally bizarre part of the jigsaw that seemed to be mapping out my existence to date. I was afraid and increasingly aware of the horrifying fact that people could be strange and unpredictable, and one could not dictate the parameters of one's environment. Life was an increasingly perplexing paradox, that which went on within your own mind and that which unfolded without. Seriously though, what were my lovely parents thinking of, exposing their precious youngest son to such barbarism. That treasured one who'd been set apart, loved above all others, handled with kid gloves, cushioned in cotton wool, a silver spoon completing the rose-tinted portrait. My dad always made out he only meant to scare the guy, but buckshot from a right barrel in a confined space is an unpredictable thing. What if the intruder had been armed? This savage scheme could so easily have had a very different outcome; one where I would have been an accessory to a premeditated murder or one where one or both of us got murdered ourselves.

13

Youth Orchestra

In the spring of 1974, I attended the first concert of my life. Don't ask me how but at a time when no musicians dared come to NI, the Galway Ensemble braved the trip and played in the Great Hall of Magee College. John Georgiadis, Roger Best, Moray Welsh and none other than the twinkling, blinking god of the flute, Pan himself, Jimmy Galway, threw caution to the wind and dipped their collective toes in the icy wastes west of the Foyle. This was a decision not to be taken lightly, as the ill-fated souls of the celebrated Miami Showband found out only a short time later. Returning from a concert in Co. Down, some delightful characters from the UVF (or was it the UDR, MI5 I hear you say…doesn't really matter, same difference) set up a phony checkpoint, stopped the Miami's coach and set about their heinous plan. They were to plant a bomb on the bus which would be detonated once they'd crossed the border. Not only would this have killed everyone on board, it would have ensured that they were perceived as nothing more than IRA bomb-smugglers. Any lingering trust of the southerners would have been dealt a serious blow and border security almost certainly, intensified. The bomb went off as they were planting it, killing two of the 'soldiers'. This sent the remainder of the gang, standing guard outside, into a panic and they sprayed the dazed musicians at close range, killing three outright and seriously injuring the remaining two. Details of this conspiracy were delivered to the grieving families, after an enquiry, in 2011.

The Galway Ensemble escaped unhurt, but for a slight bruise to their egos, given how few of us turned up to hear them. But I remain eternally grateful to them, that they made the effort. For me at least, it was a seminal moment, the first and last public concert I would get to attend until 1976.

My involvement with the Western Counties Youth Orchestra went from strength to strength. They procured a set of new instruments, which they could lend out to those in need. I was deemed worthy and thus got my hands on my first reasonable violin. I also secured my place, outside second desk of first violins. These days, Fridays were all about music. The fact that you had to spend three hours on a rickety old coach didn't seem to matter. I was making new friends, friends bitten by the same bug as me. Soon there was talk of a summer course. I did from time to time wonder why a *Western* CYO would take place in little old Omagh instead of the much more obvious choice, Derry. But then equally, why would the University of Ulster find its home in Coleraine when again, Derry had so much more to offer potential students. I of course am biased but shamefully we were used to such decisions. The second city of Northern Ireland was consigned to the second division and few tasty scraps found their way that far west.

Apart from a brief trip to London a couple of years earlier, Exmouth, wherever that was, would become my first destination outside of Ireland. The journey got off to a shaky start when my dad got me to the bus late, which resulted in him having to drive me all the way to the airport. Then he came into the check-in area! OMG, imagine the embarrassment. I was just getting to know these people; they'd all arrived together on the bus and here I was seemingly being chauffeured to the gate by some old weirdo in a brown velour Trilby who was now hobnobbing with the bigwigs. I knew we had simply missed the bus and he was just explaining and apologising to the conductor and staff. Irrelevant, it was excruciating!

Another major embarrassment was that I was carrying a fishing rod. Russell had persuaded me that a place called Exmouth, by inference, would almost certainly be at the mouth of a river called the Ex and there should therefore be some good fishing to be had. So as not to let him down, I came equipped. I survived these initial setbacks and the subsequent journey. The flight was great fun but then we had to put in some more coach hours, albeit in a considerably posher vehicle than the Omagh bus. That week away on the South Devon coast was absolutely pivotal for me. I finally got to meet real working musicians. John Ashworth, who ran the then famous Leicestershire Schools YO, took the violins. Harry Danks, principal viola of the BBCSO, who had not one but two Amati violas, and Alexander 'Bobby'

Kok, who I believe was Harry's son-in-law at the time, founder member of the Philharmonia Orchestra and principal cellist of the CBSO, tutored the violas and cellos respectively. These people had such a profound effect on me. Despite their brilliance playing-wise, they were all so personable and charming, witty and knowledgeable. Those magnificent Amatis and their gloriously mellow sound (he let me play one of them) definitely made an impression on me but it was Bobby's performance of the Kodaly Solo Sonata that really took my breath away. I sat on the front row, totally transfixed and open-mouthed at his wonderfully committed and dramatic account of that formidable work which literally blew me away. Any doubts I may have had about becoming a musician were dispelled by this single display of control, ability and panache. Add to this our furtive visit to the local pub where I and others had our first experience of scrumpy, and my future was sealed. Scrumptious indeed and for all the world like cloudy apple juice till you try standing up, only to find your judgement blurred and speech slurred. Then, on the second evening after rehearsal, I was approached by a few girls who informed me that AC wanted to see me. Ann Calvin was the eighteen-year-old Amazonian blonde who led the orchestra at the time. She came to Friday nights on a 750cc Kawasaki for God's sake and though I ended up sitting right behind her (in orchestra I hasten to add!!), it never occurred to me that she'd even noticed me. I presumed it must be some kind of initiation process, but this was not the first or last time in my life that an older woman would decide to brighten up my world and offer a little further education. It was so refreshing and not a little exciting the way in which she summoned me, took what she wanted and then, when the time was right, moved on with minimum fuss.

I remember taking my fishing rod down to the sea, but the tide was full out, leaving the bay vast and inhospitable. Why was I feeling so awkward and out of place? Almost overnight I'd gone from being embarrassed to carry my violin to being embarrassed to carry my fishing rod.

At home, the huge new piece of furniture with the tiny screen would, on occasion, offer up musical delights that would empty the room, except for me. On the contrary, I would fall to my knees and approach the great hissing cupboard in an effort get close to and decipher how it was, Stern, Ricci, Du Pre, Barenboim were producing this magic. The wireless too got put through its paces, whistling tunes it didn't know it knew, as I prized it away from Radio Luxembourg and onto what I guess must have been Radio 3, where I would catch every other bar of something or other as the old box struggled with the technological complexities of these foreign sounds as against the relative simplicity of the Top 20's latest offering. I rarely found out what I'd be listening to, I'd be way too pumped to wait around for a Brahms Symphony to end, instead I'd dash to the music room, grab my violin and start smashing through the latest piece I'd tortured Bridget to buy for me. I would play and dream well into the night. Anyone who could even half play the piano was ruthlessly abused to accompany my fumblings and myself and Brian Bergin ruined as many violin duets as we could lay our hands on.

All this activity would have to take place late at night. Days were taken up with avoiding school, rioting, blowing whistles, chasing girls and keeping up with the antics of T.Rex, Black Sabbath, Lindisfarne and Yes.

My only other trip with the orchestra was to Ayr the following year, a trip that carried somewhat different memories. Compared to the previous year's flight to London the ferry from Larne to Stranraer stirred only the stomach, not the blood and on arrival, Ayr, geographically and architecturally, was way too similar to what we'd just left. We may as well have gone to Bangor. As opposed to all the fun and cider we'd enjoyed in Devon, here we were all confined to campus. This was 1974, and war was raging in NI. News had obviously spread that a bunch of pansy Paddies were moving into the area and some local lads decided it was their chance to create a little entertainment for themselves. Even as we arrived at the gates to the college where the course was to be held, a group of maybe thirty youths had assembled, swathed in Union Jacks, chanting Loyalist songs and throwing all kinds of missiles. Police arrived and the gates were locked but these bored youngsters were tenacious and patrolled the perimeter fence for the whole week shouting obscenities and throwing missiles anytime we came into view. On one occasion it got a bit scary when they actually broke through and attacked us en masse. We were on our way from rehearsal to lunch and I remember I was wearing a black and white Beethoven T-shirt. This, coupled with my Afro hair, no doubt made me stand out somewhat and I could hear them screaming, "Get Beethoven, get Beethoven!!"

We escaped unhurt but we didn't half feel like lepers. I was amazed that even one of those losers recognised the print on my top and decidedly peeved at them taking his name in vain. Had they but known, at least 50 per cent of the people they were attacking were of their own persuasion.

Musically, two things happened of interest. We got a proper conductor. Brydon 'Jack' Thompson came to work with us and yet again one felt the enormous benefit of brushing up against real people. This guy had so much experience at a high level, a flawless technique and the best ear I had ever come across. One day the new leader of the orchestra (AC had not only left me behind, but the orchestra too) had to go to do an interview for local radio or something and I was asked to take over her position. By the end of the rehearsal, Jack said right out in a loud voice, in front of everyone, "You are really good at this, why aren't you leading this orchestra?"

To which I replied; "I don't believe I have the right figure, Mr Thompson."

This admittedly snide comment may have left Jack a tad perplexed but it most certainly struck a chord with my long-suffering colleagues.

This brief moment gave me some much-needed encouragement. In the concert performance in Derry we got lost in the scherzo of Dvorak's 8th Symphony and he just stopped us mid-flow, turned to the audience and said matter-of-factly, "Awfully sorry ladies and gents, we appear to have come adrift. It's notorious this movement, but with your warmth and positive thoughts, we're going to try it again and this time, I just know it will be thrilling!"

I loved that wonderfully commanding, laissez-faire approach. It was such a welcome and healthy attitude to life in the hair-raising front line of live performance.

We didn't get lost second time through.

I had reached a crossroads in my musical life. I was about to turn sixteen, school was a non-event, I had just got my Grade 8 violin and thanks to the orchestral experience, music was taking me over like an unstoppable wave. Meeting John, Jack, Harry and Bobby had given me a taste for something, something tantalisingly abstract. I wasn't sure exactly what it was, but I did know I couldn't find it in Northern Ireland. I don't know if it was the power of thought or what, but something was about to happen, a bolt out of the blue, which would change my life forever.

14

The Early Quartets

Earlier, I sketched you an outline of Kebroyde. Now, if I may, I would like to colour in the reality of this place and those who filled its generous spaces. As you left Derry's city boundary demarked by the old 30mph limit sign, you came upon, on your left side, a line of ten properties. Each house was unique in style and layout, their generous, elevated plots affording them glorious, uninterrupted views across rolling countryside, first down to the river, then on and on to the Sperrins in the distance. Ours was the last in this line of landmark homes. As you entered the stone gates, the sweep of the drive, flanked by rhododendrons, firs and other more exotic trees, skirted a majestic two-tiered lawn interrupted by an enchanting rockery. The scene was decorated with stone paths, Monet arches, huge ornamental flowerpots, a sundial, birdbath, and various shaped rose beds. A summerhouse in the same style as the house sat overlooking all this and the formal gardens that straddled the main house were punctuated at the rear by laurel hedges. Gravelled carriageways encircled the back garden in a long-extended horseshoe. Immediately behind the house was a raised grass tennis court bordered by a high beech hedge. On the right side was a lawned area with espaliered fruit trees along the boundary wall. To the left were a vegetable garden and three kennels. Behind the central beech hedge stood the orchard, crisscrossed by romantic little paths, arches and a central pergola. There was an old-style water pump, which would eventually fall into disrepair and become home to a family of blue tits. This area ended with two sunken brick structures with glazed roofs, used for cultivating soft fruits and the like, the whole section enclosed by another ornamental beech hedge.

Carrying on from the right there was a large greenhouse, grape house, potting shed, three-bed house, barn, hayloft, and finally, two stables. The whole concept was from another era entirely: aimed at a lifestyle vaguely attainable back then, nowadays, pretty much out of sight. Frustratingly, though many photos exist showing the front garden, I have never seen a single shot of that most breath-taking back garden. I remember as a kid someone coming to the door selling aerial shots of houses in our area and my dad turning him away. What I wouldn't give for one of those shots now.

For the most part we, the family, kept that whole garden working and pristine, just as we did the house. Hedges clipped, fruit trees pruned, lawns mowed, paths and rockeries weeded, flowerbeds dug and manured. It was an 'all hands on deck' approach, which I must say, I'm not entirely averse to. All too often these days, kids are given way too easy a ride in respect of their familial duties. Imagine telling your twelve-year-old that he had to get up at 5am, milk two dairy cows, then herd twenty-five bullocks the two miles up to market before walking the usual mile and a half to school; something I had to do regularly.

Over time, my dad took a couple of characteristically odd decisions, in that the precious lawn-tennis court gave way to goalposts, easier to keep, I guess; tennis moving to an all-weather surface, i.e. the forecourt of the house itself, a summer seat taking the place of the net. And on the lawned bit up the right side of the house, he erected fences for the horses and riders to practice jumping.

Every Sunday morning after Mass there was a bit of a ritual whereby the boys would take to the back lawn for a spot of footy while the girls prepared lunch. These games were one-way traffic, in other words, just one net. We were very fortunate in that we had not one but two keen goalkeepers, so that eternal problem was always happily avoided. The kickabout was taken very seriously, half the Man Utd team were represented there on that makeshift pitch and the pressure to perform, mixed with the relentless, feverish, ongoing commentary made the experience thrilling.

So, what was life really like out there in Kebroyde? Well from my perspective, the first thing to realise is that, with the whole hospitalisation process, coupled with more and more of the older ones getting married and moving on, I, the youngest of sixteen, increasingly spent my life with an ever-diminishing set of siblings or even more amazingly, alone.

Rather in the way that the great quartets of Beethoven seem to naturally divide themselves into three distinct periods; early, middle and late, so the Cassidy family seemed to adopt a natural classification. You will be relieved to hear that I will now immediately ditch this patently fanciful analogy given that it already, quite clearly, holds little or no credence, in as much as the late quartets of Beethoven have six Opus numbers whereas the Cassidy elders numbered only four. The middle five quartets correspond to six of us (seven if you include our deceased William). And the glorious six early works have as their counterparts only the four youngest (five if you include Andrew, who disappeared). Besides, I'm already trying to figure out which quartet that means I would correspond to, since one would have to flip Beethoven's output on its head to begin with for it to make any kind of sense (oldest to youngest). You'd then have to dispense with that annoying arrangement, Op.14/1, no bad thing in my opinion, and decide that the Grosse Fuge was the last movement of Op.130, thereby ignoring the last thing he wrote; its inspired replacement Rondo. To conclude all this futile nonsense, I am either Op.18/3 or Op.135. I can live with that!

The Cassidy family was nothing if not horribly predictable in the upholding of all the fine family traditions. Love, laughter, admiration and camaraderie lived happily alongside hatred, anger, jealousy and antagonism. Relationships within the family were complex and often, friendships seemingly forged in steel one minute, could become a rusty, crumbling mess the next. Things never got talked through in my family. No effort was ever made to reach a mutual understanding in troubled times. It was and remains a frighteningly black-and-white situation. This archaic approach to relationships, in which you are the judge and jury, where decisions are taken and acted upon based on your own solitary perception of events, inevitably results in endless division. My mum was the exception to this rule. Though formidable in so many ways, she certainly didn't suffer fools gladly, she was infinitely forgiving. In our defence, there were simply too many to please, think chamber orchestra playing under quartet rules.

The four oldest siblings would have essentially been '50s kids. They would have been blossoming at a time of post-war austerity. Derry was the number one port in the Battle of the Atlantic and of enormous strategic importance. It was no accident that those who drew the border line didn't just use the natural mark made by the River Foyle but instead managed to include within their boundary the massively important asset which was located on Derry's very own West Bank, i.e. the city itself complete with deep water harbour. This is where the German Navy surrendered in 1945 for goodness' sake! One hundred and twenty 'U' boats and their crews brought into Lisahally, not a mile from Kebroyde itself. The humiliated crews were marched off to various PoW camps whilst their Churchillian cigar-shaped vessels of death were taken off to Inishtrahull Sound just a few miles round the coast to the northwest and systematically scuttled in a frenzy of anger and excitement. Quite extraordinary is it not, that no one thought to keep even one of those most notorious of sea-going crafts. Now that could have made a tidy sum for someone; all polished up and positioned where else but opposite the Railway Bar.

I only found out this remarkable piece of recent local history when I chanced upon a BBC programme about Ulster's part in WW2. Though my dad did often talk about the sailors from all over who came into the bar, the bloody fights and general mayhem, never a word was uttered about this mammoth historical moment. Hardly surprising therefore that Derry became a target for Nazi air raids during this time and there was more than one occasion when my dad would bundle his young brood into the Humber and head for the relative safety of the Donegal Hills.

Anyway, as I was saying, this austerity that my elders faced must also have been laced with an infectious sense of happiness and optimism. Dad's business was in its prime and the family had finally settled in an imposing home. It was at this time that my dad was fully indulging his passion for cars. He had not one, but two Armstrong Siddeleys, saloon and sports, both in racing green and several horses (we would always have at least two jumpers in the stables out back). His love of shooting was also enjoyed to the full. Top-of-the-range Webley and Scott shotguns kept a steady stream of pointers, setters and spaniels at the top of their game.

As a boy I would love nothing more than stealing into the girls' bedroom as they prepared for a night out. They would be so happy, getting dolled-up, discussing their prey, singing the current hits and dancing around the room in anticipation of their evening escape; I would curl up in a corner, wide-eyed, open-eared, feeding off all that intoxicating positive energy. In short, the family had eased its way into a slightly different echelon of society, opening up, if only for a brief moment, the relics of a Jane

Austen scene; a veritable potpourri of tea dances, balls, shooting parties and gymkhanas.

On one famous occasion I almost let the cat out of the bag as it were, briefly puncturing this fake middle-class idyll when, aged about seven, I was playing, as I often did, in Dad's majestic Armstrong saloon. I had somehow managed to release the handbrake and before I knew it, the colossal machine had begun to edge forwards, gathering momentum under its own considerable weight and in a heartbeat, had ploughed through bushes and a wire fence, coming to rest on next door's carefully manicured lawn. The adorable Mrs McFarlane, owner of that gorgeous, granite, Georgian home, hearing the commotion, came running down the garden to see if I was OK. She hid any feelings of anger at the mess I'd just made of her beautifully manicured front garden, and I, largely unaware of what had happened, happily took her up on the offer of a glass of lemonade and followed her into the house. The McFarlane household was considerably more civilised than the madhouse next door and the proud mother of two would forever relish telling the story of what happened next. Apparently, as I sat quietly at the kitchen table with my refreshing glass of fizz, I became increasingly perplexed and bemused. Fearing that I was maybe suffering from a bit of shock, she once again asked me if everything was OK. I, not used to such calm serenity, replied; "Och aye, I'm fine thanks. But tell me, where is everyone?"

Already, within this early crop there was a natural selection process at large. Only the chosen few, well two actually, would have access to this glamorous Polaroid of what life could be like. Real life has a nagging way of asserting itself and there certainly was work to be done, abundant work, both at home and in the bar. These places did not look after themselves. I've often pondered what determines this unsavoury favouritism between parents and their children; on the one hand you think, "So and so is just like his dad. Loves horses, boxing and cars," yet by the same token it is often said, "Oh they've never gotten along, too similar, like 'peas in a pod'."

It's a curious phenomenon that sometimes, no matter how hard one child tries to be the model son or daughter, the parent they are so desperate to impress remains indifferent whereas the other child can seem oblivious to such efforts and yet garners delight in said parent. Same rules apply the other way round. The whole equation seems to boil down to chemistry, that most fundamental yet bewildering reaction which can take place between two people causing the heart to flutter or the brow to furrow.

I must say, I do not subscribe to the widely held belief, shamefully endorsed by that sickening parable about the prodigal so and so, that absence makes the heart grow fonder. Enforced absence, absence where the choice has been taken away, maybe; but in instances where people freely choose to spend time away from their loved ones, that I just don't get. Why should the return of one child be celebrated any more than the constancy of another? The child who went away and came back is simply the child who went away and came back, and the child who remained close, the child who remained close. We all have our ways and needs of getting through and all should be treasured equally. To my way of thinking, absence in this scenario merely throws a false light on things, momentarily lending any relationship a glossy patina, which will inevitably fade. Rather like the glorified post-row sex routine. In all honesty, just how many times is that little spurt of confused emotions followed by another row, often more vociferous and depressing than the last. Surely, any dictum putting itself forward as a moral compass would do better to suggest embracing the true picture of your relationships. Encourage one to learn to understand and accept, even love, all the aspects of your chosen few and realise that they will patently have to do the same if the relationship is to stand the test of time and flourish.

15

The Middle Period

Continuing the Ludwig analogy for a moment, much in the way the Middle Period is divided into two sets; the three towering Op.59 Razumovskys and the two slightly later solitary works: Op.74 'Harp' and Op. 95 'Serioso', so our middle brood divide up into 'the secret four', a strongly bonded gang whose exploits became legendary within the family and the two slightly older girls who bridged the gap between middle and late.

These two could not have been more different. Mary was an out-and-out force of nature. An elegant '50s belle, she was always impeccably turned out and loved the high-life. She was the one who, whilst preparing for a night out, would be singing at the top of her lungs and dancing with chairs. She was multi-talented. A consummate horsewoman, she could turn her hand to any number of things, including painting, needlework and baking. The other side to her character was equally happy and able, mucking out stables, herding cows, helping with the lambing, digging flower beds, or pretty much any chore required about the place.

Margaret on the other hand was more of a cuddly little doll. Though every bit as competent in her own way, she was much more geared to home life. She was somehow a carbon copy of Mum and in fact became like a second mum to me. We had a special bond, an unspoken closeness. Though she enjoyed the craic as much as anyone else and could hold a tune with the best of them, she was uncommonly self-effacing and endlessly generous with her time. She was the one who would visit me in hospital. She was the one who would buy clothes for us younger ones out of her own hard-earned cash. If anyone were to brighten up another dreary teatime with a mouth-watering collection of pastries, 'nyimmy-nyims' as she called them, it would be her.

When eventually she started turning up at the house with her husband-to-be, Billy, I would be that infuriating younger sibling who would just stick around, refusing to leave the room when it was clear the courting couple were desperate to be left alone. Billy quite quickly figured out however that I had a bit of a sweet tooth and soon bribes of sweets, chocolates or biscuits would lead to mutual satisfaction. I must have been *so* annoying! Not averse to popping up from behind the sofa at the most inopportune moments squeaking… 'Bicky! Bicky!' (biscuit, biscuit) and not leaving until the deal was done. I find it forever touching that that whining demand was somehow greeted with a certain amount of affection along with the undoubted irritation in that Billy's pet name for Margaret to this day is 'Bicky'.

And so to those Op.59s, or Razumovskys as they are called, though I must concur, the 'Secret Four' does have more of a ring to it. Here's where life at Kebroyde must have started getting almost impossibly complicated. Don't forget, we're now up to ten brats running around the place, and this last lot would be the '60s kids.

Not even the walls surrounding Kebroyde could possibly keep out the fever that was taking hold of the world at that time. If the '50s saw the aftershock of the second Great War, then the '60s witnessed the enormous release of tension. If the '50s was a black-and-white still of prim and proper diplomacy, the '60s was a fast-moving image of carefree abandonment in glorious technicolour: a dizzying, psychedelic riot of optimism buoyed on a magic carpet of music, art and literature. A utopian snapshot of a world that unfortunately couldn't last. A world where the words and sentiments of 'peace, love and understanding' were released from a carefully folded sheet of paper, furtively placed in the inside pocket of a tailored, double-breasted pinstripe, to be written large on tie-dye T-shirts, schoolbooks, placards and banners proudly waved openly on the streets of the world.

Whereas the Earlies and Lates were for the most part quite independent, this little quartet in the middle range of the brood were joined at the hip. Back in those days, my dad and even some of the more cynical elders were vehemently enforcing the rules of Kebroyde whereby family members weren't allowed outside of the walled compound and certainly, no outsiders were allowed in. This feeling of imprisonment led to, on the one hand, extreme boredom, but on the other, a vivid imagination. I would spend hours plodding round the back garden on our poor old knackered pony, Demon, sporting one of Dad's cast-off Trilbys and singing 'Shenandoah' to myself or after a much anticipated episode of *Garrison's Guerrillas*, race to the cutlery drawer and hunt out that special paring knife Uncle Charlie had given my mum before sneaking outside and recreating the entire plot alone. Funny how something so simple as the way in which Brendan Boone (the Chief) despatched his switchblade underarm could inspire such awe.

These were the conditions under which the Secret Four (Joe, Peter, Bernadette and Joan) conducted their operations. As with most gangs, all four contributed in their own way but it was Joe who emerged as the natural leader. He was the ideas man and the others pretty much fell in line. They developed a sign language that enabled them to furtively communicate their next move across a crowded lunch table; vital if they were to slip away and reconvene unnoticed.

Without wanting to simplify their objectives, one of their main goals was to get away from everyone else, above all, Dad. To this end for example, when they were on gardening duty, a common occurrence, they would engineer it so that they were deployed at the same time. Then, whilst two of them weeded, raked or dug, the other two began work on a hugely ambitious project, an underground hut. They started by carefully slicing a sizeable area of sods and placing them to one side on a discarded sheet of corrugated iron. They then proceeded to dig down, depositing the waste soil in the undergrowth outside the back gate. This impressive feat accomplished, the corrugated sheet, complete with sods was re-employed as the perfectly camouflaged roof. Once installed, a makeshift periscope was fashioned from wine boxes and mirrors, a light was run on an extension lead from the potting shed and the *Derry Journal* was recycled as smoking material, essential for that all-important cool factor. How smug they must have felt, kicking back in their subterranean shelter watching those left above them going about their business, oblivious.

Joe was the gentle giant of the family; the classic strong, silent type he was nevertheless a natural comedian, excellent company and a real ladies' man. He was also a consummate sportsman and it was probably this fact that led to the Secret Four's infamous Sports Days; a kind of Family Olympics mostly made up of activities Joe was particularly good at. He devised, ran and dominated proceedings, winning most, if not all events.

Joe excelled at football and though he could play in most positions, his physique and disposition saw him gravitate more and more to the role of goalkeeper. He soon progressed from those Sunday morning kickabouts on the back lawn at Kebroyde to being a key member of what many say was the best ever St Columb's Gaelic Football team. They were virtually unbeatable and won all before them in the early '60s. He then went on to soccer and forged a formidable career playing for many of the best clubs nationally, including Derry City and Glentoran. We watched him play many times with great pride but perhaps most notably when the Glens faced Benfica in the European Cup. Benfica was a world-famous team and a real force to be reckoned with in those days. They had within their ranks a legendary No.10 by the name of Eusébio who on the night of their visit to the Oval, unleashed a free kick with such power, it actually broke the crossbar. Joe of course had it covered! He would even go on to represent his country and have a trial with none other than our beloved Red Devils, Manchester United. Much in the way people say how unlucky Andy Murray was that he found himself in the era of Federer, Djokovich and Nadal, so our Joe was vying with Harry Gregg at United and Pat Jennings in the Northern Ireland goal. Not easy competing with a Busby Babe and arguably one of the greatest of all time. Still, he did remarkably well and when in 1970 he headed off to make a new life in Canada, he played for many years with Toronto Italia. Joe was the sibling I looked up to and not just physically. He just seemed to have it all. He was charming, easy-going, witty and sporty. He had a certain notoriety because of the football, drove a coffee-and-cream Riley Elf and he played the guitar. It was he who taught me all the Beatles songs, a priceless service. Whatever he did, I tried to copy; still haven't forgiven him for giving up sugar! It was a dark day indeed in 1970 when he and his beautiful new wife, Nora, headed west to Toronto and my beloved Margaret and her hubby, Billy, east to Perth, both sets of people on the £5 one-way ticket. A fire blazed in the music room, The Carpenters sang 'The Carnival is Over', we hugged and danced, the tears flowed freely and many lives, mine included, would never be the same again.

16

The Lates

And so we arrive at the Lates. Rose, Clare, Denis, Andrew and me. Remember, at this stage, that in order to shoehorn in my ill-conceived analogy, we must imagine that the Grosse Fuge loses its singular place in the great man's Opus numbers and instead, nestles happily back in its original place as the finale of Op.130.

It's worth mentioning that Bridget and I were not the only members of the family pursuing some sort of a life in music. Joan, one of the Secret Four, took the cello to LTCL standard and went on to be the cello teacher of choice in Derry and its environs. Joan, a stunning Rita Hayworth-style beauty was a soft, gentle soul with an impressively athletic frame. Her appetite for life was matched only by her appetite for food. You did not want to be seated next to Joan at the dinner table, at least not without some serious defence strategies in place. Boys were jibbering wrecks in her presence; our post was delivered regularly, and we often had three deliveries of milk daily from that rather cute but hopelessly forgetful little milkman. Try though he might, Joan had her own ideas on the romantic front and in time, met and fell in love with the irresistibly handsome Tom. A match made in heaven apart from the sinister presence of that most destructive of pastimes, religion. You see, Joan and Tom dug with opposing feet and in those dark, fearful days, this was unthinkable. Thankfully, though goodness knows they were severely tested, their resolve stood firm. Even when, at their wedding, one of the invitees actually stood up in the service and asked Joan if she was sure of what she was doing, the couple graciously ignored this unspeakable affront, took each other's hands and embraced their new life together. Joan blazed a welcome trail in this respect and no fewer than three of her younger siblings would go on to play away from home.

Clare was another one who pursued music. Her exemplary dedication, spending hours of every day after work practising the piano, inspired me enormously at that crucial time when music was taking over my being. She actually got a degree in music but would ultimately follow a different path, utilising her considerable business prowess in the field of fashion.

People always make out that the youngest sibling is the lucky one, the one who gets all the attention. This scenario could not be further from the truth. Coming so far down the line, what could that child do that hadn't been done countless times before? As the youngest, you can never be one of the gang. Regardless of your experiences, they had it rough, you had it handed on a plate. Though loved I'm sure, in some Victorian sense, I had little or no parenting in the conventional sense. Ask yourself, if your twelve-year-old hadn't been to school in weeks, was regularly arriving home from 'school' two or three hours late, stinking of tobacco and covered in filth from rioting; was continually out galavanting till all hours, in a war zone and coming home smelling of booze: would you feel you were fulfilling your role as a parent?

A dear friend recently asked one of my sisters what I was like as a child. Instead of replying, oh he was a happy, warm-hearted, talented little terror, she came up with the stock answer.

"Ah well you see, Paul came along and ruined Denis' life. Up until that moment, Denis had been the apple of everyone's eye, the baby (aged six!), but then Paul arrived, and Denis just got dropped in favour of the new arrival."

So, let me get this straight, none of the others ruined any lives, this privilege was reserved for me. Even though I had allowed him six years of adoration, my timing could not have been worse. I had it in for him from the start. Most of my siblings who carry on this perverse and extremely hurtful myth have their own families. Do they burden their precious offspring with such emotional baggage I wonder?

Anyway, I digress. In that six-year period between Denis and me, there was another birth. Mum endured pregnancy number fifteen, notwithstanding any miscarriages, of which we were aware of three, and made the familiar journey up to the little nursing home on the Northland

Road in the Rosemount area of Derry City. She always maintained that things went absolutely according to plan. The birth was straightforward, a healthy boy bounced out into the world with an unfalteringly raucous cry, and the cord was duly cut.

It was at this precise moment that things took a sinister twist. Instead of the baby being placed in his mother's arms, the bundle of joy was unceremoniously whisked away whereupon a doctor entered the room and gave my mum an injection in the leg, which knocked her out for a full twenty-four hours. Upon waking, my mum was told that the baby had died, the death certificate states death by asphyxiation due to the umbilical cord being wrapped around its neck. At no stage did she ever lay eyes on that son she had carried around for the first nine months of his life. It's a well-known fact, indeed I experienced it myself with my daughter Holly, that a baby with the cord around its neck does not cry until that problem is dealt with.

Throughout our childhoods this incident was never referred to and we were strongly discouraged from talking about it 'for fear you upset your mother'. Extraordinarily, exactly forty years later, after my dad had passed away, Mum became totally fixated on this event. She became agitated and fiercely driven to find out what exactly had happened. This obsession was not short-lived; for the best part of two years, Mum spoke of little else. It was truly humbling to witness this old lady's trauma as she struggled to explain and comprehend what had taken place all those years before and why she and others had just let it happen. It was unbearably upsetting also to realise that she had clearly been struggling with these events for forty years but was unable to vocalise her feelings. Some progress was made in unravelling the mystery but you know, Ireland is a funny place, riddled with fear and superstition; couple this with the terrifying complexities of a big family, where taking the initiative on almost any matter requires either great courage or foolishness, and things can often end in tears. A combination of these two traits resulted in the situation never being satisfactorily resolved. This worrisome incident took place at a time when the Catholic Church was engaged in money-laundering involving babies. Babies born to single mothers, babies born out of wedlock or just simply mistaken or unwanted babies were taken away and sold to more deserving couples. All records altered or destroyed. My dad insists there was a funeral and it is true that in those days, often only the parents would attend such a harrowing event.

Mum was apparently too weak to go, was she so weak she couldn't open her eyes though? She never even saw the body.

Mum always insisted, "your daddy changed." If she said it once, she said it a hundred times. This mysterious, all-encompassing and irrevocable change was always blamed on a certain incident involving one of my siblings. I will not speak of this in these pages because that would only give credence to such a pathetic claim. Somewhat hurtful though this incident may have been at the time, it was not life-changing, it was the sort of circumstance we all have to deal with regularly in our daily lives; which leaves me wondering, was there something more sinister going on in his life. One can only hope that he was not involved in any horrible conspiracy, though it is not beyond the realms of possibility that tremendous social pressure may have been brought to bear upon him in light of them already having fourteen children.

My sister Bridget did pay a visit to the city cemetery and spoke to the gravedigger there who, would you believe, had worked there for forty years and said that there was in fact an unmarked plot where he believed two children had been buried. He promptly took her over to the spot. Subsequently, Bridget and Mary tracked down the midwife who had been on duty that day. Strangely, she lived not a stone's throw from Mum's family home, Drumaweir, and when they arrived at her front door to ask her what had happened that day all those years before, all she had to say was that she did remember the incident clearly but that it would break her confidentiality code to divulge any details. If the baby had died, why wouldn't she just say so, this would hardly contravene any privacy laws. The two girls walked away none the wiser and that particular lead bewilderingly dropped.

One fine evening, on Mum's request, a number of us made our way to that bleak spot overlooking the Bogside, Mum armed with two simple, wooden crosses, each one bearing the name of a life she had borne and lost. We duly marked their resting place and stood around the tiny plot. Flowers were laid there, we all sang some hymns and I played a couple of tunes. Just then, there unfolded a most poignant and magical moment. As I played and we sang 'Nearer My God to Thee', Mum's favourite hymn, we all witnessed a piercing dot of light in the distance, like the brightest of stars shining out from exactly where Kebroyde stood. It remained there, uncannily vibrant for a good few moments before its light faded, extinguished as the sun moved relentlessly west, forcing this enormously emotional day to a close and pushing us all, however reluctantly, towards a new dawn. A new dawn without our two beloved siblings, Liam and Andrew. Mum never mentioned them again.

If you ask me, somewhere out there, there is yet another one of us and I have a bone to pick with him. If he hadn't gone and jumped ship, *he* could have taken the lifelong flak for ruining my big brother's life.

17

Homelife

Truthfully, you can't have so many children and expect any real nurturing or education. It's a dog-eat-dog situation, a survival of the fittest scenario. There wasn't a single book in Kebroyde save the ancient, riveting, leather-bound chronicles on tropical diseases and the like, which came with the undeniably lovely, revolving bookcase my old man picked up in some local auction. TV didn't show up until the late '60s, the radio was frowned upon because it wasted electricity, and the only newspapers that made it through the front door were the impossibly erudite *Derry Journal* and, once a week, the even more enlightening *Belfast Telegraph*. Life was about avoiding confrontation; not worrying Mum and not pissing off Dad. This, I can tell you, was easier said than done. This fear of doing or saying the wrong thing quickly led to a mind-numbing state of inertia and silence. We kids could never be seen to be idle; to this day, I have to be doing at least two things at once. Mum busied herself from morning to night with household chores while Dad hung around the place like a dark cloud, a dark cloud which, being in Ireland as we were, appeared a tad too regularly.

Quite clearly, with these sorts of numbers, there were no family holidays or meals out, heavens above, the older ones used to wait patiently for the clothes parcels to arrive from distant cousins in the States. On the very rare occasion we were forced to eat out, it would only ever be as a last resort and only if there was one or two of us present rather than a 'whole handling' as we would say. It would always be the same scene; Mum would hate the experience and become meek to a ridiculous extreme, making out that every little thing any one of us did was wrong in some way. Obviously deeply uncomfortable and in a heightened state of terror, she would unwillingly give up her coat and hat. Under great duress and with the appearance of a frightened bird, she would pretend to peruse the menu, unable to take her eyes off the staff. Given half a chance, she would have gladly swapped places with them. My dad, on the other hand would milk the situation for all its worth. His embarrassing behaviour, which I loved by the way, would start at the door.

"You don't have a record of my reservation? [he hadn't made one]. Well, I sincerely hope my usual table is available [first time in the place]."

He would then flirt outrageously with the waitress long before we'd get to the order; "I'll start with a generous double of your finest Irish whiskey, with just a dash of chilled still water, slice of lime… you do have lime? No, oh well I guess lemon will have to do. Put that in a nice chunky crystal tumbler will you, please. Before you disappear, may I just check a couple of things from the menu today; the mussels are from Mulroy Bay I take it? The salmon is of the wild Atlantic variety I presume, not one of those farmed blighters? Was the pheasant shot locally? How long has it been hanging? I'd like my steak medium rare, verging on the rare side but nicely charred on the outside, you think you can manage that?"

Mum, by this stage would have paled into insignificance, mortified by the display that had all been put on for her benefit. Amazingly, Dad was able to do all this without upsetting anyone other than her. This was way before PC took over our lives and his show was performed in a naive spirit of good nature. Everything on the table had to be finished; this included the salt, pepper, milk, sugar and butter. This mortifying approach to dining out was borderline serious but in fairness, always carried out with more than a hint of self-awareness and humour. At least, I cling on to this hope when I recall the thud of his Grensons as he dropped them over the bannister on a Sunday morning to be cleaned.

It was always the same deal, absolutely no build-up or warning. You'd be pfaffing around, getting on with your day when Dad would suddenly appear.

"Would you like to go to the races?" he'd whisper, out of the blue.

This meant, we're going to the races. Problem was, this meant, now! Great for anyone who had any interest in standing around freezing in the company of horses, while he got a skinful and had fun, placing bet after bet. I didn't mind the inevitably long drive, on the contrary, that was the exciting bit, sitting there, looking out the window, daydreaming. It's when you arrive and he drives straight up to the owners' enclosure, somehow blags his way in, then while he's busy distracting the guy on the turnstile, you have to have gotten yourself under or over the fence, otherwise you spent the day in the car. He was not paying the entry fee. Whilst it was embarrassing, I couldn't help finding it also kind of intrepid; in many ways, it was my helping of adventure for the day.

What's worrying is that I find the same trait appearing in myself. If you want to get into something that's sold out, have arrived late at a restaurant and they're telling you the kitchen's closed, are desperate for a cup of tea on a remote beach, I'm your man. I seem to be able to make the unlikely a reality.

I recently got tickets to a Boxing Day game between Sunderland and Man Utd and invited my brother-in-law, Tony, a fellow Red. As we approached the Stadium of Light, he kept saying we should probably park. Look, there's a space or that side road looks promising. Instead, I found myself unable to control my actions as I completely ignored all his clever suggestions and continued edging through the crowds, talking my way past the police cordon by saying we were guests of the board, and finally parking right outside the front entrance next to Roy Keane's (the then manager) Range Rover. It's something I'm good at, call it charm or bullshit, and I owe it all to my dad.

Back to the feeding of the masses, the more regular method involved the use of the double-barrel. A constant supply of game was provided but never dealt with. Dad and some of the older boys would happily go out shooting but that's as far as it went, the carcasses were hung in the back pantry until they were ready to be prepared by us lowlifes. There were frequent visits to the wholesalers, Sterritt and Henrys, where everything came in huge containers, buckets of jam, chests of tea, vats of butter. On the way home, we'd stop off at Hunter's Bakery, Dad would reverse the car up to the doorway, open the boot, and we would literally throw the loaves from the counter, through the open door into that seemingly bottomless pit.

Birthdays and Christmases were completely ignored but for the fact that the poor old turkey still got it in the neck. I remember one notable exception, however. It was the year I got out of hospital, I came down on

Christmas morning to find, to my utter astonishment and delight, a bright red pedal car parked in the middle of the kitchen floor. It was a simple mechanism made out of tin, but to me, it was heaven on wheels. This turned out to be money well spent, I don't think I bothered my parents for most of the next year, all I did was hurtle around in my mean machine. You can imagine my devastation when I came down one morning in the following November to find that someone had stolen my precious chariot from the front garden where I had parked it, as usual, next to my dad's inferior Armstrong. I was distraught and totally inconsolable. I passed a thoroughly miserable month till it was once again time for the jolly red giant to hitch up his deer and perform his most impressive annual task; I mean, talk about loaves and fishes... I reckon this guy drew the short straw. This feat was rendered all the more extraordinary in that, firstly, Kebroyde wasn't even on his itinerary, and secondly, how was he to know what the child who lived there yearned for more than anything else in the world. Be that as it may, all I can tell you is that the sulky boy who opened the kitchen door that morning was confronted by the only miracle that would have fully restored his normally upbeat disposition. There, in exactly the same spot as before, was an identical pedal car, only this time, in classic, racing green. Green, what did I care. Overjoyed, I jumped in and disappeared for the best part of another year.

I was in my early thirties when one day Mum nonchalantly told me that the whole thing was a conspiracy. They realised they had struck gold with this little car. I loved it so much that they decided to take it away, let me suffer for a month or so, and then reintroduce it as a brand-new model, in a very flattering green. Even by Kebroyde standards, I find this pretty reprehensible behaviour. I mean, we were used to getting nothing. That car was an admirable gesture, a lovely way of signalling a new start after all that hospital business, but to then take that away and watch me mope around all day and cry myself to sleep at night, for what? To buy another year's childcare? I would probably have continued to enjoy it for that long anyway and missed out on the purposefully inflicted trauma.

Mum was a painfully shy, saintly sort of a character, her level of self-worth didn't even make it onto the scale, but she was impossible to impress and equally impossible to please. Other than a good cowboy film, or a 99 from Fiorentini's, all efforts fell short of her exacting standards. Things society normally viewed as achievements were ignored in favour of what one might term the mundane. Winning was irrelevant in that she would immediately feel sorry for the loser, nay chastise you for even wanting to win. She was consumed with fear and almost embarrassingly self-deprecating.

If, for example, I was telling a joke about someone with a stammer or a hunchback or something, she would immediately get visibly nervous and interrupt me saying; "Paul, stop that, or you'll end up like that yourself!"

She slaved away from morning till night, monk-like in her demeanour; one always felt she was a uniquely pure soul from another time. These people who go off looking for themselves in far-flung places could have learnt a lot from her; I have never known anyone less materialistic than Celia.

"You'll have as much as'ill do you," was her take on money. She plucked that evil root, laid it bare and sneered at its exposed powerlessness. This is a mantra for which I am eternally grateful. I am not so foolish or fickle as to suggest that money has no worth. It's nice to be warm and clean and we all have to eat, but to have it as your goal in life is surely misguided and ultimately, a vacuous endeavour. Thanks to Mum, I have an impressive capacity for existing on very little and no fear of being without. Curiously, though I know she loved me, she never once hugged or kissed me in her entire life. I would hug and kiss her, but she would remain passive, made limp by a world she didn't understand and a life that robbed her of her worth.

Dad, on the other hand, was an innately gregarious rogue whose natural tendencies were suppressed by circumstance; circumstance he had brought upon himself of course. Though he liked to socialise and possessed an effortless charm, we never ever had people round our gaffe. I do not remember a single time when someone outside the close family came for dinner, or anything else for that matter. In the early days of their marriage however, things must have been rather different, if the famous quote from Dad's father to my mum is to be believed;

"Close your door missus, they're making a doormat outta'ye!"

By all accounts, Granddad was a sensitive soul and this statement about his own sons certainly shows an awareness of Mum's kindness and their penchant for taking advantage. Dad was the so-called successful one in his family, with his thriving business, big house and fancy car, and his brothers were not averse to hanging around, on the lookout for whatever slim pickin's might come their way.

Indoctrinated by an allegedly detestable mother, whom I also never met, Dad trusted no one, least of all his own children. In the '60s, when he was getting weary and unable to keep up with social changes and how they impacted on the pub business, one or two of the sons suggested he should relax a bit and let them take over the everyday running of the premises. His infamous retort was; "If I can't run it, no one will."

In many ways, my parents could have enjoyed a golden old age. There were enough of us who loved them and would have done anything to make them comfortable and happy, but that's the stuff of dreams. That's not how big families work. Fear, mistrust, competition and endless comparison are highly corrosive and combustible materials. Instead, Dad stubbornly ran the pub into the ground and sent said sons packing. In fairness, he sent most of us packing. There was an unspoken yet very real consequence, that when you reached the tender age of sixteen, your days were numbered at Kebroyde.

Strange how these people so revered the priests, the doctors, the teachers, yet never once considered that any one of us could easily have become one of those. Oh no, those positions were unattainable by the likes of us. Keeping up with the Joneses and a terror of doing the wrong thing paralysed the whole society, and yet he, in his own way, had achieved so much in that small community. Fear and lack of trust, yet again, were his downfall. Had he but opened his arms and embraced the goodwill of those around him, all could have been so different, instead he poured scorn on most of the in-laws, choosing on several occasions not to attend the weddings of his own children. Some, who had overstepped the mark entirely, were no longer welcome at home either. At least here, Mum stood firm in her resolve that she would never shut out any of her children. This resulted in my daily life being punctuated by lonely rings on the doorbell, whereupon my heart would sink. A sense of fear and doom would rise within me, Dad would fake sleep on the armchair and Mum would answer the poor soul, left only half-wanted on the doorstep. He or she would enter and leave without their father saying a single word.

Why did we all stand by and let him get away with such despicable behaviour? I take some comfort from the fact that I was still only a lad but frankly, some soul-searching needs to be done, responsibility taken and apologies made. Fights were commonplace, sometimes fisticuffs but more often than not just horrible, silent standoffs that could go on for weeks. I remember vividly, after one particularly violent encounter between my dad and one of my brothers, in which the double-barrel was employed where words failed, Mum donning her coat and hat and leaving home. I watched, imprisoned in that hellhole by my plaster of Paris and my dad. I was never allowed to forget that my mother's reappearance some days later was only because she had to look after me. She would have finally escaped this beast, if it hadn't been for me. Another life I had unwittingly managed to ruin, and me only six years old too!!

Children are resilient… so say the adults of this world. The poor wee souls don't exactly have a choice now do they. They simply have to accept their lot and get on with it as best they can, inevitably picking up unwanted baggage with which they will in turn burden their children. And so it goes on. Most of my father's appalling behaviour could be explained and understood on some base level, but one or two things pushed even the most forgiving of minds to the brink and indeed, over the edge. Selling the site of the Railway Bar after forty years without consulting his wife was stooping pretty low but quietly selling their own back garden from the dining room, again without so much as a word to his devoted spouse, really was scraping the barrel. He would continue to bewilder and disappoint from beyond the grave, but that's another story.

Having sacrificed music at O Level in order to carry on with art, the plan was to then drop art and take music at A Level. A substantial proportion of this exam is taken up with the 'set works' which have to be studied thoroughly. For mere mortals this entails listening to the pieces in order to better understand them. Given that there was no mechanism for listening to recorded sound in Kebroyde, Bridget asked my dad whether, if she arranged for the school to put the works on tape for me, he would be prepared to buy even the most basic cassette player so that I could listen to them. He refused. It was shockingly plain to see that his interest in my education didn't even stretch to the couple of quid required for such a device.

In short, I had no shortage of reasons for wanting to get away from that place and when on the eve of my sixteenth birthday, I found my beloved best friend Bonzo lying dead in the summer house, I had one less good reason for sticking around. Bonzo was a glorious mix between a black Labrador and a springer spaniel. He was cleverer than most of the people I'd met up to that point and infinitely more loving. He never left my side and was a constant joy for the ten years we spent together. I was devastated but got little or no sympathy for losing my best friend.

Though I had wonderful mates in Russell and Brendan, a special girlfriend in Deirdre McCaul and an angel in Mum, my life was going nowhere. The despair surrounding dear Bonzo's demise only served to strengthen my resolve to escape and accelerate its employment.

18

Daily life

Those halcyon days of playing with catapults and bows were firmly behind us, far too dangerous. Even going fishing, one had to be extremely vigilant. If you appeared from a ditch or a hidden gateway as a foot patrol was going past, those guys shot first and asked questions later. This led to us having to spend more of those interminably dull days when we should have been in school, in more urban areas for fear of being caught out in the open as it were. One such day, Brendan and I found ourselves holed up for warmth in the stairwell of a small block of flats at the edge of Shantallow, when the door burst open and in came a masked man carrying an Armalite. He was up-to-high-doh, breathing heavily and fidgeting manically. He went mad when he saw us in there and screamed at us to get under the concrete stairway; he would not let us leave. He opened a window that looked out across open countryside towards the neighbouring housing estate, Carnhill, and took up his firing position. Brendan and I were terrified, yet curiously did not huddle together for comfort. Instead, shock had prepared for us, individual isolation units in which various horrifying scenes of what was about to happen were played in fast forward and at full volume, rendering us silent and frozen. Within moments, an army patrol came into view in the distance and our lone ranger began shooting. The noise of the shots in that cavernous acoustic was ear-splitting and shocking enough but when bullets started coming back, ricocheting off walls and shattering windows, we really thought this was it. We were going to die right here with this guy. Then, just as suddenly as he'd entered our lives, he turned, dashed back out the door he'd come in and threw himself into the back seat of a car that had screeched to a halt on the pavement outside. The car sped off and all we could hear was the army, screaming orders from afar and mothers and children wailing with fright in the nearby homes. Brendan and I still felt trapped; if we so much as moved, the army guys who were still in position might see us and start shooting again. We sat tight, riveted to the spot until the Land Rovers moved off whereupon we grabbed our chance and made our getaway before that stairwell became a crime scene.

In our everyday Fianna gatherings, we could sense they were upping the ante. There was talk of training camps and the like. More and more friends were getting lifted in army raids, never to be seen again; or getting killed in action. Things were becoming horribly real and I was closing in on my sixteenth birthday. Panic set in.

Every single day there were fierce riots with an ever-increasing number of casualties and though I only ever got hit with one rubber bullet, the army had recently brought in new plastic bullets and on the first night of their employment, a friend of ours had been hit in the head with one and subsequently died.

The local supermarket, Superfare, had been bombed more than thirty times over the years. An insignificant little place, it seemed to me a remarkably mindless activity unless it was some sort of training sortie. One day, a local lad was sent off on an ill-fated trip to that glorified corner shop. Halfway there, he found his path blocked by an army spot check forcing him to retrace his steps and go the long way round to his destination. This would have been little more than an annoyance had it not been for the fact that this was a warm summer's day causing the gelignite in his backpack to sweat and prematurely explode blowing the young man to smithereens fifty yards short of his target. Incredibly, no one else got hurt but that kid's visit to the shop should have been for groceries not martyrdom.

And so, the fear intensified, the claustrophobic feeling of being trapped in an ever diminishing, ever more dangerous environment made life intolerable. We were picked up and thrown into cells where we would be beaten, interrogated and generally scared out of our wits. Often, late at night, an army patrol would corner you, throw you in the back of a Saracen and drive off. You'd be in that confined space with a couple of soldiers who would intimidate you mercilessly; roaring and shouting they would put guns to your head threatening the unimaginable. They liked to show you photos of your friends saying that they had just picked this one up, leaving him in such and such a place with a bullet in his back. They knew everything about you and therefore just what to say to scare you. After some time driving around, when they'd had their fun, they would open the back door and kick you out, usually on a remote, disapproved border road, miles from home.

One Monday morning in the summer of '75, I was making my way to school, over the back field and down through Shantallow and Carnhill to the dreaded building on the Buncrana Road. The night before there had been a particularly fierce riot, starting in the early evening and going on into the night but that could not explain the unreal and eerie quiet I encountered in the estate that morning. The extensive, open playing area next to the flimsy community centre where the rioting usually took place was knee-deep in glass, stones and other debris. Lone dogs wandered about as usual, yet there wasn't a soul to be seen. Sparrows chattered, crows cawed, but not a vehicle moved. It was so weird, I consulted my trusty dark-blue Timex thinking I'd somehow arisen and left home at too early an hour, but no, everything was as it should be, timewise. Only as I neared the gates to Coulterditz did I finally encounter some life in human form. I immediately began to enquire as to what in heaven's name had happened, why was Shantallow a wasteland? Most of the other students also had no idea as to what had gone on and in the end it fell to the teacher of my first class to inform us that, early that morning, twenty-two lads between the ages of fifteen and eighteen had been lifted in a highly organised dawn raid.

Twenty-two boys suddenly disappearing from a small community like that is seriously shocking. I knew every single one of those kids, most of them I would never set eyes on again. Seven of them got life sentences, the others receiving eight, ten, twelve years each. All the younger ones were fellow Fianna members. Of course, we all knew that the British Army intelligence was far reaching but even by their lofty standards, this was uncanny. Word on the street was that one of the lads who'd been picked up the night before had foolishly kept a diary in which he had carefully detailed the names and ranks of all his mates in the IRA. He was a kid you see, hadn't even the awareness to realise that this was no game. In a bizarre quirk of fate, my name was not in that book and nor was Brendan's because we, on account of where we lived, i.e. outside the real trouble spots, were given the lamentable, embarrassing, ludicrous rank of IOs; Information Officers. We were deemed to have the desired distance yet insider knowledge to be able to keep a considered eye on things and report anything unusual to the appropriate authorities. What a joke. In all our time we never once reported anything other than who was going out with who, or who had fags to tap. As is so often the case, it's on whimsical details such as this that lives are lost or saved. Not knowing this crucial fact at the time, myself and Brendan, in a state of absolute panic, headed for the hills or rather, the small town of Moville.

Moville is on the mouth of the Foyle about twenty miles north of Derry, across the border. Much as I disliked the place, it wasn't far, and I knew it well. I told my parents that I was invited on an extended holiday with Brendan's family and off I went. We thumbed a lift and set about trying to survive in our adopted home. We quickly made friends who helped us with food; we literally begged on the street corner and slept in the Lough Swilly buses that would park up overnight in the town square.

Life had become surreal. It certainly wasn't choice that had brought these two kids to this perilous dead-end, rather a set of circumstances too complicated for ones so young to rationalise. Life can cut you adrift. Caught in the wrong place at the wrong time, and with no one around to nurture or advise me, I was flailing around, drowning in a quicksand of consequence. Which ladder would see me clear of this pit of vipers, which hitherto hidden path could I take that would offer an escape to a higher plane? That place I had glimpsed, in Omagh of all places.

After some weeks, we heard through the grapevine that the story of the infamous diary was indeed true but learnt that our names were not in it. We gingerly made our way home. My lifestyle changed from that moment on. I stayed in evenings, other than meeting up with Deirdre, always away from the danger spots. I walked to school the long way round and practised the violin endlessly. I turned sixteen that September, this was the moment of no return and I lived in constant fear that one day that creep in the cheap suit would come knocking, reminding me of my pledge and handing me something other than a whistle. It was during this same month that my sister Rose would arrive home on what was to be, for me, a fateful and life-changing visit. She would bear news of a potential saviour in a far-off land. Though hardly a wise man, and bearing no gifts, my escape plan was in place and I set my sights firmly on visiting that gentleman the following Easter.

19

London

My sister Bernadette had gone to London to pursue a career in nursing. Starting out at Charing Cross in the late '60s, by 1975 she had become a peripatetic, private nurse. This meant she would visit mostly old people who were recovering from one ailment or another but able to convalesce at home. In the spring of that year she was assigned to an all-too-typical case. An elderly lady in South Kensington had fallen over and broken her hip, or should I say, an elderly lady's hip had broken, and she had fallen over. In any case, Bernie cycled off to No.38, Princes Gate Mews and into the lives of the Burn family.

Mrs Marjorie Burn was a quirky little aristocratic, bird-like creature in her eighties. Her customary cardi had more holes in it than material and the foundation and powder, applied around her spectacles, was slapped on with the sort of careless disdain that would have made a Celtic Tiger plasterer proud. She spoke with a veritable punnet of perfectly plump, purple plums in her mouth and sported an ever-present cigarillo, which she balanced masterfully, Andy Capp-style, irrespective of what she might be doing. We used to place bets on when the ash might fall. It was a constant source of fun as she performed her daily chores, of which answering the phone was arguably the most entertaining. She would invariably say hello and rhyme off the telephone number long before she'd actually got the receiver to her mouth. Something in the design of the contraption meant that she then almost always got the speaking bit and the listening bit the wrong way round. Upon realising this, she would get in a frightful tangle and the phone would come crashing to the ground. She would quite calmly ignore all this hullabaloo but for a series of swear words, reposition the receiver, this time correctly, repeat the hello, followed by the number and then wonder why there was no one on the other end of the line.

Like all her patients, Marjorie soon grew very fond of Bernie and would look forward to her daily visits. One day, Bernie asked her why she had a grand piano, pride of place in the front room. Did she play?

"Oh no, that's my son John. He's a wonderful pianist/composer and the Registrar of the London College of Music," said Marjorie proudly.

"Really," said Bernie. "I have a little brother who's crazy about music. He plays the violin and I believe he would like to pursue it as a career."

"Oh but my dear, he simply must meet John. Do you think he'd like to?"

"Well I'm sure he would jump at the idea," said Bernie, enthusiastically.

"Let me know when the boy can make the trip and I'll speak to John," Marjorie concluded.

This whole story was related to me by another sister, Rose. Rose had followed in Bernie's footsteps by taking her RSN diplomas at Charing Cross but then decided to branch out a bit, career-wise. She was at that time an IFD for that pioneer of modern aviation travel, Freddie Laker. This was the man who paved the way for Branson, Stelios and O'Leary... cue fanfare! To an impressionable teenager from Derry, Rose was impossibly exotic. This was a woman who flitted between London, NY and LA, shopped in Carnaby Street and the Kings Road and was recognised at London's top night spots. I would eagerly await her visits home and waltz around in her perfumed wake enraptured by tales of a life I could only dream about.

John Burn, someone I'd never laid eyes on, was about to make that dream more of a reality. My plan was clear. It was September; I had just turned sixteen. There were auditions in the spring for the London College of Music. If I found odd jobs and saved every penny, I could probably make my way to London during the following Easter holidays. Rose said I could stay with her, and Bernie went about arranging a time for me to meet John.

Those months went by so quickly, yet the minutes were interminable. My thoughts were razor sharp, reality confused. I existed in a rarefied zone trying to sidestep everyday life and practising long hours into the night. When the time came, I told only Mum of my plan. School, my friends and family thought I was off to the big smoke for an Easter break, I on the other hand had booked a one-way ticket. Gosh, those were difficult days. In light of the situation back home, I knew I wasn't going to be returning there anytime soon. The drive into London from the airport felt a lot like that drive home from hospital with your first bairn; all familiar yet entirely alien. The feeling when you close the door to your new digs, similar to when you arrive home with your baby and realise that this is it. You, the parents, are alone and totally responsible for this life you have created. In the other scenario, it's not a life that you've helped to create but your very own life that you're suddenly alone in and responsible for. People are all around, you eat and drink, day turns to night, yet nothing is the same. You need something, *you* go and get it; you're hungry, *you* prepare something. Only time can provide that longed-for familiarity, the hitherto unacknowledged security of your parents just being there. Regardless of your relationship with them, that comfort blanket has been taken away.

My mum's words in that first phone call home; "I went into your room this morning to make your bed and you weren't there. It's not the same here without you."

Those words will stay with me to the grave. Though she'd had many, I was her last. I was leaving the nest empty. She was so brave to not only let me go but to encourage that flight in the positive manner that she did.

There was another horrid phone call. Brendan called me one day after work, it was only my second week away and I was finding the experience challenging to say the least. During the course of our chat he mentioned Deirdre. This was a particularly difficult topic for me, we had been together for nearly two years and I missed her terribly.

In a fit of teenage bravado and trying my best not to cry, I said something flippant and not true, "Aw, I wish she'd back off and leave me alone. She keeps writing and phoning…"

A deafening silence ensued.

Deirdre had been listening in on the call. She was about to surprise me with what would have been a most welcome hello. Instead, she overheard my clumsy attempt at just getting through another hellish day. It must have been horribly hurtful but there was nothing I could say to retract my cheap words. They put the phone down; I was a wreck. It was some years before Deirdre and I spoke again. It was not a fun moment and certainly not how I would have liked our wonderful time together to come to a close but in truth, it probably helped us deal with the situation. I'm happy to report that Deirdre eventually forgave me, and we are close friends to this day.

It turned out that Rose no longer lived in her flat. She had moved in with her boyfriend so instead, my brother Denis was occupying it. I would be living with him, not her. The tiny one-bedroom flat was the top floor of a Victorian terrace in Shepherd's Bush. It was as basic as you can imagine and presented one of two new odours in my life. Gas. In Ireland, everything was oil or electric. This new gas smell signalled a new life in every sense. Garlic was the other new nasal-assailant. What was this seductive smell that seemed to be on the breath of this new breed of women I was beginning to meet? I know vampires are a weird bunch but truthfully, what was the problem with this stuff, get over it will ya!

I very gradually began to get out and about. My first sighting of a catholic priest on foreign soil was a heartwarming experience. There was I, ambling along Oxford St. nodding and saying, " 'bout ye, hi," to every passerby and thinking to myself how rude these Brits were, not replying, when I spotted him coming towards me. I honestly stood there aghast as this insignificant being, dressed like a down-at-heel version of one of those smug disciples of old, scurried past me. Eyes down, visibly twitching, he disappeared into the jaws of Oxford St. tube station, exhibiting the pitiful characteristics of the second-rate, life insurance salesman that he was. This was an encouraging sign that I was moving in the right direction, even if my fellow pedestrians seemed to lack a certain degree of common courtesy.

Rose took me all the way across town to meet her man, a giant West Indian bass player called Eddie. To say I felt somewhat out of my comfort zone was an understatement. The closest I'd come to anyone like this in my short life was on the sleeve of an LP. Eddie looked different, sounded different, even smelt different. He dressed like Jimi bloomin' Hendrix and next to his larger-than-life persona, I shrank into insignificance. Breaking the silence, he asked me how I was enjoying my new life in swinging London.

In my mortified state, all I could think to say was; "Well, it's fine except no one can understand me. Coming from Derry, I just speak too fast so I'm constantly having to sloow doownn my speeeech."

"Tell you what kid, take a toke on this. 'At'll slow ye down a bit!" he said handing me something that resembled a 'secret four' special. I managed to avoid taking the toke because Eddie was by now spinning around in hysterics, his beaded dreadlocks creating a veritable merry-go-round scene. At the time, I couldn't understand what could possibly be so funny about what just happened but in time, I'd figure it out.

Though I was extremely lucky to have this flat to come to, it was clearly not ideal, and I would have to go about finding a place of my own. My meeting with Mr Burn wasn't for a couple of days, so I thought I may as well concentrate on preparing for that before trying to find some employment. I couldn't waste too much time though. All my savings had gone on buying the airline ticket and my dad's generous gift of a fiver as I left wasn't going to go very far. Fast-dwindling resources and the unpopularity of horsehair on catgut with the neighbours meant that that audition couldn't come soon enough.

On the appointed day, I jumped on the No.49 bus and met Bernie outside the Royal Albert Hall. Though I was feeling alone and afraid, the sight of such an outstandingly beautiful building, flanked by those majestic crescent-shaped apartment buildings, bordering the park and overlooked by Albert's Memorial helped strengthen my resolve to follow this challenging path I had chosen.

Unlike Rose and Bernie, who were full of encouragement, Denis just wanted me to fight the battle with our dad that he hadn't had the nerve to fight. He was adamant that I should go home and finish my education. That's all very well in normal circumstances, but things in Derry were anything but normal. I was vulnerable and needed support to resist the lure of giving up. The outcome of the next hour or so would hopefully answer some questions and clarify the situation.

Bernie and I walked down Exhibition Road and turned left into that quaint and charming former stable block, Princes Gate Mews. Tarmac gave way to cobbles as we wound our way towards No.38. These were not grand houses but given their location, hugely sought-after. The Burn household had been arranged as follows: front door opening onto a generous open plan space with grand piano, seating area and endless floor-to-ceiling shelves containing books and LPs. A door on the immediate left took one to the small garage beyond which was a tiny, dark study with just enough room for a sofa, coffee table, desk and upright piano. A spiral staircase from the main room arrived at the first floor which consisted of a bedroom to the front, doll's house dining room, galley kitchen, bathroom and box-room, then continued up to a further bedroom, like a ship's cabin with roof terrace.

The feline creature who opened the door to us, and I, could hardly have been more different. Our countries at war, he a besuited, ex-public-school, establishment figure with an ostentatious, bejewelled signet ring which I imagined to be an Agatha Christie-style pillbox, housing capsules for every occasion. I, an anti-establishment misfit in DMs, parallels hanging mid-calf and a Wrangler jacket, sporting little more than Timex's cheap and cheerful and half a box of Anadin.

Despite the odds being heavily stacked against us, we instantly clicked. Of course, our mutual love of music threw us a lifeline, but this went beyond that, we just seemed to gel. I was nervous as hell and felt utterly unable to do what I'd come all this way to do. My chaotic state of mind was focused considerably when John said he would accompany me on the piano. This alleviated what is a strange and uncomfortable situation at the best of times, that of playing only the solo part of a sonata or concerto.

Having played for twenty minutes or so, John got to his feet and said: "OK, I think I've heard enough. Now let's hear what you can do on the piano."

"But I don't play the piano, Mr Burn," said I.

"Oh, so what is your second instrument then, guitar?"

"I only play the violin."

"You do realise that to get into music college you have to have a second instrument."

This was a bit of a bombshell to put it mildly.

"I tell you what, let's do some ear-tests instead," said John, in an effort to keep the scene alive.

I was reeling from the devastating news I'd just heard but somehow managed to get through this next ordeal relatively unscathed.

"OK Paul, let's sit down. You show undoubtable promise as a musician. You've got an excellent ear and your violin playing holds great potential. What should we do about the second instrument issue? Given the facts, what instrument would you choose to learn?" asked John.

"I suppose I'd go for the piano," I replied, trying to put a brave face on things.

To cut a long story short, I immediately started piano lessons with John. Within a fortnight he had found me a delightful violin teacher from the LCM called Peter Turton and six weeks later I moved into the box room on the first floor. It was only big enough to house a single bed and I was living in a house with two ancients, but the rent was reasonable, and it felt great. I had my own place and thanks to John my education began in earnest.

I was already in my third job by this point, at the Fidelity Radio Factory up in North Acton. This meant leaving South Kensington every morning at 6am and getting two buses. I'd get home around 6pm, practise the violin before dinner, the piano after, and then sit with John till all hours, either playing through repertoire together or listening to his vast LP collection. There was little sleep to be had, but I had some catching up to do.

20

RCM

All this relentless hard work must have paid off because one day, less than a year later, John took me aside and said, "Good news Paul, we've got you an audition on the seventeenth of February."

"Oh, but I thought my audition was the twelfth. I've asked for that day off work," I replied.

"That's your LCM audition. I'm talking about your audition for the Royal College of Music," beamed John. "The College is where you belong, Paul."

This news came as such a shock to me. I had never even dreamed of trying to get into the College. My feelings of excitement and trepidation were overwhelming. Despite this sudden, added pressure and with only two months to go till my big day, something crazy happened. I started taking seriously my recent, inexplicable attraction to the, dare I say it… viola. Funnily enough, there had been an old viola back in Kebroyde, languishing in a dark corner, almost out of reach, beneath the piano. I had, on occasion, fished it out and drawn a bow across its three strings. I couldn't pretend there wasn't something seductive about that darker, chocolatey timbre, something beguiling about the voluptuous curves of its more generous body. I know not why these adulterous feelings should trouble my conscience at this time, but they were sufficiently strong and persistent for me to have to address and ultimately, act upon them. So taken was I with this notion that in my very next violin lesson with Peter, I plucked up the courage and told him of my evil thoughts. Peter, being the wonderful man that he was, saw immediately the positives in this potential situation. He said he thought it could be an excellent idea and enthused about how I had the physique and sensitivity to be a great viola player, and assured me that he would have a viola for me to borrow in time for our next lesson. He was true to his word, it was love at first sight and with six weeks to go till my audition, I took up the viola.

Together, Peter and I perused the syllabus and chose some unknown repertoire that I would now have to make my own. One of the works we chose was a mundane load of predictability known as the Handel/ Casadesus Concerto (probably something in the name got me!). I was loving this new sound world I had embraced but as anyone who has been there will tell you, learning to read a new clef on a new instrument is one thing, but a new clef on what at least feels like the same instrument can be testing. My way of getting over this problem in the short term was to learn my audition pieces from memory. It impressed Peter no end when, at the next lesson, I stood there in front of him, moved the music stand to one side and let rip. Dear Peter let me saw my way through the entire first movement before pointing out, with characteristic diplomacy, that I had learnt whole, random sections in the wrong key. Those early stabs at the Alto Clef turned out to be suspect, and without the aid of the piano accompaniment, I hadn't even realised that I had periodically strayed by a minor third. As if time wasn't in short enough supply, I now had to go back, undo and relearn whole swathes of this nonsense.

 Nerves are unpredictable little blighters. There are the blatant ones that taunt you mercilessly; they're the ones that feed the gremlins that hang out just under the surface of your mind, the ones that take pleasure in convincing you that you're a no-good imposter. Then there are the sneaky ones, the ones that lurk in a darker place; they can disturb you to such an extent that your brain, arms and fingers become sausages and cauliflower drowned in a Jack cheese sauce. These guys make you doubt every note just as you're about to play it. On the day of my audition, they all came out to play. Nerves, by the way, are not only the scourge of the inadequate; they say Casals felt sick before every performance, but they can ruin performances and, as such, one has to learn how to control them.

 Entering an imposing Victorian building, meeting your accompanist for the first time and being called into a soulless room where a few people sit po-faced behind a desk, sipping tea, is not necessarily conducive to giving the most convincing account of yourself, musically. At the precise moment my new accomplice sounded the A, a motor car blared its horn so loudly and angrily that it completely obliterated the 440 vibrations. Perhaps it was the palpable tension within the four walls of that sanitised space but, whatever the reason, that moment took on a hilarity beyond its comedic content and all of us roared with laughter. I will be forever grateful to that passing, raging road user for his momentary musical contribution, which so comprehensively broke the ice for me.

If the viola felt a tad unfamiliar under these stressful conditions, imagine what the piano felt like. I had never played the piano to anyone other than John, yet somehow, I managed some kind of an account of a Bach Prelude and Fugue and a Beethoven slow movement. Whatever went on in that room that day seemed to work. Not only did I get accepted to the RCM but Michael Gough-Matthews, the then Registrar, seeing my distress at the thought of six more months in that mindless job, broke with protocol and allowed me to begin my studies a term early. Things were moving at such a pace it wasn't easy keeping up with it all. Within weeks, I was a bona fide student at the College. I could barely contain my excitement and must have appeared like a kid in a sweet shop. I had arrived at this junction in the road by means of a windy dirt track compared to most of my contemporaries, who had been travelling on the straight and narrow for much of their lives. For them, their being there was an inevitability; for me it was an endless source of wonder.

Around this time, Denis and I went to a party thrown by a little bundle of female perfection called Dolly. Dolly worked for BCAL or British Caledonian Airlines and whilst she did carry some of Ms Parton's healthy attributes, she was more reminiscent of Goldie Hawn. As she opened the door, it was immediately obvious that we hadn't read the invite properly; this was a fancy dress do with the emphasis on sleepwear, a pyjama party. We were decked out in jeans and granddad shirts, the de rigueur of fashion statements in those days.

"Never mind," said a bubbly Dolly, "you can just take off your jeans and you'll be fine."

Nervous laughter.

"Come in. What can I get you guys to drink?"

"I'd love a beer," said Denis trying not to sound too keen.

As it turned out, the beers were nestling in the bottom of a fridge right there opposite the front door. As our scantily clad hostess bent over to release one from its box, not a lot was left to the imagination. Instantly transported to a heavenly, if rather uncomfortable place, that place of a racing mind, pumping heart and no voice, the now upright Dolly had to ask me another three times what my beverage of choice might be before I managed to blurt out, "Could I have one of those too, please?"

I can only imagine I must have kept my strides on because I'm sure that, had I taken Dolly's advice, I would not have been so eagerly and expertly seduced by a Sandie Shaw lookalike. Barefoot, twice my age, oozing confidence and sensuality in her red silk PJs, this unexpected gift of femininity took my hand and introduced me to the big bad world. What Jacqui Andrews saw in me I have no idea. Me, a clueless teenager, she, a savvy grown woman who drove a sports car, but she stuck around for a while and saw me through those potentially awkward first adult steps for which I am forever indebted to her.

She was a bit of a conundrum in more ways than one however, because she certainly smelled of garlic, yet had an impressive set of incisors, though neither characteristic seemed to dull my enthusiasm. Mind you, I do remember on my first return visit home two years later, sitting down to a plate of mince and spuds only to find something distinctly unfamiliar. Looking up, I saw Mum proudly showing off a jar of garlic salt. Ironically, she thought it would make me feel more at home.

Sorry Dracula, I take it back, you're right. That damned garlic is the devil's own herb. Some things are not be messed with!

2 1

Salou

Airline travel was very different back in the 1970s, an altogether more laid-back and pleasurable affair than it is today. My sister Rose, who was still under the employ of Mr Laker, worked mostly long-haul and boy did I take advantage of her perks. At every opportunity, I would skip off with her to LA or NY for the weekend. Toronto too, because of Joe and Nora, was a popular destination. Basically, wherever she happened to be going, if it fitted in timewise, I would be a willing stowaway. I have flown in jump-seats, cockpits, even on occasion in the galley, though there were also times when not even Rose could get me on board and I would have to trudge back from dreary old Gatwick, downhearted.

Just before the beginning of my first proper year at the College my brother Denis and I were hanging out round at Rose's flat. My summer job had come to an end and apart from the usual practice routine, I was effectively kicking my heels, waiting for term to start.

"You two fancy a week in Spain?" said Rose, out of the blue.

In a flash, the decision was made. She was operating the weekly flight down to a place called Reus early the next morning. She'd already checked the load and there were plenty of empty seats, we could easily jump on.

Reus airport was a tiny tin structure in the middle of absolutely nowhere. Descending the aircraft steps, with that feeling of having a hairdryer stuffed in your face, was already enough to make us want to turn back, our feet having not yet even touched the molten tarmac. I remember turning around in a panic just in time to see Rose wave goodbye as the aircraft door shut and they were gone. We were already burning in the fierce sun and headed for the relative safety of the single-room terminal. It was not the sort of place that might possess an air-conditioner however and was consequently like a sauna. If outside was a scene from a Spaghetti Western, inside was a horror show with frantic people tripping over each other in a mindless frenzy trying to retrieve their luggage which had just been dumped in a pile over in the corner.

What were we to do? Where was the beach? Where were the bars and the girls?

Oh, and where were we going to stay by the way?

This hut was emptying fast and before we knew where we were, well actually, we had no idea where we were, a brusque, uniformed lady informed us (I guessed from her gestures, because she was speaking with forked tongue) that we had to get out now as she was closing up. It was at this moment of moderate desperation that I spied a short queue of people lining up next to a nice young lady who was holding aloft an advertising board which read; 'Thomas Cook Holidays'. They promptly started boarding a small coach. I grabbed Denis and dragged him over to our getaway vehicle, instigating a pretend family squabble.

"I told you this was our bus. Can't you see the sign? You nearly made us miss our transport. Then what would we have done!" I blagged.

Denis played along with a few choice expletives.

"I'm so sorry miss," I said to the nice young TC rep who had now taken her place on the front row opposite us.

"I hope we haven't held you up."

Our improvised ruckus had thrown her off guard and soon we and our fellow holidaymakers were being whisked off to God knows where. We kept her busy with lots of inane chit-chat until the bus reached a traffic light and we could see, right in front of us, sand and sea. This was our moment; we suddenly got up and jumped off the bus leaving our young lady and all the other passengers totally bemused. So far so good but we still had no idea where we were. It was blisteringly hot, and a quick reckoning of our monetary resources revealed the terrifying news that, between the two of us, we had the grand total of £27.50.

I'm not ashamed to admit that we were scared. To say we hadn't thought this through was an understatement. All we could think about was how to get home, an obsession quickly dampened at the nearby travel agent's office where we found out that there was only one flight in and out of Reus to London every week. That was the one we'd come in on, and that's the one we'd be going out on, if we were still alive. After the initial panic and subsequent depression, a surge of resilience coursed through our veins, helped along by a draft of the cheapest alcohol we could find. Suddenly, we were commandos on a mission in enemy territory. We'd found the booze, now we had to sort out sleeping arrangements and concoct a diet that we could afford. We soon settled on a baguette and a couple of beef tomatoes to get us through the day and after a brief recce of the place, we found some upturned boats that would provide a place to sleep. We sat there on the sea wall as the sun went down, with our cheap fizz and dry tomato sandwich quietly trying to hold it together. People were extremely friendly, and we effortlessly struck up many a conversation, but when they naturally dispersed back to their hotels or to have dinner, we had to make our excuses and were eventually left alone. It wasn't too late when we sidled off down the beach and furtively scampered into our chosen burrow.

My luggage was my trusty blue plastic Adidas bag, half of which was taken up with my… I can barely believe what I'm about to write… my alarm clock. Yes, why would you go anywhere without your enormous alarm clock, you know, the big round colourful one with the giant pair of bells on top and a tick that would wake the dead. Bizarrely, that timepiece would come in very handy on this trip. We were in a Spain that had only just lost Franco, and as we found out the next morning, soldiers on horseback still patrolled the beaches every morning, presumably rounding up unsavoury characters like ourselves. They made it very clear, even with our non-existent Spanish, that we were not allowed to sleep on the beach, but where else could we go? Suffice to say, for the rest of our sojourn, the old timebomb was set to awaken us in only a marginally less aggressive manner than the *Caballeria*.

We quickly fell into a routine and by day three were getting quite cocky. The sea was a bit cold and salty for a couple of Derry boys more accustomed to the North Atlantic (Derry boys don't swim!) and the absence of a towel left us with that irritating sand issue. What we needed in order to keep cool was a pool, a pool and a shower. The lure of this vision fired us into immediate action. We scoured the entire town before carefully selecting our target. We purposefully aimed low, a three-star joint, with plenty of guests enjoying its choice of pools, numerous sunbeds and few, if any, potentially troublesome staff. Heads erect, eyes to front, stepping proudly together, we entered the pearly gates, cruised past reception and made a beeline for a secluded corner of the garden by one of the pools. We commandeered a couple of stray sunbeds and struck dumb with a mixture of smugness and trepidation, settled down for a much-needed siesta. We had barely closed our eyes when a wee gaggle of giggly girls returned from frolicking in the pool and took their places right next to us.

"Fuck sake, that's great craic that, so it is!" said one.

"Aye it is, but I'm gettin' burnt to a cinder so I am," cautioned the next.

"Och would you give over Mairead. Just slap on a wee bit more o' that there suntan oil an' you'll be grand," came the reply.

Denis and I fixed one another with a one-eyed stare, like two mice who had chanced upon the cheese store. There was no doubting it; these were Derry girls. Now this was a lingo we were fluent in.

"That's not a Derry accent I hear is it?"

Our opening salvo was met with a sudden silence and a stony stare.

"What brought yousens to this place then?" was our second pathetic offering.

"Freddie fuckin' Laker!"

That's more like it girls, that's the spirit. Let the banter begin.

"We're from Derry like, but we live in London," said I, nonchalantly easing myself up on one elbow.

"Aw I'd love to go to London, so I would," said one.

"Dear God, naw. Must be wil' big, and dirty, and full o' Brits!!" laughed another.

"Hi Theresa, it's nearly one o'clock, so it is," said Mairead excitedly.

"What happens at one o'clock then?" we asked.

"Every day at one o'clock, they bring us a pitcher of Sangria, so they do," answered Theresa.

"Fuckin'ell, that's not fair that. Taunting you wi'a picture of a lovely, cool drink. That's just to get you to spend your money," says I, winking sideways at Denis, who was already drooling.

"A *pitcher* of Sangria ya fuckin' eejit. Not a picture. And it doesn't cost a penny. It's all part of the deal you see," said Mairead. "Are yous not on the same package then?"

Before reality got a chance to become pleasantly blurred, this was the moment when we had to come clean. There was little point in some cock and bull story, so we told them honestly, exactly what had happened. These girls could not have been nicer. The infamous Irish hospitality immediately kicked in and our stars aligned.

Theresa sorted us out with the following orders; "First of all, yous must be starving so yous can have our lunch tickets, cause we never eat lunch anyway. When you're ready, you can have showers in my room, and you can take our towels, we always bring our own. Wouldn't dream of using them cheap hotel rags. Now Mairead, we'll be needin' extra glasses when that Ribena shows up!"

In typical Derry fashion, the girls had sorted out the boys. It's amazing how luxurious three-star accommodation can feel after just a couple of days roughing it. We still had to brave the beach come night-time, but JC had cut us some slack, and our remaining days, hanging out with the girls at the Don Carlos, were heavenly.

Our last day in Salou (we had finally figured out where we were) just happened to be my eighteenth birthday and the girls invited us to a knees-up at the hotel, which had been organised for their last night. We decided we should break with tradition and actually do something to celebrate the occasion. After luncheon at the Don Carlos, exhibiting all the invention of a pair of mules, we bought a bottle of cheap vodka, a bottle of Coke which wasn't even cold and a family-size packet of crisps, and headed off into the hills just out of town to the west. We soon found an impressive vantage point where some thoughtful local had recently tipped the unwanted contents of his front room, which rather conveniently for our purposes, contained a pair of armchairs. We made ourselves comfortable and started in on my birthday treats of Larios, Coke and Lays. Coming from Kebroyde, birthdays meant nothing to me but sitting there, looking out over the hills to the left and sea to the right, did strike me as a moment to remember. It was two years almost to the day since Rose had arrived home and told me about this guy Bernie had met, a little under four years since Derek Bell had teased out that achingly beautiful Grieg tune and put colour into my hitherto black-and-white world, and in two days from now I would be properly entering the Royal College of Music; for me, the beginning of a new era.

I think the disco was fun, though my memory of it cannot be wholly trusted. The next morning, with the help of Theresa, Mairead and co., we managed to sneak onto their coach back to the barn that masqueraded as Reus Airport and soon, the front door of the solitary aeroplane opened to reveal our sister, standing waving just where we'd left her a week before.

22

Employment

The various jobs I had, from arriving in London to starting at the College were mind-numbingly dull. I soon ditched the inevitable outdoor, building-site experience for some delightful indoor pastimes hopefully better suited to the delicate hands of a budding violinist.

First up was a menial job at Olivetti, the typewriter people, for which the interview consisted of spelling the word 'chrysanthemum' (quick spell check!). Several suicide notes later, I entered the world of drugs, securing an intoxicating job at the Hoechst factory in West London until they mercifully relocated to Milton Keynes, allowing me the opportunity of getting my foot in the door of the music world by joining the ranks of Fidelity Radio at their factory in North Acton. Every race has a tendency to stick together in a foreign place, and for the Irish of the 1970s, there was no more foreign place on Earth than England. I witnessed those barely believable signs outside hostelries which read; 'No Blacks, Dogs or Irish' not a stone's throw from my new front door. It was at the interview for this coveted position, loading hi-fi goods onto a lorry, that I first witnessed the old Irish mafia at work. The waiting room was packed at 8am with guys who all looked much more able than I to fulfil just about any given task. When it came to my turn to be grilled, I entered the foreman's office feeling very much as though I was wasting my time and his.

"Paul Cassidy is it?" asked the foreman in a strong Cork accent.

"Ah, yes, that's right," I answered.

"So, you're Irish, Paul, are you?" he continued.

"Aye, I'm from Derry, so I am," said I, relaxing a bit.

"*Failte go* London, Paul," he said, with a smile.

"*Go raibh mile maith agat. An la deas ata ann inniu,*" I rallied in my best O level Gaelic.

"Have you done much work like this before, Paul?" he asked.

"Ah, naw I haven't I'm afraid," said I, truthfully.

"You start Monday morning. The name's Joe Whelan. See you then," he said, shaking my hand firmly and calling in the next in a long line of candidates for a job that was now, presumably, no longer available.

As I said, the job was ridiculously straightforward and consisted of nothing more than loading and unloading various items of hi-fi equipment. After only a few days in the job, our stocktaker phoned in sick. Bill was a very proper English gent in his sixties, with an enviable head of wavy grey hair, all gelled perfectly in place. Whereas the rest of us worked in our everyday clothes, Bill had a pristine white coat with an impressive display of coloured pens, all lined up, caps protruding from the top left pocket. As we filed into the tiny room for our coffee break, Joe appeared in a bit of a state.

"Fuck sake!" exclaimed Joe, lighting up another Major.

"What's up, Joe?" enquired one of the guys without lifting his eyes from page three of his rag.

"Bill's phoned in sick, that's what's up. Fuckin' disaster," scowled Joe. "With no one to do the stocktaking, yous are gonna have to take pen and paper and make a note of everything you move, load or unload."

"Aw, fuckin'ell," came the chorus of disapproval.

"Why don't you just get someone else to do the stocktake?" I blurted out without thinking.

"Jaysus, would ye listen to fuckin' Einstein over there," laughed Joe, and throwing me a clipboard and pen said, "Go on then, if you're so fuckin' clever. Get to work."

I sheepishly got up from my seat, took the clipboard and pen, and amid a sea of snide remarks and giggles, was making my way out to the factory floor when Joe grabbed me by the arm.

"Would you lot shut up. Come on back here son, sure I was only pullin' yer leg," said Joe kindly, and putting his hand on my shoulder continued, "You see, that stuff has to be right, you understand. You canny just guess at it like."

Spurred on by the potential joy of doing something even vaguely challenging, I assured Joe that my figures would be correct and asked him if I could at least have a go. What was there to lose? Joe agreed and walked round the factory floor with me, showing me what stock had to be accounted for.

When, however, I landed back in his office not half an hour later, proudly showing off my figures, the stocktaking completed, he gazed up at me dumbfounded and reiterated his caution of earlier, "Like I said, Paul. These figures have to be right. It can't just be some random, stab in the dark."

He took some convincing, but as I showed him my simple calculations and talked him through my basic methods, his blatant mistrust turned to out-and-out amazement. Finally, seeing that my figures were in the same ballpark as Bill's regular conclusions, he accepted this bewildering feat of brilliance, thanked me profusely and promptly sent me back to my old post.

It wasn't until I slotted back into my dreary, daily routine that the penny gradually began to drop. What had I done! You see, I had just taken half an hour to complete what Bill made last a whole day. He would very officially don his white coat, sharpen his pencil in readiness for his copious calculations, the final hallowed numbers eventually, meticulously penned in varying colours of ink. Tea and coffee breaks in which he would studiously peruse the crisply ironed pages of his beloved *Sun* newspaper were punctuated by carefully timed toilet stops and imperative, top-level meetings with senior colleagues in various, far-flung reaches of the facility. Always stopping a trifle shy of the 5pm moment of release in order to reverse the morning's procedure in readiness for his re-entering of the outside world. Whereas Bill had turned time management into an art form, I had shown a great lack of awareness and having blithely thrown off Bill's life's work in a flash, was now back to the grindstone. I'm not sure if Bill ever found out what went on in his absence, but my unwitting moment of flair did create an awkward dynamic between myself and my co-workers.

Being a budding musician without anything on which to play music, and working in an environment where I was surrounded by the very technology that allowed that great luxury to take place, proved an overwhelming temptation. This, coupled with the carrot of doing something to enliven the daily drudge of this mindless occupation, led one day to the inevitable. With the best will in the world, there were sometimes accidents loading and unloading pallets full of merchandise. On these occasions, so as not to keep the lorries waiting, the damaged item would be taken aside, replaced and accounted for after the vehicle's departure. The plan was a simple one. A mate of mine who worked on the factory floor had a car. They clocked off fifteen minutes before we did. The last delivery of the day would incur a minor disaster in which a few MP3s (our hi-fi of choice) would supposedly find their way to the ground, I would then take them aside just in case they'd been damaged and replace them from stock. The 'damaged' items were stacked on a pallet off to the side and when the lorry was ready to depart, I made sure I was the one to go down the end where the switch for the giant electric doors was located. Right next to this switch was a door that led directly to the outside where my mate was sitting ready in his car with the back door open and positioned perfectly in line with this door. I, on my way to carry out this operation, simply picked up two of the MP3s (my mate got one for the use of his wheels) and one by one, chucked them into the waiting back seat. It was scary as hell, and though it was all for a worthy cause, it was not a feeling I enjoyed. It would take Bill a couple of days to even get to the point where he might question his maths, at which stage he would no doubt furtively make the figures work. Impossible to believe, in this day and age, with cameras everywhere and computers but the mission went off without a hitch and later that evening, we sat excitedly, favourite LPs poised to play, while Denis hooked the thing up. I'll never know what exactly he managed to do while performing what one would imagine should have been a straightforward task, and no doubt, the Good Lord had a hand in it, but when he plugged it in and flicked the switch, there was an almighty bang and the brand new music box burst into flames. We couldn't exactly take it back to the manufacturer and I was not for trying to repeat that manoeuvre, so we put out the fire, ditched the machine in its newly opened box, and silently returned our vinyls to their sleeves to hopefully spin another day.

Throughout college I would continue with various jobs in order to get some pocket money. Every Christmas and Easter I would become a postman, working out of the Fulham Broadway branch. A more regular employ however were my twice-weekly visits to the home of Dennis and Joan Wheatley. I never hear his name nowadays, but back then, Dennis was an enormously successful writer of best-selling novels. They lived in a very grand apartment just off Sloane Street and I would turn up there around coffee time, invariably have to enter their bedroom where Joan would still be languishing in the lavish four-poster like someone from one of those vile Peter Greenaway films, sipping champagne and nibbling chocolates, a bevy of nasty little excuses for dogs all around her, barking and snapping and whining and greedily slurping up any remnants of discarded soft centres. I would gather together a stack of library books in large print to be exchanged, an envelope containing cheques and various other instructions, which I would then take to the Kensington Library and the Knightsbridge branch of Coutts and Co. respectively. Sometimes there were other equally mundane chores to do, dry cleaning or the like but mostly that was it. I don't mean for my description of Joan to be unkind in any way, on the contrary, both Joan and Dennis could not have been nicer and were always very appreciative. It was just a snapshot of a lifestyle that I could only make sense of in terms of the movies.

Gradually, musical jobs began to take the place of these random sources of employment. I was so completely, totally and utterly wrapped up in playing, that I had little room in my mind for anything else. It always amazes me how little pop music I know from that period and how, during my year-long stay in Manchester, I never once visited Old Trafford. I had so much emotion inside, so much love and excitement and awe for this magical art I found myself at the edge of, but I had to broaden my knowledge and learn how to share this euphoria. The arts are a great escape; they provide each and every one of us with our own personal magic mushroom. Whether it be a painting by Goya or Kandinsky, a sculpture by Giacometti, a bowl by Lucie Rie, a garment by Yamamoto, a piece of Debussy or Bach. Often a child's drawing or an amateur performance can equally stir the senses, it's this abstract effort to demonstrate what's going on inside that is so powerfully moving. We poor artists however cannot simply inhabit this dreamy space. It is our job to understand the science and structure of these sights and sounds so we can better translate them. It's a constant balancing act, remaining sober enough to carry out the very exacting techniques required to realise works whilst being drunk enough to plumb the depths of emotion therein. I find it telling that Bach's last utterance was a colossal fugue, The Art of Fugue. One of the last things Beethoven wrote was the Grosse Fuge and when Shostakovich set out to write his own epitaph, he spelt out his name in a fugue. In the last year of Schubert's life, he was taking counterpoint lessons… Schubert for God's sake! Picasso, towards the end of his life, was reading some horrible review of his latest work in which the critic ranted that the old man had finally lost it and let's face it, had never really mastered the basics of art anyway, turned to his friend and asking for paper and pencil, proceeded to draw with one stroke a perfect circle.

Undoubtedly some convoluted consequence of being child number sixteen but curiously, though I'm very much a team player, I'm useless at being in gangs or clubs of any description. Happily, one can be an enormous asset to any team without forfeiting one's individuality but that said, I don't react well to rules or being told what to do. At college I won many competitions, was the principal viola in all the orchestras and had endless groups but I never once felt accepted, never once felt part of the team. I carry this ridiculous feeling with me to this very day. Somehow all these other people have a right to be there whereas I'm just an imposter, an incompetent fraudster waiting to be found out. And yet, I firmly believe that no one on the planet can play the viola part of a string quartet better than me, no one can possibly feel the nuances as keenly as I do. This is the weirdness that I have to live with every day in life, at once feeling absolutely incapable and utterly invincible. One thing that was very clear to me from the outset was that I had to be a driving part of the creative process; it was not enough to just take a passive role. Certainly, sitting in orchestra in my first term, playing Rachmaninov's Symphonic Dances and being paralysed by the sudden entrance of, what even was that, what could possibly make a sound like that? The thrilling sound turned out to be a saxophone (played by John Harle by the way). Taking part in Mahler's 10th Symphony, Elgar's 'Dream of Gerontius' or the Janacek 'Sinfonietta' were all unforgettable experiences but they were not what I was about. Instead I was that annoying little busybody who went around constantly forming groups and organising concerts. I would stumble upon forgotten repertoire, get a group together, dream up a programme involving those players, often commissioning fellow students or composers we happened to bump into along the way and organise concerts for us to play. Learning concertos was OK and fun up to a point but if it involved playing with someone else, interacting in some way, like Mozart's incomparable

'Concertante', then I was hooked. I used to wonder, as I crept into the college canteen, how all these groups of people seemed to know each other so well, even on day one and I knew no one. It took me a while to figure out the power of the National Youth Orchestra clique. I had never even heard of the NYO yet here I was, surrounded by fellow students almost all of whom had spent the last few years of their lives wrapped up in it. Also, the gangs from the Menuhin School, Chetham's and so on, in one way or another; it wasn't all just in my head, I really was an outsider.

Despite this polarity, I managed on day one to meet three beautiful people, three people who, like me, had never been to any of these institutions, three people who would instantly become lifelong friends; Jackie Shave, Richard Tunnicliffe and Anya Kubrick. Jackie played the violin, Richard the cello and Anya was a singer. We formed a little satellite band of gypsies and were practically inseparable from that moment on.

One employee of the College who grabbed my attention was a lady called Viola Tucker. It wasn't solely her name which attracted me, it was the fact that she was the Appointments Manager, in other words, she was in charge of all the outside enquiries to do with students being engaged to perform, out in the big bad world. She was basically the headmistress of St Trinian's, impossibly prim, matron shoes, tweed two-piece, horn-rimmed glasses, hair in a bun and an accent straight out of a P.G. Wodehouse novel. If she was Joyce Grenfell's school mistress, I was George. I badgered and bullied her incessantly, insatiably desirous of opportunities to perform, and our quartet, Jackie, me, Richard and A.N. Other, cornered the bulk of what was on offer.

Thirty pounds all-in was considered a fortune for one of these gigs, and though the money was extremely welcome, that's not what it was about for us, we wanted the thrill and experience of performing chamber music in a public setting. Often it was just weddings or parties but sometimes we got proper concerts as part of local festivals or the like. These were what we really craved but that's not to say we didn't occasionally have a laugh at the background gigs. For example, we played at the American Ambassador's residence on the eve of Diana's marriage to Charles where I remember perfectly timing my return from the washroom to coincide with the grand entrance of Margaret, the Dame of Grantham, expertly cutting across her just as she was being greeted by Ronald, the B-movie cowboy.

On another occasion, I unwittingly became a McAlpine Fusilier, when we were sent to play at his birthday party. McAlpine was a glorified builder who made it big and gained an unenviable reputation for making slaves of us Paddys. My fellow countrymen famously built most of what we know as England, leading to such exchanges as;

"Jaysus boys, we're making a terrible mess o' this place altogether," says one man leaning on his shovel.

"Keep digging Sean. Sure, 'tis only England!" came the typically astute reply.

I'll never forget arriving at this man's big day, all four of us packed into Nick Roberts' (our cellist for the day) Morris Minor van in amongst a flotilla of Bentleys, Bristols and helicopters. It was the night of the horrific Ali v Holmes fight and I remember watching that distressing event on a tiny black-and-white TV in the kitchen whilst the Roux Brothers prepared a breath-taking raspberry mille-feuille. The manner in which the whole team constructed that mouth-watering edifice of impossibly thin pastry, fresh berries and as much cream as you always secretly wish for but rarely get, the giant bowl of which was feverishly whipped up as it got passed from one to another round the kitchen till it was just the right consistency to be lathered onto the biscuit base, was an education in itself and momentarily helped take one's mind off the tragic events unfolding on screen.

I got offered a job teaching at the RCM Junior Dept which took place on Saturday mornings and this, coupled with my increasingly frequent visits to the Ulster Orchestra, meant I was gradually beginning to earn a crust from playing music. That seemingly indefatigable drive to gather people together, dream up programmes and put on concerts was a feature of my student life and would certainly come in handy in my future career.

I often wonder where certain people have gone, people who were stars at college but don't seem to be in the profession. Did they peak too early or perhaps they were such capable beings that having done music, simply chose another career? My fellow gypsies didn't do so badly I have to say. Jackie Shave is one of the most sought-after violinists in the UK today. She was first violin in the Brindisi Quartet for many years and is currently the concertmaster of the Britten Sinfonia, to mention but two of her activities. Richard Tunnicliffe turned his considerable talent to Baroque music, playing principal in every major ensemble in the country and also joining the Fitzwilliam Quartet and Fretwork. Anya Kubrick built a career in recital work and opera, forming her own Palace Opera Company before her life was cut tragically short by a lengthy and horrible illness. Death is rarely an easy thing to deal with but when a beautiful person who has so much to give, so much to live for, is wrenched away at such a young age, it's really tough to take. Anya was a particularly kind person and an invaluable friend, always there for you. She was great fun, gregarious, highly intelligent, warm-hearted, supportive, serious, loving; a downright cracker of a girl whom I continue to miss terribly.

You would never guess from meeting Anya that she was the daughter of a legend. This is a credit to everyone involved, both her and her parents. Stanley Kubrick was not one for galivanting; he was a real home bird and always longed to have his family around him. When Anya threatened going off to London to share an apartment with friends, he tried everything to persuade her against it. I remember her ace was that she had to practise not just her singing, but crucially the piano and that commuting three hours a day was not a clever use of her time. No problem he would say; we'll get a van customised with a piano in the back and a driver, that way you can practise for those three hours. When he lost that lengthy battle, he insisted that if she was determined to move to London, she at least had to have a reinforced tank-like vehicle to get around in, they both eventually compromised, and an old second-hand Volvo was acquired.

Both Stanley and Cristiane, Anya's parents, were wonderfully generous hosts and gave us so many happy memories. Both workaholics, I never once visited that house and found them lounging around. Cristiane was invariably in front of her easel creating another one of her magnificent, tremendously detailed paintings while Stanley was always off in the bowels of the house, in one of his studios. That's not to say they wouldn't come and join in the craic.

Guy Fawkes was one of their unmissable annual events. The stupendous kitchen-cum-conservatory overflowing with heavenly food and drink lovingly supplied by the wonderful Celia Brooks-Brown, and Stanley out enjoying himself as master of ceremonies. The year he brought in the special effects people from *Full Metal Jacket* was a particularly memorable one.

Stanley was always very sweet to me; often concerned that life in a string quartet couldn't possibly pay the bills (as always, he was right there!), he would offer to have a word with Sid Sax, the then Mr Big of the London session world. A quick call from Stanley Kubrick would indeed have gotten me on to Mr Sax's coveted list of slaves but I always declined these kind offers knowing that, despite the undoubted financial rewards, I was not cut out for that world and also very aware of the sickening fact that, if you said no to Sid once, you never got asked again. This always struck me as a short-sighted, self-defeating strategy; surely the best players are the busy ones and therefore the ones worth having.

Stanley was fond of gadgets and was always keen to be at the forefront of technology as it moved forward. He was one of the first people I knew with a home computer and a mobile phone, such as they were back then. There was a rumour that he actually got Orange to install one of their transmitters down the end of the garden so that his signal was strong and dependable. He also had every TV channel known to man, which came in very useful for me when the football was on. I would often call him up and get invited over to watch the United games, only problem was, Stanley would come and watch them with me. Much as I loved him, Stanley was not the guy you wanted next to you on the football couch.

"Why do you think Liverpool have chosen four in midfield? How does this United team compare to the old Busby Babes do you think? Why wouldn't you just leave two speedy guys up front and hoof the ball into the space behind the defenders for them to exploit?"

This level of questioning would go on ceaselessly until you had to beg to be allowed to just watch the game.

When Anya married the baritone Jonathan Finney (together they would produce the adorable Sam) they had their wedding reception in this same splendid room. For some reason, Jacky and I were the first guests to arrive back at the house and as we entered the space, who was standing there but Stanley.

"Paul, you're just the guy I was looking for. We need a special drink to get this party going. I'm outta ideas… what do you suggest?"

"Well, it rather depends on what you have available," I replied, buying myself a moment.

"We can get anything you need. What'll it be?" he enquired impatiently.

"In my experience, the best drink for getting a party going is a champagne cocktail," I suggested.

"OK, sounds good. But what exactly is a champagne cocktail?"

"You need brandy, champagne and a sugar lump."

"Can I try one, right now?" he asked.

"Sure," said I. "Easy."

"Get this guy what he needs please. We're running out of time," said Stanley in a panic.

Hey presto, the ingredients arrived as if by magic. It was at that moment I made a fatal mistake. Taking the champagne flute in one hand, I took a sugar lump in the other and throwing it up over my shoulder, caught it in the glass before administering the alcohol mix. Stanley's mouth dropped open and without even touching a drop he said, "Fantastic. That's it Paul."

People were now beginning to arrive.

"Please just stand right here and keep doing that. This is the perfect welcoming drink, and with the theatrics an'all. You're a star!"

Yep, Stanley Kubrick called me a star. I did my best to recreate the sugar lump trick 150 times but regardless of my proficiency, the party was a humdinger.

23

Ben's Viola

Though I unfortunately never got the chance to hear Cecil Aronowitz play 'live', his reputation went before him. His overly generous, swashbuckling approach to the Alto Clef was just my cup of tea. Being the butt of relentless, cheap jokes (here's my tuppence worth);

Q. Heard the one about the Irish viola player?

A. Joined the Brodsky Quartet!

can dampen the spirit and drag the viola world into an all-too-serious, reactionary and paranoid mindset. That's why people like Cecil are so precious. They come along and sweep all of this nonsense aside both with their laissez-faire attitude and their ability to tease an unparalleled sound from the most unlikely of places; a place where physics plays second fiddle to character. It's a sound that doesn't come easy, it requires tremendous patience and sensitivity but once produced, has the power to melt even the coldest of hearts.

As in life, Cecil's demise was nothing less than operatic. With consummate timing he brought his life on Earth to a close on stage, in the middle of the slow movement of Mozart's glorious G minor Quintet. He bowed out with a sudden, dramatic lurch forward, collapsing in a mini explosion of chair, stands, music, glasses, instrument and bow. Though clearly overshadowed by the great man's passing, it was nonetheless upsetting that he had landed his full weight on his viola, thereby smashing it into a thousand tiny splinters. These remnants were dutifully collected and delivered to the door of one Charles Beare, who saw to it that the instrument was painstakingly reconstructed in a display of brilliance and devotion.

Some years later, this dizzying task completed, Nicky, Cecil's widow decided that the instrument should be played and not lie gathering dust.

This was an extremely fortuitous circumstance as far as I was concerned. Having never had an instrument of my own and coming to the end of my time at the College, I would no longer be able to use the viola they had leant me and was on the lookout for a replacement. Somehow Cecil's viola found its way to me. I was so excited the day I went to pick it up. I was finally going to get the opportunity to move up a gear in the instrument stakes. I was going to play on a proper old-Italian instrument. In reality, this could not have been further from the truth. Though colleagues of Cecil's subsequently confided to me that his viola had always been referred to as 'the cigar box', I refuse to believe that anyone could have been happy with such a thing. I can only conclude that despite Charles' heroic efforts, the trauma and damage caused by the fatal accident had been too severe to repair. I tried my best and fought with it for many months but to no avail. This match would not ignite. It was in this increasingly depressed state that I nervously put my name down to attend a series of masterclasses with none other than William Primrose.

About ten days before the legendary William Primrose was to give masterclasses at Snape he tragically passed away. As you might imagine, this horribly sad news came as a terrible shock to the ten students who were coming from all corners of the globe to fulfil a common dream; to meet and play for the great man. Among viola players, Primrose was quite simply without parallel, but many would argue, myself included, that he was one of the greatest string players to ever draw bow.

Clearly, replacing such an icon was an impossibility but Hugh Maguire, the then Head of Strings at Snape, called us all in turn and pleaded with us to still come on the course. It's true it wasn't going to be our great idol, but he had managed to secure the services of Bill's right-hand man, a chap by the name of Donald MacInnes. Despite the obvious disappointment, we did all converge on the Maltings on that Monday morning as planned. In actual fact, Mr MacInnes couldn't get there till the Wednesday so for the first two days we had the not inconsiderable pleasure of Gerard Causse's company. He was so lovely, an excellent teacher and a fantastic player and we were all sad that he was only going to be with us for two short days. Anyway, that was the deal, so on the Wednesday morning, this suave, dark, handsome, very considered Frenchman was replaced by the open, fresh-faced, Californian swagger and infectious smile of Don. In so many ways, he was a welcome ray of sunshine; he brought openness and warmth and was wonderfully brash and to the point. He and I hit it off immediately. I remember I played last before lunch on that first day and as I was putting away my viola, he came up to me and asked me what plans I had for the summer. It took me all of one second to mentally flash through my cramped summer schedule and answer, "Well… nothing!"

"How would you like to come to California and study with me?" he asked matter-of-factly.

"Wow, I would absolutely love that of course but I have no money," said I.

"I'll see to that," he replied confidently.

Amazingly, he was true to his word and by tea-time on the same day, he presented me with all the necessary forms to sign for a totally unexpected American experience. I eagerly scrawled on the dotted lines and instantly found myself with a full scholarship to the high-flying, all-guns-blazing, three-month-long summer festival at the Academy of the West in Santa Barbara.

The classes at Snape highlighted the fact that my lack of a proper instrument had reached crisis point. Something or someone had to give. These days, the standard of instrument and bow making has risen so much that it's reasonably easy to begin to think about getting kitted out for a vaguely manageable amount of money. Back then, it seemed the only route to acquiring adequate tools of the trade was to take out a mortgage and pitch a tent. The 'cigar-box' had long since lost any hint of the appeal it may have had initially and was instead causing me great anxiety as I entered this extremely important stage in my musical career. Towards the end of the ten-day course there was a concert given by the students. Each one of us had to play something and I was asked to perform Britten's haunting set of variations, 'Lachrymae', to finish the programme. Picture the scene;

There I was, playing Britten's swansong in the Maltings, on Cecil's reconstructed viola, with Nicki, his widow, at the piano and a front row of all the great and good from Don and Hugh to Rostropovich and Peter Pears. As I came down the home straight, that simple, serene statement of the John Dowland theme, things got pretty emotional and when Peter reached for his handkerchief, it was all I could do to rein it in and hold it together. In the salty aftermath the heady mixture finally got the better of me and I quite spontaneously decided I needed to get away from it all. I promptly did a runner and went to stay with a friend who had a place nearby.

Next morning was the final class and upon my return I was greeted by several of my fellow students who were in an unusually agitated state and clearly concerned about something.

"You OK? Where have you been? You're in trouble. Peter Pears wants to see you, pronto!!"

It transpired that I had been summoned to the Red House at my earliest convenience and so it was that at lunchtime that day, a car was sent to pick me up and ferry me there and back. The Red House was the home of Benjamin Britten and Peter Pears, a magical, rambling sort of a place approached via an enchanted lane. It backs onto the golf course on the outskirts of the seaside town of Aldeburgh. Britten was a Suffolk man born and bred and when he and Peter decided to settle down together, they quite naturally chose this supremely atmospheric corner of the county. What an exceptionally magical and inspirational institution has grown and mushroomed from this routine lifestyle decision. It's always been one of the big regrets of my musical life that I wasn't around in those intensely heady and formidably productive days. Witness the polar extremes of the Jubilee Hall and Snape Maltings as a central stage and you get some idea of the interstellar journey the whole scene has taken. What must it have been like to experience the birth of such monumental creations as *Noye's Fludde*, *Peter Grimes*, *Les Illuminations* and so many others in the very place that inspired them? It's a priceless shot of artistic adrenaline to any budding dabbler, any sensitive spirit, to feel the proximity of such a creative mind. Their brilliance casts an intense light, which courses through your veins and has the power to lift you to a higher plain. The trick is to harness that energy and insight and make it part of your own creative self.

Gravel can be infuriating stuff to have around but at the same time, there's something undeniably satisfying and seductive about the crunch of it as you swing your Bentley Convertible into position 'neath the flowering wisteria. The mere fact that I cannot remember the make of the car that brought me to the door of the Red House leads me to believe that it was neither a Bentley nor a convertible. Why had Peter sent for me? We often bumped into each other about the place so, had he wanted to say something about the concert, he would have had ample opportunity so to do. What could I possibly have done to upset him? It was a mystery. Gingerly, I administered the heavy brass knocker on the thickly glossed, red front door. It opened almost immediately to reveal a beaming Peter.

"Ah, come in dear boy, come in… in there." He pointed his cane in the direction of the music-cum-sitting room.

"It's in that black case."

I stood there somewhat bemused.

"Sorry Peter but…"

"Under the piano there, do you see? Fish it out, there's a dear."

I, none the wiser, got down on all fours and crept under the old grand piano to the furthest corner where, reminiscent of Kebroyde, nestled a forgotten shaped viola case.

"Is this what you mean, Peter?" I enquired.

"Yes, that's it. They tell me you don't have an instrument of your own. Is that true?"

"Well yes, I mean no… I… "

"If that's of any use to you, I'd like you to have it."

In a bit of a daze I negotiated the broken zips and dodgy clasps. What was I to find there? First thing I noticed was the bow. It would be hard to imagine a worse example of the fine and cherished art of bow-making. Its substandard and impossibly warped stick had many years ago, perhaps when it had last been used, been attached to the sorry little frog by means of Sellotape. No fancy stuff, just the absolute bog-standard kind. This had by now turned brown and lost any adhesive qualities it might hitherto have possessed. I decided it might be best to leave that well alone. Upon lifting the red velvet cover and undoing the silk scarf that was protecting it, I unveiled the instrument itself. Despite the fact that it had no bridge, no chin rest and had managed to cling on to only one solitary, ancient gut C string, my eye was taken by the handsome f-holes and proud, fiery scroll, like the nostrils of a steeplechaser.

I could sense that the thick layer of black grime and resin was masking a more colourful soul with a story to tell.

"It was Ben's, you know. He'd be thrilled at the thought of it being used again. What do you think?"

"I don't know what to say Peter," I stuttered.

"Nothing to say my boy. If it's of any use to you, I'd like you to have it. Clearly it will need a lot of work."

"That's not a problem. Indeed, it will be my pleasure to see it properly restored."

Peter thanked me for my performance from the day before and escorted me back to the waiting car. As if in a dream I waved goodbye. I sat somewhat furtively on the back seat with my new friend under my arm. The engine engaged, the gravel announced our departure and the driver ferried me back to reality. I love it when life deposits you in a surreal bubble; time stands still, sounds fuse, colours intensify and bleed, thoughts are crystal clear yet totally muddy. It's like a legal high. This was one bubble I was not in a hurry to pop.

Upon initial inspection the instrument appeared to be in reasonable condition. There were no horrendous sound-post cracks or anything, which was reassuring, and the label revealed the maker to be one Francesco Guissani of Milano, dated 1843. Though I hadn't heard that name before, it seemed more plausible than if it had read Antonio Stradivarius. My excitement was at fever pitch.

Upon my return to London the next day I didn't even bother to go home, I just made a beeline for Beares. Beares was the most respected violin shop in the world and its owner, Charles Beare, the undisputed god of all things strung. Regardless of the fact that I could hardly claim to be one of Charles' most valued customers, he always made time for me. For whatever reason, he liked me, and I liked him. So it was that on this day when I arrived unannounced, dishevelled, awkwardly taking up too much space in the shop with my suitcase and two violas, he simply smiled and invited me into the consultation room.

"What can we do for you?" he enquired, cordially.

"I've got a viola here I'd like you to take a look at. It's in a bit of a state but…"

As the silk scarf fell away, Charles immediately said, "But that's Ben's Landolphi. My goodness, it's ages since I laid my eyes on that," he said, taking hold of it.

"Oh, it says it's a Guissani on the label," said I.

"Ah yes, well how much do you know about the instrument?"

"I know it was Ben's, because Peter gave it to me yesterday, but that's all really."

"This instrument was indeed made by Francesco Guissani in Milano in 1843. He was a viola player in the La Scala Orchestra and though he made many violins and cellos, this was his only viola, which he made for himself. I always maintain however that there must have been a Landolphi around that he liked the look of because this is a carbon copy of one. Anyway, when he died the instrument came up for sale and was bought by none other than Frank Bridge, himself a violist. Then during the Second World War when Ben and Peter were shipped off to the US on account of them being conscientious objectors, Bridge, who had retired from playing, went to say goodbye to his life-long friend and star pupil. Fearing he might never see him again, he sneaked down and left this viola on Ben's bunk as a going-away present."

I stood there, rendered speechless by the details of this astonishing story.

"My dear Paul, this makes you only the fourth person to have this instrument in its one-hundred-and-forty-year existence, and given its owners to date, that's really quite an honour."

Continued stunned silence.

"You leave it with me, and I'll personally see that it gets restored to its former glory."

Charles obviously had a bit of a soft spot for this instrument because I can't imagine it ever looked more gorgeous than when I next laid eyes on it. I wish I could say that it was the greatest-sounding viola ever but in all honesty, it was actually frustratingly mediocre. Being an old romantic however, I persevered with its shortcomings, preferring to embrace the amazing history of this viola. We fought and argued and put in the hours, forging a relationship that would last twenty-five years.

Undoubtedly, the most poignant moment of our many memorable times together would be recording the Britten Quartets in the Maltings, with Colin Matthews producing.

Colin became Ben's right-hand man, helping him finish many of his later works, the Third Quartet included, so to have his expert guidance and delightful company was invaluable. Ben, like so many of the great composers, was a viola player. He would undoubtedly have tried out certain passages from his towering quartets on this very instrument. He transformed Aldeburgh from a sleepy little seaside town into a world-renowned destination for music lovers, and the nearby Maltings at Snape from a crumbling, deserted barn, into a critically acclaimed concert hall. Aldeburgh has become a formidable artistic force with the Maltings its beating heart, and thanks to Peter's warmth and generosity, I got to feel a part of it.

24

Three 5s and a Sandwich

Throughout its forty-year existence, the Railway Bar was run by my dad and various members of the family. This was no mean feat and something that could only be realised by considerable sacrifice. Every one of us saw some pub action. I myself remember spending many nights in there from the age of ten, illegally serving up drinks in the lounge to a bemused clientele. Sunday mornings after Mass, those of us unfortunate enough to be around were dragged in to clean the place and stack shelves. Inevitably, some of the older ones were leaned upon much more heavily, often against their will and two of my brothers ended up spending their lives in the pub business as a consequence of this enforced labour.

My brother Peter was one of these homegrown publicans. Peter was a boy who loved school and was never happier than when he was double-ruling a new exercise book in readiness for the next eagerly awaited homework. All too often however, I remember him being told to put away his beloved worksheets and get into the bar for another long shift. It was abundantly clear that these kids' lives were being mapped out for them, leaving them no choice in the matter. Their school days were numbered and a life behind the bar was beckoning.

After many years slaving away for little or no money in the Railway Bar, Peter was invited to join another brother, Marcus, who had suffered a similar fate but was now running his own place over in the Waterside area of the town. This was to be another ill-fated family venture however and Peter eventually headed off in a southerly direction to find his own way in the world of liquor.

He surfaced in a grim little one-horse town called Portarlington about one hour south west of Dublin. Here, he took over a sorry establishment by the name of The Port Bar. This place was obviously down on its luck, at least one could only hope that it had seen better days. Nevertheless, one was sure that with Peter at the helm, its luck was about to change, and the good times would return once again. Peter was a tireless worker and an absolute natural when it came to sales. He could entertain the troops from dawn to dusk, holding forth on every subject from sport to politics, music to gardening. He would forever reassure his congregation of the healing properties of his 'medicine cabinet'.

"Guinness," he would say, "sure isn't it full of iron and other goodness, great for pregnant women, the calcium and suchlike. Nursing mothers, helps with the milk production. All manner of men, to give them strength; sure didn't Popeye himself wash down his spinach with it!"

Or;

"You have a cold do ya… a great big hot toddy's what you need. And as for you, a port and brandy will settle that stomach of yours."

Peter seemed to be preaching the sort of gospel the inmates of Portarlington wanted to hear.

When I was about eighteen years old, I became acutely aware of the fact that Peter hadn't really had a holiday in years. I decided to try to put this right and booked myself on a flight to Dublin. I told Peter that he was not needed for the next week and that he and his small family should make for the hills; I would be opening up tomorrow and for the next few days. I knew my way around a pub and so it was with complete confidence that I unbolted the front door the next morning at 10am. Even at that unlikely hour there was quite a gathering of seasoned professionals pacing the pavement, a neatly folded copy of the *Racing Post* tucked under their arms.

"Good morning," I declared to the impatient gathering.

"Where's Peter?" came the unison reply from this bunch who had already taken up their regular positions along the counter.

"Oh, Peter's gone fishing in the South Seas for a week or so. He sends his best and hopes you can put up with me while he's gone. Anyway, so… what can I get you?"

"Tree foives 'n' a sienwich," said a little man with a cap at the foot of the bar.

"I beg your pardon," said I, though I'd heard him clearly.

"Tree foives 'n' a sienwich," came the request once again.

This was the first order of the first day of my reign in the Port Bar and despite my experience I was completely flummoxed. I hadn't realised that Peter did food of any kind apart from the standard crisps and nuts etc. and as for the three fives… What was I to do!? The assembled were getting fidgety and no doubt already doubting my genes. By now, Peter would have been asking these guys if they wanted a refill and here I was, rooted to the spot like an eejit. There was nothing else for it; at 10.01am on my first day I would have to go upstairs and enlist the help of my poor brother having his first lie-in in God knows how long.

"Peter, Peter, I'm really sorry but there's someone downstairs asking for three fives and a sandwich and I have no idea what to give him," I whispered.

Peter looked so strange without his glasses… I couldn't help thinking what a great goalkeeper he would have been with working eyes. A croaky voice came out from under the duvet.

"Little guy with a cap, down the foot of the bar?" he asked.

"Exactly. That's the very boyo," said I.

"OK. Three fives is twenty Benson and Hedges 555 and the sandwich is his breakfast; half a Guinness, a tot of Jamesons and topped up with another half of Guinness. A sandwich!!"

"Of course," I said.

Welcome to a rural Ireland baptism of fire.

Unfortunately, my well-intentioned plan never really recovered. Apart from anything else, living on site with a young family and no money, where was Peter going to go? I remember I did take him trout fishing one evening to a local lake. Even with our vivid imaginations, the South Seas it wasn't. Hopefully I managed to break the monotony briefly though and certainly for me, it was an eye opener.

There was one other incident that I simply must report from that same visit. It was late Sunday afternoon and little or nothing was going on down at the bar. Bored with playing darts and pool we were just passing time, mindlessly doing damage to a leftover Christmas tin of Quality Street when two coaches pulled up on the street outside. It was the team and some supporters of a local Gaelic football club returning from an away fixture and looking for sustenance. The door was flung open.

"You don't do food, do you?" enquired the stranger.

"Course we do," said Peter without a second thought. "How many are y'ese?"

"Oh, about one hundred and twenty," came the reply.

"Come on in lads and make yourselves at home."

"You're a life-saver. We're starving. Have you a menu or what?"

"Look lads, we'll deal with all that in a minute, sure you must be parched. Let's get the drinks order and then we'll see about the food."

While Peter and I saw to the liquid refreshment, Peter's wife and kids went next door to raid the supermarket, closed yet amenable, thrilled in fact to be suddenly and most unexpectedly bought out of bread, cheese, butter and all manner of things required to produce a somewhat reduced post-Sunday lunch menu out of thin air. Once the sports stars and their entourage had had their second pint, they had totally forgotten about the idea of food to the extent that when a Himalayan range of freshly made sandwiches arrived with great bowls of crisps and the like, they were as happy as Larry. At last orders, the whole gang were still there joking, singing and generally raising the roof, when one modest winger approached the bar.

"Two halves o' Guinness please Peter."

To this Peter replied; "Sorry sir, but we're all out o' halves!"

Two pints were promptly sold. What a result. It will hardly surprise you to learn that Peter went on to manage three of the biggest pubs in Dublin.

25

Giuranna

Around this time, the name on every young viola player's lips was that of Bruno Giuranna. He was the current 'chosen one'. The one who had risen to the top of the pile of worshipped gurus. This status lead to him having teaching posts in both Berlin and Detmold and though I'd never even heard him play or teach, I decided to join the bandwagon and try to get to study with him. Rather conveniently, I found that he was about to play in London, one of those BBC Lunchtimes from St John's Smith Square. I made it my business to get a front row seat and eagerly went along to suss this guy out.

If this was to be my new teacher for the next couple of years, I was willing him to be God-like, to come out in a blaze of passion and blow the place away. In reality, a beautifully presented Italian took to the stage and executed his recital with consummate poise and elegance. All was perfectly in order but I, at least, was not blown away. Yes, but hang on a minute, wasn't this exactly what I needed? Someone who could harness all my raw, often wasted energy and carefully hone it into a method by which I could translate my thoughts and emotions into music. I decided there and then to go for it.

Because of the enormously long walk from the stage to the stairs that lead to the crypt and dressing rooms, the BBC used to erect a curtained-off area to the right side of the stage where performers could wait unseen between curtain calls. It was in this extremely closeted space that the unsuspecting Signore Giuranna got accosted by an overly pushy young Paddy. I did at least wait for the applause to die down, but only just. I badgered the perspiring maestro as he was putting away his instrument.

"Oh, Mr Giuranna, that was amazing!" I gushed.

"Thank you," he replied, only mildly irritated.

"Mr Giuranna, I want to study with you, please. How might I go about that?" I went on.

"Well, have you auditioned?" he asked, showing some agitation.

"No."

"I see. Well, my classes for next year have closed."

"Oh dear, that's terrible news. I didn't know how to get in touch with you, you see. That's why I came along today when I saw you were playing here. I came along in the hope of meeting you."

"I'm afraid it's not enough for you to meet me, young man. I have to hear you play."

"Is there any way I could play for you now?"

"No, no. I don't have any time right now. You'll just have to wait till auditions come up for next year."

"If I came to Detmold when you're next there, would you listen to me then?"

"Look, there's really no point in you doing that. Please just go through the normal channels."

"But would you listen to me if I showed up?"

"I suppose so. Now you'll have to excuse me."

I arrived in Detmold on the first morning of his next visit there and duly knocked on his door as he was preparing for his class.

"Yes, come in."

"Mr Giuranna, hello, I'm the guy from St John's. You said I could come and play to you."

"Good God, I'm sure I really did say that, but I certainly never imagined that you would actually make the trip."

"Well, here I am. When would be a good time please, Mr Giuranna?"

"Look, I've got fifteen minutes right now. I'll listen but I promise nothing."

I played him some Bach and after five minutes or so he stopped me.

"What is it you want from me?" he asked, visibly worn out by my persistence.

"A technique, I want you to give me a technique," I replied eagerly.

"Very well, you can start in September," he said, leaving the room.

"But I thought you said you were full next year."

"I like you. The class just got bigger!"

26

A Fishy Tale

In the '80s and '90s the Germans began to discover Ireland. The West in particular seemed to offer tremendous appeal with its extreme beauty and its people, so affable. One such *fräulein* was a steely blue-eyed blonde called Karin. Karin was a psychiatrist, living in Berlin and recently happily divorced from the renowned abstract painter, Bernt Koberling. They were both fly-fishing enthusiasts with a particular love of salmon fishing. Their pursuit of the King of Fish inevitably brought them to places like Iceland, Norway and Ireland; Bernt actually ended up living in Iceland and Karin spending more and more time on Ireland's West Coast. She would head off in her VW Camper in search of the bars of silver who were themselves on that miraculous trek, retracing their path from the Arctic Shelf where they had gorged themselves on prawns to the very spot in the very river where they had spawned some years earlier. These fish are notoriously stubborn and for reasons best known to themselves, don't give themselves up easily. Indeed, it's extraordinary that any are ever caught at all, given that they don't actually feed in freshwater. The whole phenomenon is therefore potentially down to either an involuntary reaction or a moment of anger and frustration. Astonishing how many people will spend a lifetime in this pursuit, often with little or no success.

During one of these Irish trips, Karen decided she wanted to extend her knowledge of these elusive creatures and in particular their capture. She went into the little angling shop in Ballina, which overlooks the Moy river in Co. Mayo and asked the proprietor if he knew of anyone who could help her achieve her goal. The chap took her by the arm, out into the street. He pointed to a solitary figure, up to his chest in the middle of the fast-flowing stream, who was effortlessly casting a 30m line into a stiff breeze.

"If you want to know anything about fishing, he's your man!" he said assuredly.

Intrigued, Karen donned her waders and made her way along the bank towards this vision of *'nature sauvage'*. She tried calling to him from the safety of dry land, but he was so lost in concentration on what he was doing that any attempt to capture his attention was futile. He could be there for hours. There was nothing else for it; gingerly, she edged her way into the freezing rapids. Russell's complete disregard for self-presentation and his reliance on *'la cuisine paysanne Irlandaise'*, that of wee frys and erm... big frys, had afforded him a disarmingly wild appearance. Feeling more and more unnerved by the relentless, bubbling mass of water now lapping the top of her waders, Karen let out an almost primal scream. It stopped the traffic on the bridge, spooked an entire rookery which peppered the leaden sky and, albeit momentarily, disturbed the focus of the angler. Karen always says that it was in that very instant, when the startled mountain man turned to face her and she was transfixed by his steely blue eyes, that she fell in love with him.

"If you don't mind, you're right in the way of my casting," he protested.

"I'm so sorry but I'm looking for fishing lessons and the man in the shop there said that you could help me," she screamed, coyly.

Still visibly irritated by this unwelcome intrusion, Russell fished a business card from the inside pocket of his Donegal tweed jacket.

"Here's my number. Obviously can't do anything today, as you can see, I'm busy," he answered dismissively.

Little did Russell know, Karin had his number all right. Many lessons followed, not all on fishing and not all from Russell. The great man's diet was overhauled, and he eagerly embraced a newfound worldliness. The happy couple would soon be married, and these days spend their time between Berlin, Fuerteventura and a beautiful home overlooking Lough Corrib, not a million miles from that famous spot on the Moy.

27

National Symphony Orchestra

As I was coming to the end of my time at the RCM, I got my first real taste of life as a professional musician in the London orchestral scene. I got invited along on a European tour with an ad-hoc band calling itself the National Philharmonic Orchestra. The programme was to be Wagner's 'Tristan and Isolde Overture', Mussorgsky's 'Pictures at an Exhibition' and Bruckner's 8th Symphony all conducted by a highly-strung Argentinian by the name of Carlos Païta. The orchestra was vast and star-studded, the unusually reasonable fees attracting many of the top players. I was by far the youngest member of this great gathering, a role I took to quite naturally. After a couple of rehearsals in London we set off on our short but prestigious tour. I arrived in plenty of time for the horribly early flight from LHR to find that, to my amazement, the bar adjacent to our gate was not only open at 6am but doing remarkably good business. A great many of my colleagues were, shall we say, limbering up in readiness for the trip ahead. I had heard stories of the drinking culture prevalent among the touring orchestras in England, but to witness it first-hand was something altogether different. My sister Rose had told me of the terrifying amounts of alcohol consumed by various groups on flights. How on one particular flight which had undergone a short delay before take-off, crazed passengers (a London orchestra) had drunk the bar dry before boarding. Stories of musicians going to so-called dry countries, getting permission to carry 40oz bottles of spirits, vital for keeping their instruments clean during their two-day visit to the Middle East! The people who are particularly lumbered with the insane drinking reputation are the brass and percussion players and this early morning at LHR proved no exception. There's no doubt that the partakers came from all corners of the band but the guys who were loudly propping up the bar hailed from those notorious sections, and within them, one gentleman in particular stood out. Who knows how long he'd already been there but by the time I spied him he had a half-drained glass in hand and no fewer than six Blue Diamond super-strength beers lined up on the bar next to him. Incredibly, these were duly dispatched before boarding whereupon I found myself sitting in the row behind this giant Horatio Hornblower. To my utter amazement, as we taxied towards the runway, this very same guy opened a bag stowed beneath his seat, unearthed a litre bottle of Smirnoff Blue Label and put it to his head. Slightly unnerved by this behaviour I entered into a little light-hearted conversation with myself.

Oh, he's got some kind of a blue thing going on here. I hope he has more sense than to carry that on into his all-day drinks menu. I mean, the thought of a vat of Blue Nun with dinner washed down with a bottle of Blue Curacao left me retching at the mere thought of it.

The passenger to my right, dear old Hugh Bean, must have become aware of my open-mouthed gaze and sought to reassure me.

"Jim's terrified of flying," he said.

Outwardly, I nodded and gave a wry smile. Inwardly I was thinking, *this guy's in the wrong profession. How can anyone start a day like this and end it by playing first trumpet in such a demanding programme?* This level of abuse went on all day and well into the night. The concert seemed to go well and I, being a pathetic lightweight, would have been tucked up, snug as a bug, before these guys even got serious.

By day three however there were stories of unruly behaviour and dodgy shenanigans ending in Jim badly hurting his hand. Evidently, he had finally gone back to his room on the fifteenth floor, found he'd forgotten his key and rather than trek back to reception, tried putting his first through the door.

The next night was the final concert in Señor Païta's hometown of Geneva. It was clearly a huge deal for Carlos, and he was more sweaty and agitated than usual. There were TV cameras, radio mics, family friends and countless VIPs from this beautiful lakeside town in attendance. Into this highly charged situation, propped up by a couple of his mates, staggered our first trumpet complete with a balloon-sized right hand. It was clear he was in no fit state to play but it was still several hours to showtime. After much shouting and whispering, strops being thrown and accusations levelled, it was agreed that Jim's bumper would basically play the entire programme, but that Jim would still be expected to not just sit there but take the main solos, in particular the big trumpet variation in the Mussorgsky. Occupying the back desk of violas, I was seated just in front of this bizarre scene. Come curtain-up, our still-inebriated trumpeter spent most of the proceedings slumped in his chair, often with his head between his knees, till it came to the all-important Picture. You see, Señor Païta, knowing he had one of the great trumpet players of the world at his disposal, indulged himself by taking this infamously tricky solo at breakneck speed. By all accounts, only Jim could deal with this whim satisfactorily, and so, comatose or not, this was his moment. As it approached, the tension on stage was palpable. With seconds to spare, the bumper gave Jim a kick and with a superhuman effort, plumbing the depths of all his experience, the big man came to, sat upright and delivered the impossible fanfare with a hitherto unmatched gusto. Jim did not reappear for the Bruckner and sadly I believe he had to be hospitalised upon his return to England.

Maurice Murphy was called in for the subsequent recording of the repertoire back in London. I think I witnessed the great man at a low ebb. Thankfully he recovered from this madness and continued his formidable career. This sort of approach to orchestral life is, I believe, a thing of the past. Any such behaviour these days would either be reported or sniffed out and harshly dealt with. As far as I was concerned, I scurried back to the relatively sober environment of string quartets where the technical demands, soloistic style and need for team commitment renders the very idea of doing rehearsals, never mind concerts, in an inebriated state impossible to imagine.

I remember a colleague once saying to me with great glee; "You know, we shouldn't worry so much about the old booze. I mean, after all, we never drink on the day of a concert so, if we're doing eighty-odd concerts a year, that's at least eighty days of the year when we don't drink."

"Oh, and what do we usually do after a concert then?" I enquired.

"Aw, darn it. Back to the drawing board!"

28

The Molitor Cocktail

It's a well-known fact that the Irish adopt shall we say a colourful approach to the use of language. I am certainly a fully paid-up member of the 'why spoil a good story with boring facts' club, other than in the hallowed pages of this book, obviously.

Lough Neagh's the largest freshwater lake in Europe.

The Foyle's the fastest flowing river in Europe.

The tallest sand dunes in Europe are at the Five Finger Strand.

Or, my personal favourite is the sign on the dramatic approach to a particularly stunning beach in Donegal that reads;

'The second most beautiful beach in the world.'

These are only some of the random facts that a Derry boy grows up with. Another tale was the one about a certain Willie Anderson, the guy with the Stradivarius. These were such heart-warming notions, why would you want to go and prove them false. This last fact however, I viewed with more than a little scepticism until much later in life when it came up in conversation with the violinist, Hugh Maguire. Not only had he heard about this man, he had actually visited the house and even played on the fabled instrument. With this unquestionable endorsement I decided that on my next trip home I would make it a priority to pay Mr Anderson a visit. Bear in mind that even though this man lived with his sister Muriel, both amateur musicians, in quite a nice townhouse just a few doors up from where we had lived before Kebroyde, he walked the streets dressed in tramps' clothing, investigating the bins as he passed. I don't think he was expecting to find the great violin maker's recipe for varnish within these receptacles, lunch was probably closer to the awful truth.

The long-awaited day finally arrived, and I made my way unannounced to the yellow door totally unsure of what my reception might be. I need not have worried. An animated pair of siblings greeted me.

"Well, well, if it isn't Paul Cassidy himself. We wondered when you might show up," they chorused, grinning widely.

"You'll be wanting to see the violin," they went on, as one.

"Come in, come in. Upstairs, follow me," said the sister. The brother went off into a back room to fetch the prize. Even before I got to the stairs, I could see that the two reception rooms on the ground floor each had two pianos in them. A cursory glance elicited a Steinway Upright and a gorgeous Bosendorfer Grand. There were stringed instruments everywhere, on top of the pianos, in glass cases, propped up against the walls. I was shown into the front room on the first floor and soon the man of the house reappeared laden with instrument cases.

"OK, shall we begin? First of all, what kind of bow do you like to use? French, German, English perhaps?" he asked.

"Well, given the choice I would always choose French," I replied.

"Fine, I have Henri, Pecatte, Tourte…"

"Oh, the Tourte will do fine, thank you," I blurted out, slightly hysterically.

I was already overwhelmed, and he hadn't even opened a single case. Upon opening, I could see that here was someone who really knew what he was doing. Every instrument was cosseted in velvet and fondly wrapped in a colour-coordinated silk cloth. Each and every case carried a full complement of bows and the instruments themselves were all in pristine condition, recently strung with the latest fashionable brand.

"Let's start with the Rocca," he exclaimed, like a kid in a sweet shop.

And so, this extraordinary exhibition began. The Rocca was followed by a Pressenda, then a Testore. A Gagliano was barely given the time of day before a Guadagnini was produced. It took some getting your head around. Here was a figure who I'd only ever glimpsed raiding the city waste bins, standing in his own rather beautiful living room, handing me one priceless relic after another. Dumbstruck and fast running out of party pieces we came to the big moment. Mr Anderson left the room and returned this time with a double case. How odd, I thought to myself. Why with so many options would you choose to keep your *pièce de résistance* in a double case… strange. Sure enough, the opened case revealed not one but two violins. This guy sure had a flare for drama. The anticipation was well-nigh unbearable.

"Here's what you've come to see. It's the Molitor Strad. Golden Period of course. It dates from 1.6.1707 and originally belonged to Napoleon who subsequently gave it to one of his favourite generals, Count Molitor. As you might imagine Paul, you're not the first person to come to see this violin. Many of the great violinists of the world have made the journey here, including Yehudi himself, in an effort to get their hands on this beauty."

It was magnificent. Everything you might expect and more from such a revered work of art. Once again, the mint condition of the instrument was mind-blowing. Over the years I have often found that Strads can be a bit of a disappointment, maybe because they have such a reputation to live up to, but not this one. When one put bow to this string the possibilities were endless. Clarity, sweetness, power, intimacy. Seemingly all emotions could be teased from this magic box. What excited me most, was the feeling as you approached the bridge with the bow, the sound appeared to have no end of intensity. There was an almost deafening hiss close up, but you could tell that the core of this sound was hitting the back of any hall. It's an exhilarating feeling, much as I imagine coming down the home straight in a F1 car. I could have spent the rest of the afternoon enjoying this rare thrill, but I could see that the Andersons were not done yet. What possible trick could they have up their sleeves at this stage of the proceedings? How on earth could they possibly trump this?

Mr Anderson politely waited for a natural lull in my infernal scratching before intoning; "And now for my pride and joy."

With that, he unveiled Molitor's bedfellow. It was without doubt the most beautiful violin I had ever seen before or since. It was an immaculate Amati. Nicolo Amati was the teacher of Stradivarius and the maker who, for some unknown reason, held a special place in my heart. It was a humbling experience to handle such a piece of history. I found myself unable to actually play it, preferring instead to just gawp at it in wonder.

When the owner produced a letter from none other than Charles Beare himself that read; "This is the finest example of Nicolo Amati's work I have ever seen," the whole experience became all the more fantastical.

I left that unlikely address that afternoon, punch drunk. Just when I thought I'd rode his famous uppercut, he caught me with the killer right cross. I have no idea where Mr Anderson got his money or what drew him to acquire such a collection of instruments, but what a collection it was. Despite their warm welcome and insistence that I come back at any time and spend as long as I wished in their wonderland playroom, I never did return. Someone sent me an article from the local paper years later reporting the death of the sister; he had already passed sometime before. The article outlined how the collection was to be sold and the proceeds given to the Red Cross, whose Meals on Wheels service she had used for years. The Molitor went on to fetch a record breaking $3.6m in 2010. As for the Amati, I know not of its whereabouts.

29

Slava

Musicians basically fall into two denominations. Us mere mortals (who range from routine interpreters of an abstract language, to enormously gifted individuals who have a deep understanding of this nebulous artform and an enviable ability to communicate it), and the rare and precious gods of music. These are beings who transcend all technical barriers and effortlessly use music, as it flows through them from another dimension, to strike at our very souls, making us laugh or cry, eager or nostalgic. Music identifies nations, incites revolutions, charts love affairs, signals birth, provides requiem, balms wounds and calms the mind.

When Terry Waite was released from captivity, we played at his welcoming home event. We played, at his request, my arrangement of Elgar's simple little 'Chanson de Matin'. There wasn't a dry eye in the house. One thinks of the power of such ballads as 'Free Nelson Mandela', 'Do They Know It's Christmas', 'All You Need is Love', or 'We Shall Overcome', all of which did arguably more than anything else to further their relevant cause. What finally crushed the spirit of the Nazis after two years of encircling Leningrad? Not the extreme cold or the screams of the starving. It was the premiere of Shostakovich's 7th Symphony, played by the near-death band of besieged skeletons and relayed via loudspeakers to the outside. The side-drum player who led the famous march had literally been found in the morgue not a fortnight before... they had mistakenly thought he was dead!!

I consider myself most fortunate to have brushed shoulders with one such musical god, in the form of Mstislav Rostropovich. The first time I encountered him was when he came to conduct the Britten-Pears

Orchestra. In the run-up to his visit, Hugh Maguire would regale us with stories of Slava, whom he knew from his days as leader of the London Symphony Orchestra. One mind-boggling tale recalled a US tour when the great man played thirty concertos in ten concerts. Basically, the entire such repertoire for cello in little over a week. As if this wasn't already a super-human feat, each night Slava would be the last to leave the bar. Now this, on an LSO tour, really is remarkable. Upon vacating the watering hole, he would retire to his room and practice for the next night (he used a practice mute btw!). This was someone who inspired a doubling of the cello repertoire during his own lifetime. He was friends with the likes of Prokofiev, Britten and Shostakovich, all of whom wrote major works for him.

I love the story of when Shostakovich sent him his Second Concerto. Slava excitedly and instantly committed it to memory and four days later, the two men met to play it through, Shostakovich taking the part of the orchestra on piano. It went swimmingly and both men were ecstatic. Vodka was produced… much vodka.

"Let's play it again!" bellowed Dmitri.

This performance, at least of the cello part, was a tiny bit wayward. Shostakovich was thrilled however… More vodka.

"Again!" insisted DSCH.

On the third run-through, Slava reckoned that though the composer once again faithfully reproduced the orchestral part, he was reduced to playing excerpts from the Saints-Saens concerto.

This level of drinking sounds like a tall story I know and I too would struggle to believe it had I not witnessed it with my own eyes; at dinners where we lightweights would be having beer or wine, Slava would be tidying up a bottle of vodka on his own. Such was his colossal energy he just seemed immune to something so trivial as mere fire water. This guy was coming to Aldeburgh to conduct us kids… Wow!

I cringe when I think back on it now. Coming back from a fortnight's holiday in Spain, travelling on a coach through the night and stopping off only to pick up my viola, I landed on my seat under the maestro's nose. On the stand was Prokofiev's fiendishly difficult Classical Symphony, which came as a rude awakening to a sunburnt, threadbare, unprepared twit like myself. Rather like when the violinist Ignaz Schuppanzigh complained to Beethoven of the impossibility of one of his violin parts, Beethoven replied; "Do you think I spare a thought for your wretched fiddle when the gods are summoning me!!?"

So, Slava showed no mercy for our woeful inadequacies as we hurtled through Prokofiev's masterpiece. His authority and absolute understanding of the piece were thrilling. Next up was the same composer's ingenious 'Peter and the Wolf', which Slava narrated most entertainingly in Russian. He was intent on playing through the programme in its entirety before settling down to work. After coffee came the Haydn C major Cello Concerto whereupon our conductor morphed into the personage imprinted on the mental wall chart of everyone in that hall. Suddenly, there he was in full regalia as it were; Mr Cello. His command of the instrument was breathtaking. All piffling concerns such as intonation, phrasing, articulation and so forth disappeared under his spell. It was a brief moment in the last movement however that would make me jump out of my seat and leave an impression upon me for life. The opening phrase of that movement is a fun-filled horn-call punctuated by two triumphant gestures. These two chords, this simple pair of thirds became, in Slava's hands, something so much more. Over and above the conveyance of their inherent, unbridled joy, was the effortless display of power and masterful technique. I couldn't get over these sounds that he had produced, like silver bullets. The fact that he was sitting there, facing me, barely a cello's length away made it all the more riveting. After that morning's rehearsal I gingerly approached him and asked if he could possibly explain how he was able to make those sounds. He smiled and taking my bow, winched it up till the stick was almost parallel to the hair.

"Well, here's a start," he said with a smile.

What was he to say? Where does one begin with such a question? His answer was simplistic in the extreme and didn't address the issue in any depth whatsoever, but the tremendously complex physics of the bow arm cannot be dealt with in a rehearsal break. His answer was good enough for me and to this day, I tighten my bow Slava-style.

A couple of years later, Slava was to furnish me with another unforgettable musical memory. Through his close friendship with Ben and Peter he had become increasingly attached to their chosen corner of Suffolk, even buying a house there at one stage. He and his wife, the soprano Galina Vishnevskaya, became more regular visitors. This particular year saw them both take a very active role in the festival. Imagine my delight, terror, excitement, when Hugh asked me to play in a performance of the Mendelssohn Octet at the Maltings in a group containing none other than Rostropovich. Hugh's colleague from the Allegri days, Patrick Ireland, would play first viola leaving me on second, seated right next to his highness. The solitary rehearsal was an intimidating experience to say the least. As I recall, Slava was playing all the Bach and Britten Suites over the few days, as well as conducting a concert or two and this performance of the Mendelssohn. He turned up late, having been held up by a press conference that inevitably overran and then, contrary to all things real, took his place next to me. I was literally shaking with fear and happiness.

The piece unfolded as it always does, a swirling, turbulent sea of imbalance and un-togetherness. But it was in the calm after the storm, within the development section that danger lurked. Mendelssohn switches the focus to deep within the group; a tranquil, misty moment where the fourth violin utters one of the most poignant lines of the whole play. It was here, among a sea of bars rest, that the cellist to my left found himself adrift. Not used to the piece, his mind on a million other things, he had completely lost his bearings. After several aborted attempts to clamber back on board, I decided to take charge of his rescue. Unnerved myself and wary of losing my place, I managed to catch his eye just at the moment where that momentous, musical wave begins to lift you and sweep you along. I gave him a nod and a smile, signalling where he should join in, and he jumped on board that glorious white horse which ultimately crashes you onto the beach, which is the recapitulation.

We had weathered the storm. Not a word was said as we turned the page and embarked on the slow movement. We weren't eight bars in when Slava once again showed signs of being elsewhere. As Hugh tried his best to weave some magic in that most touching opening phrase, Slava was intent on interrupting it with an inappropriate bass line. This time my idol turned to me, his glance silently asking if I could possibly help him out again. I duly obliged and we continued on our way. It was a perplexing and somewhat underwhelming experience. Nothing was ever said between us on the subject, but I could see in his eyes he was grateful for my gentle nods of reassurance as we negotiated the concert performance.

This was Rostropovich for God's sake! He was arguably the most formidable musician on the planet; he dined with royalty of every kind. Whilst for me, this was probably the most prestigious gig of my life to date, for him, it was nothing more than an annoying late-afternoon bash which completed the overall picture of a festival theme. He, and he alone, had filled the Maltings that afternoon and for every other concert he was involved in; few in the auditorium knew or cared who we were. While we were downing Adnams in the Plough and Sail, reminiscing, he was busy delivering memorable accounts of the Britten Suites to another packed house. While we drove back to reality in our second-hand motors, he was on his private jet winging his way to play for the Pope or a president or maybe to a G8 summit. He had long since become way more than just a cellist; he was a major character of the world. Sadly, I never got to meet him again but at least I have my memories of a force without which the world is a lesser place.

30

The Brodsky Quartet

It was in the September of 1981 that a piano student by the name of Dina Bennett arrived at the College from the RNCM to do a postgraduate year. Word soon spread that she was an excellent player and was particularly interested in accompanying. These sort of people were like gold dust so I quickly hunted her down and asked if she fancied doing some playing together. She immediately agreed, pointing out how much she loved the viola repertoire and we started a partnership that would last throughout my remaining days at college.

In May 1982, I received a phone call from the first violin of the Brodsky Quartet, Michael Thomas, asking if I would be interested in auditioning for the group. Given that to play in a string quartet had become my dream, I jumped at the opportunity and we agreed that I would come to Manchester, where they were based, the following weekend. I remembered that I had in fact once heard the Brodsky Quartet. It had been at Snape, during a Lutoslawski Symposium in which I and various colleagues had performed the Prelude and Fugue for 13 Solo Strings and they had come to play the String Quartet.

I remember thinking how cool that seemed, already a proper, full-time string quartet and only eighteen years old. That had been it however. They came and went in a cloud of resin dust; we didn't even get to say hello.

Suddenly, these people were making a reappearance in my life. Who were they, I wondered? Then I thought of Dina, my trusty piano player. She had spent four years studying in Manchester. She must know all about them. I quickly got on the phone and invited myself for dinner that same evening.

By the time I got there I was impatient and full of it; "So, who are they? Are they any good? Are they nice people? Why is the viola player leaving? TELL ME ALL YOU KNOW."

Dina was unusually reserved in her response to all this haggling; oddly considered and professional somehow. She did however leave me in no doubt that this was a special group of people, enormously talented and completely driven in their quest to be the very best in their chosen field. They had already been focused on this lofty goal for ten years. I was so excited.

It was only much later in the evening that she divulged the information that subsequently explained her initial reaction. She had had a four-year relationship with Michael Thomas and even shared a house with him and some other students, among them Mike's sister Jacky, the cellist of the Brodsky Quartet.

It was to this very house (5 Edge Lane, Chorlton-cum-Hardy) that I was destined to go just a couple of days hence.

"How should I be?" I asked Dina.

"Just be yourself," she replied.

"What should I wear?"

"Wear a suit. That will impress them," she said, after some thought.

I only had one suit… But what a suit! It was a cream Yves Saint Laurent number with a fine pinstripe. The cream shirt underneath was twinned with a brown silk tie and the whole ensemble of out-and-out dandiness was made complete by the addition of a pair of maroon, patent, alligator-skin ankle boots. Take into account that in those days, my hair was a veritable explosion of curls, springing high above my head and cascading onto my shoulders, what a sight I must have presented as I stepped off the train in Manchester's Piccadilly Station. Mind you, the sight that confronted me was arguably just as comical. Mike was sporting a striped T-shirt that had seen, well… days. And what little remained of a pair of shorts, which had also obviously seen, well… a few more. He had with him another viola player, which unnerved me somewhat. Was this some sort of weird strategy, or were there several people turning up for this audition? I never really found out the answer to this, but I did learn that, though several people had already auditioned without success, neither Mike's pal nor anyone else was going to be intruding on our weekend together. The more I got to know Mike; the first option was undoubtedly the more probable explanation.

We made our introductions, jumped in his old Saab (*he's got his own car... cool*, I thought to myself) and made our way back to the quartet house (*doubly cool*, I thought to myself). This short journey was surprisingly adventurous as Mike, quite naturally, took to pavements and grass verges to nullify the pressures of annoying traffic. Sooner than expected we were screeching to a halt outside an imposing Victorian semi in the leafy Manchester suburb. Upon entering the abode, my ill-chosen attire was made to feel even more ludicrous. The entire place was in a severe post-party state with discarded debris on a grand scale. I was shown into the kitchen area, which appeared to be ground zero. I stood there, all creamy silk and bounce, knee-deep in bottles, cans, crisps and nuts. Streamers fell untidily from every surface, and the remains of a large cake stuck resolutely to its stand in the middle of the table, its many candles, which had been carefully arranged to spell out '21', now buried within its icing and filling. It was at this moment the door opened to reveal the object of all this merriment. Her slightly-the-worse-for-wear look only added to her instantly overwhelming appeal.

"Hi, you must be Paul. I'm Jacky!"

It is perhaps a trifle fanciful to suggest that at that moment I fully understood the dramatic effect this young woman would have on the rest of my life, but equally, there's no denying that her infectiously sunny demeanour and charismatic energy did have a profound impact upon me. This was only to be reinforced when later that same day I sat next to her for the first time and experienced at first hand her total command of the cello and extraordinary knowledge of the quartet repertoire, never mind the sheer allure and mesmeric quality she would quite clearly bring to any stage.

I could stand it no longer and asked if I could possibly change out of this ridiculous suit, using the false excuse that I had had an exam earlier in the day in London, and no time to go home before my train left. I was shown to my room on the second floor and quickly ditched the YSL car crash (thanks Dina!) in favour of a T-shirt and jeans.

My big audition day continued somewhat falteringly. Jacky, Mike and I stood around for quite a while talking about this and that, which was very nice and all, but it did become increasingly obvious that we had a slight second violin issue. This was way before mobile phones but Ian Belton, being an extremely reliable sort of chap, had clearly come up against some insurmountable problem. Lunch slowly morphed into tea and more and more sleepy-eyed, hungover students began to appear from every recess of the house. We retired to the adjoining park to play football, Jacky too, which made me happy, as I already felt the world a lesser place without her around. This simple kick-around was an important initiation process and when I subsequently suggested booking a table for later at a well-known Indian restaurant downtown, I unwittingly moved myself a baby-step closer to the Brodsky Quartet without yet playing a note.

At about 5.30pm we had returned all hot and sticky from the park and put the kettle on again, when down the hall, behind a wave of apologies and excuses came not a white horse, but a black horse. From what I could make out of Ian's features, he seemed to be an immediately likeable fellow. Completely covered from head-to-toe in a grimy film of black oil, he explained that he had spent the whole day under his dad's hand-me-down green Hillman Hunter, which had broken down, leaving him stranded on a remote stretch of the M62.

All of a sudden, a different dynamic fell upon the place and in the blink of an eye, we four had taken our places in the pre-arranged front room, a veritable mountain of quartet literature stacked silently by our sides. I found these initial playthroughs absolutely thrilling. To actually be a living part of these great masterpieces, the recent loves of my life, was almost unbearably exciting.

I had been in quartets before, having spent the last four or five years focusing on little else, but those experiences, though magical in so many ways, were not like this. Up until this point, pretty much everything my friends and I had learnt, we had learnt together; finding our way, together. But here, I was in the midst of musicians who had been studying these towering works for ten years already. People who knew their intimate details and could negotiate their many pitfalls. The Mozart D Minor, Beethoven Op.18/1, Schubert G Major, Brahms A Minor, Janacek 2, Bartok 5 all seemed to effortlessly and faultlessly come to life in their young, yet experienced hands. The ability to move seamlessly from intricate dialogue, to restrained *accompagnato*, to devilish bravura, was staggering and completely intoxicating. Before I had coiffed my first glorious Kingfisher, or dipped my mouth-watering Rajdoot papadam, I knew without doubt I wanted to be a part of this formidable band.

We spent the whole of the next day locked away in that room, perched among the foothills of Durand, Breitkopf and Peters. We barely took time for a cup of tea as, one after another, we shouted out our next favourite quartet. There was no discussion or murmurs of disdain; as soon as someone called out their choice, the music was found, and the entire piece dispatched with feverish alacrity. In the late evening, exhausted both mentally and physically, we retired from the chaos of the music room and reconvened in the sitting room on the first floor. This was a very pleasing space with a bay window, impressive original fireplace, and one of those light shades made up of little squares of coloured glass. This particular one was in various shades of green, which, coupled with the well-matched sofas, curtains and carpet, made the whole scene reassuringly cosy and grown-up. I would later come to realise that this homely scene was unsurprisingly the handiwork of none other than Jacky.

We had arrived at what was inevitably the treacherous part of the weekend, the part where we have to talk, and talk not of music but of the more mundane, nitty-gritty aspects of what we might be embarking upon. The fascinating fact is that you can tell in a heartbeat whether or not you can live with someone's playing, they have only to put bow to string and you instinctively know. Talking is a whole other can of worms. Communicating your feelings, on even a basic level, can prove to be a challenging endeavour but when the issues under discussion involve not only your future and your livelihood, but your precious art; the skill you have devoted the vast majority of your waking life to, then the often ill-equipped protagonists face a wickedly unfair task, alone. It makes my blood boil when people go on about the amount of time surgeons, lawyers and the like invest in their chosen field. Pit it against the input of a top-class instrumentalist and it pales into insignificance. The three youngsters before me in that room, though barely out of their teens, had already, collectively invested thirty-three years in their chosen field of excellence and that doesn't include the many years of individual toil that predated the quartet's formation.

That evening's conversation went on for hours, as people tried to voice their anxieties. It came to a natural close when at a certain moment, sensing the trepidation in the room, I just opened my heart to these newfound friends in an effort to alleviate the pressure and show my already resolute commitment to the group. What effect this emotive outpouring might have on the others I had no idea. I only knew I had to follow my gut. If such an honest gesture backfired, then perhaps I was in the wrong place after all.

On a positive note, we all agreed that we were very happy with each other's playing but quite rightly, shouldn't rush into anything. We decided to let the dust settle and meet up the following weekend at my place in London when we would focus our attention on one work. We could spend the two days rehearsing just that piece and give an informal playthrough to a few friends on the Sunday evening. That piece was to be Janacek No.1, a piece none of us knew.

Becoming a Brod

I had recently moved from what was arguably the wettest flat in London, to what was indisputably the coldest. From an early age I had dreamed of living in London and now, as an older man, there's still nowhere I'd rather be, but I guess like all great metropoli, London inevitably has its ups and downs. Sandwiched between the Swinging '60s, when London was spearheading the revolution and was seen as the yardstick for all things cool, from music to art, literature to fashion; and its glorious resurgence in the '90s, which has seen London once again take up its rightful place as the number one city in the world, lay a grey, dank, lifeless period. Wilson's ill-fitting suits, haphazard comb-overs and pipe smoke were replaced with her fearsome two-piece, matching handbag and hairspray. We were unknowingly embarking on a long voyage with an Iron Maiden at the helm and we idle Jack Tars were going to be made ship-shape. At least the Jolly Giant who had previously skippered Britannia was openly passionate about music and could therefore be trusted to keep half an eye on the state of the arts; this battleship showed no such weakness and was clearly blind to all that nonsense. She should maybe have glanced over her neat little blue shoulder pads before donning the blinkers. Was it not her most revered and successful predecessor, certainly of the twentieth century, who at the start of the second Great War, when his Cabinet had suggested scrapping the arts budget in order to release much-needed financial resources, had replied; "But then what would we be fighting for?"

I shared this ice box with a wonderful wee leprechaun called Dara de Cogan. We met at the Irish Youth Orchestra on a course where he expertly led the orchestra through some challenging repertoire including

Strauss' infamous 'Ein Heldenleben'. Though he looked for all the world like a champion jockey, he very wisely put looks aside and concentrated on playing the violin. He was a rum character and he and I hit it off immediately. Dara had just won a big competition in Ireland and first prize included a performance of the Sibelius Concerto with the RTE Orchestra. I came home late one evening to find Dara and a fellow female student listening intently to this very work. Dara was reclined on the sofa, in a sleeping bag for warmth, while she lay on the floor, wrapped in blankets, enraptured by the great maestro's playing.

"They finally sent me the tape from Dublin," said Dara nonchalantly, in between long, considered drags on his Dunhill Extra Long.

She didn't even notice I'd come in, but became more and more transfixed on Dara with every dizzying violin entry emanating from the double cassette deck. I decided not to get in the way of what seemed like a pretty sure-fire situation but couldn't help also being somewhat bowled over by the brilliance of the playing. When I eventually saw Dara the next day, I immediately congratulated him on the amazing performance and asked if I might borrow the tape so I could hear the whole thing.

"Of course you can," he said.

"My performance is on deck one; deck two is Heifetz with the Chicago Symphony. Sorry but I didn't want to take any chances with her, know what I mean!"

Absolutely priceless. Dara's performance with the RTE was actually excellent but I guess, if you want to be sure, to be sure, Jascha's yer man!

The three Brodskys turned up promptly on the Saturday morning and I had managed to commandeer the front room for the whole weekend. It was great seeing them again and I couldn't wait to get stuck into some proper work. I'd spent all week trying to get to know the Janacek, but it proved to be quite elusive. The notes are one thing, but we had chosen well because almost every bar throws up challenges of ensemble and interpretation. The rehearsals were intense and in no time, we were assembling in a friend's house in Hampstead to give our first performance.

We started the short programme with a gallop through Haydn's 'Rider' Quartet, before unleashing the Janacek. The few people there were invited musician friends and more crucially the two people responsible for getting us together in the first place, Terence Weil and Hugh Maguire. Terry had been the quartet's mentor throughout their time at college, and it was he who had thought of phoning Hugh in an attempt to cast the net wide in their search for a violist.

Terry was one hell of a cellist. A founder member of the ECO, he was also the first person the Amadeus Quartet had tried to contact when they were forming. Unfortunately for Terry, he was on tour in South America at the time, they found Martin Lovett and the rest is history. One can only imagine just how good Terry might have been had he not been seriously addicted to booze and cigarettes and a fully signed-up member of the Django Reinhardt school of cello playing; he only ever employed two fingers on both hands. Take the left; only fingers one and two were deemed viable options. The third was a necessary substitute on occasion; the fourth only made up the numbers and rarely got off the bench. As for the thumb, this was considered a ludicrous proposal and consequently never even made the team. The right had a slightly different formation. Here the thumb, being a necessary evil, was used along with fingers one and four to steady the infernal bow; neatly leaving numbers two and three for the more useful task of cradling a Weight in readiness for the odd bar's rest whereupon a quick drag or two could be enjoyed.

His great love was chamber music, in which he was heavily involved throughout his career. He played in the Melos Ensemble and one of his many quartets had the rather tasty line-up of Hugh Maguire, Iona Brown, Cecil Aronowitz and his good self on cello. Hugh would later confess to me that rehearsals in this group were remarkable in that they could barely see each other through the cloud of smoke created by their relentless puffing away. One day Terry laid down his bow on the stand whilst he scribbled in a crucial fingering, when suddenly to his amazement, the hair of the bow caught fire and swung loose. He had earlier on placed a lit cigarette there and having forgotten about it, had already lit another one. That was the last time he'd ever bother with silly fingerings.

Despite everything, he was a loveable character and a magical player. His dependency on tobacco and alcohol however did eventually get the better of him. We had to watch, sad and horrified as he, bit by bit, lost both his legs due to poor circulation. On a musical level, turning up one hour late and pie-eyed, for the world premiere of *The Turn of the Screw* in Venice wasn't popular. Nor was lighting up, in the principal's chair, mid-performance at the Proms in London. He was so drunk he'd momentarily forgotten where he was.

In retrospect, it's slightly scary that my future potentially lay in the hands of this one man. Though I'm sure the three Brodskys would ultimately decide, his say would hold some sway. I blame it on the drink myself, but for whatever reason, the decision was taken that evening. Two half-Belgians, a Paddy and a Brit would throw their caps and berets into the ring, share their dreams, pool their aspirations, share their futures, and merge their personalities in pursuit of a common goal. Yes, three hats were effectively already in that ring, but my predecessor Alex's decision to move on at such a crucial moment did rupture the initial bond. For anyone harbouring any doubts, now was the time to jump ship.

Four hats remained!

These decisions, these promises, often taken, like ours, in the heat of the moment over a pint, are colossal. Though we wouldn't have known it then, or cared, we had without putting pen to paper entered into a bona fide legal agreement. We were in what's called a Partnership at Will, which carries many far-reaching implications. News of this decision would spread through the musical world like wildfire. Changes of personnel are perceived as a weakness; you risk becoming a second-rate group, not taken seriously by the music world at large, including your peers.

At a moment when many of our friends were embarking on proper jobs, affording them a bit of security within the profession, we faced a totally uncertain future in which an unnatural degree of enforced intimacy and a perilously high level of stress were abysmally rewarded financially.

'Oh, you're so lucky to be doing something you love' or 'What do you do for a living, then?' are just two of the phrases musicians hear all too often. Both are ignorant, degrading and inciteful.

Our future consisted of three concerts, each bringing in a total of £150, and endless days of long, punishing rehearsals stretching into the distance, for which there was no recompense. Whilst the quartet did already have very respectable management in place in the form of Ibbs and Tillett, students couldn't easily commit to paid gigs in case they interfered with their all-important college duties. Instead of encouraging such extraordinary devotion and passion, the RNCM chose to quash it from the outset, forbidding the quartet to work together except on the rare occasions when it benefited them; a student exchange programme for example. Apart from these instances, the four students were actively discouraged from playing chamber music in favour of individual and orchestral work. Thankfully, the group totally ignored this foolishness, but imagine how much could have been gained by both sides had the College had a bit more foresight.

I remember there was an imminent lunchtime performance of Beethoven's Opus 127 in the College, which the quartet was not allowed to do with me. This would prove to be Alex's swansong before he struck out on his own path. As of that fairly random moment, I would be the viola player in the Brodsky Quartet. Flippin'eck, I would be in a real band. I would be playing quartets for a living.

Oddly, despite the inevitable limitations brought about by this new definition, I found it incredibly liberating; something akin to becoming institutionalised in a way. A simplification of choices and a strict regime with challenging demands seemed to sharpen my focus, lending life a crystal clarity. Suddenly, I was one of the gang, and we could talk more openly about all manner of things, past and present.

Within days of our newly forged relationship, a post was advertised for a resident quartet at Lancaster University. We decided to go for it but as luck would have it, the audition day was the very same as the day of my final recital at the College in London. Unperturbed, I found that if Lancaster was prepared to give us the first morning slot, I could catch a flight from Manchester to London and with a bit of luck, and a favourable tailwind, just make my afternoon slot.

The whole thing felt so rock 'n' roll, man! Saturday evening, last rehearsal with Dina for Monday's recital. Sunday, up to Manchester to rehearse with the band. Monday morning, on to Lancaster for 9am audition; play Janacek 1/Op.127. Then, bomb down the M6 just making BA007 back to LHR.

I ran at full pelt from South Kensington station all the way to the old recital hall of the RCM. The worst bit was that glass corridor which linked the old building to the new... gosh that was hot! Arriving literally as my name was called, Dina in a panic, me shaking and in a sweat; the opening of Hindemith's 'Der Swanendreher' can't have been pretty. Yet it mattered not. I was like one in a relationship that I have decided is over but haven't been able to finish. This whole scene was history and consequently, went by in a haze. The past and the future had momentarily blurred the present.

For what it's worth, I got my ARCM. We, yes *we*, the Brodsky Quartet, didn't get offered the Lancaster job. Life has a habit of working out for the best. These couple of days were thrilling, the results merely stamps on the passport of life. I was about to start getting that other passport stamped.

My four years at the RCM came to an end that afternoon. For the most part, I had loved every minute of it, but now and with exquisite timing, real life was kicking in. One minor detail was that I would have to move to Manchester. Jacky still had one more year of studies to complete which in a way worked out quite well since I had got myself a one-year scholarship to study with Giuranna in Detmold. It was never in my mind to actually go and live in Germany, so presumably I could just as easily commute from Manchester as London. It was going to be very sad leaving London, but it was a change of scene and the beginning of a lifetime adventure so, *tant pis*!

Before all that though, I had the summer to negotiate. I had two weeks' work with the Ulster Orchestra before embarking on my much-anticipated three-month period of study with MacInnes. This had all been cleared quartet-wise in advance, and so it was that no sooner had we cemented our futures together than we parted company. The summer would give us time to focus our minds and we would re-group in September.

In truth, that farcical final recital told a story. In many respects, I had long since become disenchanted with the RCM. Given my waning interest in both the solo viola repertoire and orchestral playing, my mundane lessons and the College's prioritising of our endless participation in their flagship orchestras, lead to my time there being more and more frustrating. A year earlier I had actually been expelled because I had chosen to do an extremely lucrative week's recording work with the Ulster Orchestra, causing me to miss one college orchestra rehearsal. How any sane person could imagine for a second that a budding musician would be better served sitting around for yet another week practising some obscure viola sonata and turning up for a three-hour orchestral rehearsal rather than flying off to a different country to record two symphonies with a professional orchestra and conductor, is bewildering. When I was refused permission by the then president, my old mate, Michael Gough-Matthews, I think I thought about the consequences for about as long as it took me to descend the marble stairs and exit the Victorian oak doors.

I took the £1,000 I eventually earned that week straight to Withers Violin Shop and bought a beautiful Vigneron bow for £999. I cherished that magic wand and played on it for the next twenty years. I was subsequently expelled but a few weeks later allowed back in after I had written some letters of apology and they had no doubt realised they were probably a bit light in the old Alto Clef department.

32

The Ulster Orchestra

A year later I would once again make that welcome journey over to Belfast for a couple of weeks' work with the Ulster Orchestra. The UO arrived in my life out of the blue, around the time I started college and my frequent trips over there proved to be financially invaluable for me. They were such lovely people and I quickly felt comfortable in their midst. My first rehearsal with them included Brahms' 2nd Symphony and in the break a slim, fresh-faced violinist with a dollop of white candyfloss for hair came over and asked me if I was OK. I was young and not a little nervous being in amongst these professional musicians, but he was so friendly and soon we were yapping away like we'd known each other for ages. He enquired as to whether I'd found somewhere nice to stay.

"Oh yes," I replied and told him of my B&B a short walk up the Antrim Road. His pallor paled and his voice took on a more serious air.

"Don't you be walking up there alone son. I'll give you a lift after the rehearsal."

"Aw it's fine," said I, "it's not that far and I could use the exercise."

"That's murder mile you're talking about. More people have been killed on that stretch of road than anywhere else in NI. I'm giving you a lift and that's the end of it."

Dennis Benson, or Benny as he was known, and I quickly became best buddies and from then on I used to always stay as a guest in his lovely house out in Bangor where I also got to know and love his beautiful wife, Muriel, and their three charming children, John, Kathleen, and Bridget. This unexpected development brought an added dimension to my ever-increasing visits north. Not only was I learning how to survive in an orchestra, but I was witnessing at first hand the lifestyle of two very different musicians. These people were hard working. Bringing up three children while holding down two jobs is not a walk in the park, as I would find out later in life. They would both practice for an hour before preparing a delicious breakfast for six, consisting of juice, muesli, fruit, yoghurt, tea and toast, all of which was lovingly homemade. Then while Benny and I would get ready to leave for our day's rehearsal, Muriel would make us some delicious packed lunch before herself settling down to a day of teaching the piano.

Upon our return in the late evening there would be tea, cheese and crackers and Muriel's mouth-watering flapjack. All this would be enjoyed, relaxing and chatting in front of a roaring fire. Great times indeed.

Benny's striking looks made him a real focal point in an orchestra not short of a few characters. There was Jeremy the cellist, who always played with neither spike nor footwear. Colin, the jolly giant of a principal flute who played on a very impressive golden flute, not unlike a certain Mr Galway, the then principal flute of the Berlin Phil. who probably came from the same pipe band! Then there was the bewitching sound of the enigmatic clarinettist Chris, who always seemed to be hiding himself behind both Colin and his almost comically super-charged bifocals.

Last but not least was Malcolm on percussion, the undisputed comedian of the band. During one of my visits the orchestra played a 'pops' concert in the Slieve Donard Hotel in the picturesque coastal village of Newcastle, Co. Down, where the Mountains of Mourne sweep down to the sea. Coincidentally, the principal conductor of the UO at that time was none other than Bryden 'Jack' Thompson, the man who had so impressed me in the youth orchestra. Jack was a formidably gifted conductor and though this programme was perfectly reasonable in many respects, it placed no great demands on his ability, and I could sense he was struggling to keep his mischievous side in check. We all undertook this evening of lollipops in the playful and light-hearted manner in which it was intended, to a packed ballroom.

It was near the end of the first half and we were luxuriating in the dreamy sounds of Debussy's 'En Bateau' when we became aware of the not inconsiderable figure of the orchestral manager, Frank, tip-toeing his way up the middle aisle from the back. Upon arriving at the conductor's podium, he rather gingerly tapped Jack on the shoulder. As you might imagine, this took Jack somewhat by surprise and the poor man looked visibly shaken. The orchestra ground to a halt and Frank took to the podium looking very grave.

"Ladies and gentlemen, I am so sorry to interrupt your evening, but we've had a phone call to say that there is a bomb in the hall."

A groan of disapproval rippled across the room but there was no stampede towards the door. This was NI in the late 1970s and people had become almost immune to this sort of situation.

"Keep playing!" someone shouted up.

"Well, unless anyone objects, shall we all just check under our chairs and around about us for any suspicious packages," cautioned big Frank.

A moment of silence fell about the place as we all diligently carried out the random search. It was at this precise instant that Mad Malc decided to run up and unleash a thunderous thwack on the bass drum. This decidedly dodgy bit of comic timing might have worked well down the pub on a Friday night but under these circumstances, it scared most of us half to death. There wasn't so much as a flutter of nervous laughter; everyone was too shocked. We, not least Malcolm, were so fortunate that given how many fragile hearts there were in that gathering, not one missed a beat.

Jack very wisely called time on the first half though, and one and all vacated that disturbed scene, shaken and confused. There was an extended interval for us all to catch our breaths and calm down.

As the applause crescendoed for the entrance of the conductor at the beginning of the second half, it became blindingly obvious where our maestro had spent his break. Fond of a drop under normal circumstances, this catalogue of events had obviously unnerved Jack, weakening his resolve and sending him the way of some spiritual fortification. He somewhat precariously took to the podium displaying an inane, permanent grin, reminiscent of another Jack, though this one was never dull, and his paltry baton decidedly less fearsome than his look-a-like's axe.

We kicked off with the Waltz from Tchaikovsky's 'Serenade for Strings', which he gleefully beat in 4 throughout. During the next offering, players were being continually cued in the wrong place. Every turn in the music brought a fresh cartoon face from our clown bringing the orchestra to its knees in fits of giggles. It was the excerpts from Bizet's *Carmen* however that finally pushed the evening's frivolity over the edge. To begin with, Jack took his two batons and placing them like horns on a raging bull, charged up and down the aisles through the audience. For his next trick, he took the sizable score and retracing his steps played the part of the matador, screeching with laughter and hollering, "Ole!" The whole place dissolved in laughter and the evening came to an early yet natural close with everyone retiring to the bar determined to catch up with Jack.

Jack was a fiery and able musician, bringing a welcome spark of excitement to an often all-too-bland world. He could effortlessly conduct five with one hand and three with the other, had a commanding understanding of even the most complex rhythms and could confidently tell the third trombone that that F double sharp was fractionally high given its place within this particular sub-dominant thirteenth chord. His career never really scaled the heights his capabilities promised. He had no doubt put some prudish noses out of joint at some stage. Anyway, his name was far too common for him to have been taken seriously in the opinionated, fear-fuelled, cynical world of classical music.

33

Summer of '82

I went from Belfast pretty much directly to LA and the Music Academy of the West. My generous scholarship meant I was picked up at LAX by a chauffeur in full regalia, driving an absolutely enormous white stretch limousine, and driven the two hours north to the chic coastal town of Santa Barbara. We were housed in student accommodation in Goleta, one of the university campus towns nearby which was straight out of a '50s Hollywood movie. A collection of purpose-built apartment blocks erected round a central courtyard and pool. There was a huge, open, grassy expanse with sectioned off areas for baseball, basketball, football and so on. There were various town centres which all looked the same; laundromats, ice cream parlours, burger joints and diners. I remember seeing *ET* on the weekend of its release at the Picturehouse there after a suitable precursor of huge pizza slices and pitchers of Bud… somehow all wrong yet just right!

Before visiting Goleta however, Parker had parked me in a very different courtyard. This was the forecourt of the Music Academy of the West, a spectacular old Palladian villa, resplendent in all manner of exotic trees, a labyrinth of well-manicured hedgerows and paths sprinkled with fountains and sculptures. The house itself was a magnificent High Chaparral-style structure, boasting endless columns, arches and balconies. Its many shutters had been flung open lending the majestic residence a wonderfully airy and transparent feel. I stood there with my instrument and cheap sports bag transfixed to the spot. Had the names Paul Newman and Butch Cassidy gotten somehow mixed up at the limo office? Was I mistakenly on the unlikely set of *The Return of Cass and the Kid*?

Reality kicked back in when I heard my name being called from one of those first-floor balconies. I looked up to see not Robert Redford, but the warm, welcoming smile of Donald MacInnes. We both stood for a moment waving and taking each other in before spontaneously bursting out laughing; We were wearing almost exactly the same clothes, a sky-blue open shirt and yellow lightweight pants.We were a good match and this summer was shaping up nicely.

In case you're thinking this is all a bit 'artsy-fartsy, airy-fairy', let me assure you it was anything but. I had come all this way and set aside this exact time solely to work on my bow arm. The viola class was made up of ten hand-picked high flyers from all over the world and in our open masterclasses, which took place three times a week, they would each stride onto the stage and confidently dispatch with admirable displays of virtuosity the concertos of Bartok, Walton and Hindemith whilst I in turn would shuffle forward, make some nasty scratching noises and have dissected the minutiae of muscle movement in my right arm. Each and every day I would find a sheltered spot in that tropical garden and try to identify the precise movements that would time and time again capture the heart of the string thereby releasing that elusive depth of sound, which would in turn capture the heart of the listener.

Extraordinary things happened there. Things that would stay with me for the rest of my life. I got to sit an arm's length from the resident violin teacher at an impromptu recital, a guy by the name of Itzhak Perlman. To sit next to the person who, perhaps more than anyone else, displayed with consummate effortlessness the very technique I was desperately trying to achieve, was priceless. It was right here in the Lobero Theatre that I first heard the 'Three Pieces' of Stravinsky played by my old friends and mentors, the Vermeer Quartet, who were also teaching there. The impact of these three, brief but oh-so-colourful snapshots, was colossal and they would go on to become a staple part of the BQ repertoire. I remember trying to convey my feelings of elation to Shmuel Ashkenasi in the green room after the show, but he was too depressed by what he'd thought was an awful performance of Beethoven's Op. 130. This is a hollow feeling that I would come to know all too well. Doing justice to such a beast is a lifelong struggle. Strangely, on the rare occasions when you think you might have cracked it, the audience is often left cold. It's usually when you've been hopelessly flailing around that you are faced with a standing ovation. That's what's so thrilling about a live performance; the chemistry, those vibes that can run amok through the concert hall cannot be bottled.

Then there was Menahem Pressler teaching piano and a truly inspiring cello teacher whose name I'd never even heard before, Gabor Rejto. It was not a name I would ever forget. The few lessons I begged off him were perhaps the highlight of the whole experience.

There was also the inevitable orchestra to mop up any slack time and a steady flow of lectures and tutorials should you feel so inclined. Ah, that's better. I've managed to clear my conscience and have hopefully persuaded you that this place wasn't just a paradisiacal commune but a place of serious learning.

Having said all that, there was down time to be had and fun a-plenty. The house was a short woodland stroll from the beach where the locals seemed to be able to spend an inordinate amount of time casually perfecting the typically Californian pursuits of surfing and throwing Frisbees.

I quickly made friends. Take Jim, for example. I just happened to be standing by the front door when a jaw-droppingly beautiful De Soto pulled into the drive and out stepped the stereotypical Texan. He must have stood 6'6" in his patterned boots, had a bull on his belt buckle, open shirt and leather waistcoat; golden shades and perfect flowing blond hair escaping from under a ten-gallon hat completed the vision.

"Well, howdy," he growled in an impossibly low voice, easing a Marlboro from the corner of his mouth and revealing an irresistible toothy grin.

"My, this Academy really is far West!"

His drive from Houston didn't seem to have phased him much, though I can't imagine he got much conversation out of his travelling companion. His cello was sitting, pride of place, strapped into the only other seat of his Cabriolet. One fact had tickled him though; he couldn't wait to tell me that on leaving his friend's house in LA earlier he had asked for directions. His friend said, matter-of-factly, "Take this road north and hang a left at the lights."

Mildly surprised, he duly obliged and fully two hours later did indeed hang a left at the first traffic light to find himself in downtown Santa Barbara. He'd been on the Pacific Coast highway.

That traffic light stood in the shade of a magnificent sequoia and in a square, just a gentle stone's throw from that spot, was an amazingly authentic Greek restaurant called La Plaka. Normally we couldn't afford to eat out and made do with the stuff they served up back at the house but one night after an orchestral concert, which happened to coincide with someone's birthday, a gang of us made our way to this eatery and commandeered a great big extended table, right in the heart of the action. There was a blue-and-white theme to the taverna. It had an open kitchen and a bustling atmosphere. Gaudy pictures of Aegean life adorned the walls and the place was dripping with ancient pots and pans and various knick-knacks. If you enjoyed your meal, you were invited to smash your plate into the open hearth. Traditional music flooded the scene and at 9pm, when the Retsina and Ouzo were playing tricks on your retina and generating a lovely woozy feeling, an impossibly snaky and mysterious belly dancer would appear on the scene as if by magic. One of these girls in particular caught my attention. Her sultry, hypnotic movements were intoxicating, as was the rather sickly aromatic herb she later shared from her pipe disguised as an old-fashioned telephone. Did she really have a secret door from her bedroom leading directly onto a diving board and pool, California Dreamin'!

One day in late August my fantasy world got a premature reality check by way of a very different phone call. Mike was on the blower from Manchester, England to say that we had been offered a cancellation Wigmore date in October. The programme was to be Bartok 3, Mozart Clarinet Quintet, Mendelssohn Amin and we needed to start work asap. Of course it was a blow but I didn't give it a second thought. Alternative travel arrangements were made; I proffered my apologies to everyone at the Academy, said my goodbyes and within forty-eight hours was on my way. Parker was called into action and my parting memory is of sipping a giant margarita, bought with my last $5 in the airport's rooftop bar from where I contemplated my future and watched the sun set on my life before Brodsky.

Arriving at Heathrow came as a bit of a shock. To begin with, I would now be renting a room in Ian's house in Manchester and with characteristic kindness, he came to meet me off the plane. My British Parker was a definite improvement on the American one, but my fancy stretch had been replaced by an ageing Hillman Hunter. As we closed in on the home of my beloved Red Devils, the temperature fell to below double figures and we were forced to pull off the road by a torrential hailstorm. It was August 22nd!

34

Quartet Life

With a pleasing symmetry, our first two outings as a quartet were in Middlesbrough and Derry. There can't be many groups who can boast such an auspicious debut as ours, the quartet plus me that is. We played a selection of pieces in the interval of the Ken Dodd Show at the Forum in Billingham. Whilst this date held no importance of its own accord, it did signal my first visit to the real home of the quartet. Middlesbrough bears an uncanny resemblance to Derry in many ways. Not only do they share the same latitude of 55 degrees north, but both harbour a feeling of being beyond the pale.

As you head towards Derry and the Wild West from the perceived civilisation of Belfast, one is well guided towards places like Coleraine and Ballymena but it is only when the M2 bafflingly comes to an abrupt end, forty miles short of your destination, that a mysterious place called 'L'derry' begins to appear from the mist and onto the rusting signposts. Derry, once the proud capital of County Donegal was unceremoniously relieved of its ancient position, had a new name forced upon it and was then cast adrift on the choppy waters of a newly designed North of Ireland.

Approaching Middlesbrough from the south, one has a similar feeling of going in search of a place somehow abandoned. Middlesbrough, once of Yorkshire then North York, Teesside, Cleveland, Teesside again and finally of nowhere, also only appears on any signposts at the very last minute. Until then, one must head for Teesside. I realise, we are in no way unique in this respect, but the people of Derry and Middlesbrough do tend to share a feeling of being outcast and forgotten. Luckily, though this can engender unhealthy feelings of anger and resentment, managed in the right way it can become a force for good.

Arriving at the Thomas household was a seminal moment for me. Jacky is the youngest of nine children and that chaotic scene which greeted us was one I was very familiar with. The big old house; all thick gloss paint, heavy brocade wallpaper and thick pile carpets: the manic, buzzing kitchen with a constant stream of people coming and going. Meals in various stages of preparation, screaming wains, endless banter. Watching Mike morph, upon entry, into the court jester, a role I myself had perfected as a means of survival in my own crazy zoo. It was seeing our cellist in her home environment however which was to have the most dramatic and long-lasting effect on me. Jacky was no longer just a fantastic musician; she was a resourceful, funny, vulnerable, stunningly beautiful, infinitely lovable young woman. Now I was really in trouble.

Within two weeks of our comic routine (our own stand-up debut would come much later!) my band and I were pitching up at Kebroyde. We arrived on my twenty-third birthday and our first proper gig together was in Magee College the next day, September 14th, 1982. This debut concert would set a pattern and begin an education in how to deal with such events. They'd chosen to put us at the wrong end of the hall and the stage they had erected was uncomfortably high, unstable and noisy. That shiny surface would cause problems for Jacky's spike (someone needs to bring a rug). It being September, the 7.30pm concert would be in daylight hours so, to provide atmosphere, we would have to draw the enormous velvet curtains everywhere, which would dampen the sound uncomfortably. What light there was seemed to be everywhere but on the stage, resulting in a tired collection of much-loved standard lamps having to be commandeered and placed in between us. The beautiful hall, where I had witnessed my first ever chamber concert (the Galway Ensemble) some seven years earlier, was beginning to look more and more like a living room by the minute. On the day, we would rehearse too long and too intensely and eat too much just before going on. The promoter would give some rambling 'introductory' speech in which she would talk about raffles, upcoming concerts and the price of interval refreshments. We, being youthful and inexperienced had chosen a massive programme, aimed at the enjoyment of the player and only extremely sophisticated members of the audience. As we were about to go on, we realised, listening to the speech, that for some inexplicable reason they had elected to have the interval after Bartok No. 3 leaving the small matter of the Mendelssohn Amin. and Schubert's massive Gmaj.

in the second half. We would nevertheless round the evening off with a fifteen-minute encore, the Slow Mov. of Beethoven's Op.127!!

On a personal note, any blemishes in my playing would have a devastating effect on my performance. The slightest inaccuracy, whether I was responsible or not, would severely dent my confidence. My mind would race, and all inadequacies would be spotlighted. It would take many years to rationalise these feelings and learn how to better cope with live performance. All the other issues listed dog us to this day. In four years at music college, one short lesson on how to deal with concert days would have gone a long way. Equally, I guess someone should write a little guidebook for promoters on how to deal with the same situation; instead we all go blindly on.

The saving grace of that first night in Derry was the wonderfully generous audience. Not only did they fill the place, but they coped admirably with the bizarre interval placement, remaining good-willed to the bitter end. When I left Derry, I had never heard of a string quartet let alone played in one, now here I was, six years later, devoting my life to one. It felt like the right place to begin our journey together and we would go on to have a strong bond with Derry over the coming years.

For the most part, I liked living in Manchester. I found myself going to concerts and the theatre much more than I had in London and I made a host of new friends. You could get out to proper countryside quite easily; I even went fishing once or twice. I was the only non-driver amongst us so I set about putting that right. Actually, Jacky gave me some lessons. Never was anyone so happy to fail a test… more lessons!

Though the life I'd left behind in London was still a huge draw causing me to spend a lot of time on that stinky train, we were rehearsing flat out and it was amazing how quickly work came in for the group. Added to this, I still had my studies with Giuranna in Detmold to fit in. Arriving in a cold, grey, rainy German town on a Monday morning to the sound of slow scales was not a good feeling. My life had completely changed in the last six months since his concert at St John's and I could tell this Deutsch experience would be short-lived. I think I endured about three trips before explaining to Bruno that I felt unable to continue my studies. Stripping my technique back to the bare bone did not sit well with having to give concerts. He was understanding and endlessly encouraging, in truth, probably glad to see the back of me, bless him.

That first year with the quartet really was a bit of a whirlwind on all kinds of levels. My feet hadn't touched the ground for months and my life, having been stable for the last five years, was all change. Ian, his girlfriend Liz and I soon agreed that their home was way too cramped for three to share and anyway I realised that for a diehard United fan, living in the shadow of Maine Road simply wasn't an option!

On the very day I'd heard about a two-bed place in Whalley Range I was taking lunch in the RNCM canteen when I spotted a familiar profile across the refectory. It was none other than Dara 'Jascha' de Cogan. He had just secured a job with the Hallé Orchestra and was about to start looking for digs. The following week we moved into our modest maisonette above a shop, overlooking the green. This was a godsend from my point of view. I wouldn't have been able to afford this place on my own and Dara and I had just been sharing successfully in London. Though basic, the place was clean and well placed for me, in between Jacky and Mike's house and our rehearsal space, the Hermitage Room at Hartley Hall. The college gave us a residency in which we did them a few favours in terms of concerts and teaching in return for free use of this rather nice room. It's just as well it was nice given the endless hours we spent in there. Real life was hitting us hard. Though we never questioned it for a minute, while Jacky was still in her last year of study, three of us were now out in the big bad world having to earn a living. At a time when most of our friends were slotting into reasonably well-paid jobs, we had three engagements as our future and those were for half nothing. Whereas our contemporaries were busy reaching out and expanding their musical vistas, we were closing in and madly focusing on our very specific goal, to become the best quartet ever. I remember signing on the dole but never going back for the handouts. I'd been used to scraping a living, doing whatever work had to be done to pay the bills. Somehow, the dole didn't seem like the right attitude to have, it just didn't suit me. Instead, I made a list of every concert the quartet had ever done and set about writing to each and every one of those promoters, reintroducing ourselves and bringing them up to date with our activities. As a direct result of those letters we played not three concerts in our first season together, but forty.

Within the first month we had played twice as many concerts as we had been due to play in the first year. By the end of two months we had doubled that figure with dates that included our Wigmore debut. On the anniversary of our third month together, Jacky and I kissed for the first time. Like an oncoming tide, Jacky had imperceptibly seeped into my very being and I awoke to this fact, already stranded.

It is my firm belief that a fledgling group needs a mentor. The pressures are too great for any bunch of kids to deal with alone. Sure, we somehow managed it, as have many others, but at what cost one wonders. The single-mindedness required to make a success of it is monumental. The incalculable amount of time spent rehearsing never mind practising, the absolute priority afforded this musical activity over all others. Honing a collective musical character, agreeing on an artistic identity, choosing repertoire, finding a common ground on how to work out what's important; intonation, phrasing, style, bowings, fingerings, tempi, technique, musicality, legato, portato, vibrato, staccato, dynamics, ensemble, letting the music speak for itself or performing with a capital P, talking, no talking, CDs, stand, sit, dress, music stands, page turns, presentation. This before you get down to riders, dressing rooms, accommodation, transport, and the extremely time-consuming and logistical nightmare of dealing with management. Desperately trying to steer a course on many levels that will prove to be wise and not too upsetting to too many too much of the time. Then there are 'the books' which have to be cooked. Though the finances of a string quartet are notoriously meagre, they still have to be taken care of. Add to this the meetings, press, interviews, teaching, yes or no to this tour that tour, this concert that concert, this fee that fee: who's properly prepared, who's not practising, who screwed up last night… and you have a brief glimpse of life in the minefield that is a quartet.

On the other hand, being a part of and helping to build a group can be enormously thrilling and rewarding. At first, it's relatively easy to close the door on whatever outside opportunities might come a-knocking but as life's pressures build and the bills mount, this resolve can get thoroughly tested. Then, the relentless travelling puts untold stress on even the strongest relationship. If you're the kind of group to be content with a diet of predictable performances of a couple of tried and tested programmes per season you should arguably think yourself very lucky. If, on the other hand, you are a group plagued with ideas and driven by curiosity then you're in for a rough ride. We would spend hours in rehearsal talking about how best to rehearse and in true democratic style, every idea had to be given credence. Democracy is a word often used in group parlance but at least on a musical level there is a very strong argument for the fact that a democratic delivery of one person's vision can often be more convincing. With this in mind, we would give responsibility of a particular movement or even, on occasion, a whole piece to one person. Another fearsome tactic we often employed in those early days was for each member in turn to stand in front of the others and play their part solo from start to finish. This was a no-nonsense approach and the criticisms, brutal. We were death on the much-aired notion that chamber music is a bit of a soft touch, a place for failed soloists to take refuge. Anyone still secretly harbouring this lamentable idea should have a look at the late quartets of Mozart, middle Beethoven, Brahms, Smetana, Bartok, Janacek, Britten, Verdi, Zemlinsky etc. etc. and think again.

Suffice to say, it is a pressured business and a little advice from someone who has travelled this path would go a long way. The first part of my musical adventure was complete, I had reached my promised land, and so, with no help of any description, we set out on our perilous journey together.

(The Quartet's exploits over its fifty-year career are chronicled in my next book, to be published in the autumn of 2021.)

35

ECO

Though generally frowned upon, we all did the odd bit of outside work just to pay the bills. The English Chamber Orchestra was kind to me in those early days after leaving college. Founded in the 1950s by the likes of Terence Weil (our old mentor), Manny Hurwitz and Cecil Aronowitz, it built up a formidable reputation, attracting some of the greatest musicians in the world. Thanks to them, I was fortunate enough to meet and work with the likes of Menuhin and Zuckerman, Barenboim and Perahia. The orchestra is fronted and basically owned by the principal viola, Quentin Ballardie. Quinn is an intimidating individual, not only on account of the fact that his ownership of the band lends him absolute power but also because he's 6'2" in his stocking feet, built like a house and has a voice that would rival any sergeant major. This being a chamber ensemble and he the number one viola, meant that one was never far from the hot seat and indeed, on many occasions, I found myself actually sitting next to the self-styled ogre. The first time I took this chair we were giving the premiere of Carl Davis' Clarinet Concerto with the composer conducting. I was keen to impress and arrived in my seat early, warmed up, sharpened pencil and virgin eraser at the ready. The second half of the programme was Tchaikovsky's Serenade and Carl had brought many ideas on interpretation for the performance. We were still on page one when I naively blotted my copybook. Mr Davis suggested a shapely ritardando, diminuendo; a tempo, crescendo, with an appropriate change to the bowing. I diligently set about putting the new instructions into the part when Shrek rapped me across the knuckles with his bow, rather like you might imagine a Victorian parody of the situation.

"Leave the part as it is, sonny," he said. "We'll play our usual version this evening."

As an inexperienced little eager beaver, I found this behaviour despicable, yet in reality, how can any conductor seriously reshape a whole programme, particularly if it's famous repertoire, in one afternoon rehearsal? Arguably better to just stand there waving your little baton and allow the orchestra to get on with the business of playing a work they know from memory. On that hugely contentious subject of bowing (this one issue alone would prevent me from pursuing a career in orchestral playing), I was particularly taken with a wonderful Quinn quote which states that you never have to worry about the bowing in Handel's Messiah. If you start up and bow everything as it comes, you'll finish with the desired down… priceless!

Another classic Quinn moment was a Sunday morning gig at the Barbican. Maurice Hasson was directing and playing 'The Seasons'. He must have had previous experience because he arrived with his own parts in which all dynamics, bowings etc. were written in red ink. This combined with the early start had led our principal viola to conjure up a decidedly ill-tempered canine in the famous solo. The cowering figure of the already diminutive Monsieur Hasson allowed this rabid creature as much time off the leash as he could bear before tentatively applying a diplomatic muzzle. He stopped, turned and addressed the Quinn Bee;

"*Excusez-moi, Quinn, mon ami. J'adore* zis dog of yours. Such strength of character. I suppose, *enfin*, I just imagined a slightly smaller dog!"

The orchestra bit its collective lip, and I, seated next to the brute, eased back in my chair in an effort to become invisible. The chastised one merely growled, bared his teeth and continued his inimitable barking to the bitter end. One final ECO memory was turning up to a venue near Euston Station for what was a financially mouth-watering ten days of recording. It was all very hush-hush, and no one knew what this ambitious project was going to be. Upon arrival, it was clear that this was a massively enlarged ECO. Instead of the usual twenty to thirty players, the stage was overflowing with more than one hundred musicians. As we took our seats and opened the hallowed pages of the crisp new score, we found it to be Andrew Lloyd Webber's latest work, Requiem. We can't have been more than one hour into the opening rehearsal when a strange little figure appeared from the stalls and approached the conductor. Looking uncannily like his *Spitting Image* puppet, his trademark way-too-tight tank-top had helped to camouflage him against the brocade backs of the seats. He stopped the proceedings and whispered some instructions in the maestro's ear, whereupon a break was called. Upon our return to the stage, it was announced that the recording would proceed as per the schedule except for the small matter of the violins not being needed. What a moment to be a fiddle player! All thirty-two of them were released there and then with full pay. Suddenly, as if by magic, that sprinkle of fairy dust, that last minute flash of inspiration and hey presto, we had been transformed into the forces used by the great Fauré for his master work of the same name and it's not like there's where the similarities end. The good Lord works in mysterious ways.

36

Love

Jacky and I falling head over heels in love was not something we had planned. Though I was more confident about the relationship on a business level, Jacky was convinced it was a bad idea and absolutely adamant it could never happen. There's no denying there were complications, Jacky was actually living with someone at the time, but the attraction was fierce and pretty soon the inevitable occurred. Our tumultuous affair was short-lived however because, although I already knew I wanted to spend the rest of my life with this girl, she was plagued with guilt and fear. I do not recommend spending most of your waking life right next to the love of your life, if she represents the forbidden fruit; the torture, you wouldn't Adam 'n' Eve it.

The next four years were nightmarish. We made sure we were never alone together and other than pleasantries and rehearsal speak, barely said a word to each other. Jacky continued her relationship while I sought comfort in every port. I always rib her that she waited till I had finally got over her and was ready to move on, before clicking her fingers and bringing me to heel; an accusation she vehemently denies. All I know is that in August 1986, we had done a couple of concerts at the Edinburgh Festival and I felt able to not only walk Jacky back to her room, but to accept her invitation to have a nightcap. We had our first proper chat in almost as long as we'd known each other and off I went to bed, alone. I spent that September in Barbados and by the end of October, hey presto, we were together again, this time for life.

We were both at a party in Cambridge, thrown by my then girlfriend, when we locked eyes across the crowded dance floor. For some reason, in that moment, all those emotions that I had been suppressing for the last four years flooded back, filling my entire body like a potent drug; in a glorious daze, I involuntarily mouthed those three words (no, not 'paint my house' or 'fancy a …') but those three words that you only get to say in a truly meaningful way if you've been lucky enough to meet that special person without whom your life seems not worth living. I'd played my ace and it seemed to be working, luck was on my side. Jacky held my gaze, could it be possible that she felt the same? In one of those extraordinary Bjork moments, the room emptied, and the din subsided, we silently consumed each other, body and soul, from a distance. Though we went our separate ways that night, something in the chemistry of that aching look erased any uncertainties. In that instant, we both wiped the slate clean and embraced our fate, the unavoidable truth that we simply had to be together, come what may.

Nothing was said, however. After the party, Jacky returned home to London while I remained in Cambridge for what was the longest weekend of my life. I could hardly bear to turn up for our rehearsal the following Monday; was it all in my mind, did that moment even happen? As we caught sight of each other in the car park before the rehearsal, any doubts were banished. We somehow fumbled through yet another six hours of purgatory before finally allowing ourselves to be together. Plenty was said that night all right. Though still a scary prospect, how could anything that felt so right, possibly be wrong? I could not have been happier. We have not left each other's side since.

This time, there was no secrecy, no furtive hand holding in the back of the communal car coming home from concerts, no turning up early to rehearsals so we could steal five minutes alone together, no refresher course to hone my driving skills. We would brave the wrath of our colleagues and our own not inconsiderable trepidation about entering into the well-trodden, treacherous path of mixing business and pleasure. We went to ridiculous extremes to keep things as they had been in the workplace. Separate rooms, never sit together in cars, aeroplanes, restaurants; always communicate as individuals; agreeing on anything workwise threw us into a panic, for fear we were seen to be ganging up. It's gratifying to know that our colleagues have commented many times over the years that no one would ever know we were a couple.

37

Jacky Meets the Lads

We moved in together almost immediately, renting out Jacky's pad in Highgate and living in my Hampstead basement. It was such an exciting time. I couldn't wait to show Jacky off to all my friends and re-introduce her to my family, who only knew her as 'the cellist'. I was also particularly keen for her to meet Russell and Brendan.

Whereas my fishing days effectively ended with that Easter trip to London, my two esteemed colleagues had only just got started. Having already put in a lengthy apprenticeship, they now took to the task of becoming professional anglers, in earnest. Consequently, it was well-nigh impossible to catch up with these guys other than on the water. Jacky on the other hand, had never been fishing in her life. She was however an outdoorsy kinda gal with a deep understanding and love of nature. My plan was to hijack Jacky and sneak up on these two tight-liners when they might least expect it.

Ephemera are one of those miracles of nature that must surely bring a life-affirming glow to even the iciest of dispositions. Though they can be spotted anytime from March–October, the mayfly, as the name might suggest, seems to favour the month of May to put on a song and dance, or a dance at any rate. If you're in the right place and the conditions are favourable; warm, dry spring weather, clean, clear water; just sit back and let the show begin. Seemingly as one, these beguiling insects hatch on the lake or riverbed. As nymphs they make their way to the surface whereupon they emerge as beautifully coloured, long-tailed, elegant creatures, the arched body resembling that of a ballerina. Once their wings have dried, they ascend into the nearby trees for a brief moment of respite before performing a hypnotic mating dance. This completed, they return to the water, lay their eggs and die.

This annual event usually lasts five to ten days with each individual life cycle unfolding over a thirty-six-hour period. At its conclusion, the lake surface becomes a thick carpet of gently twitching 'spent gnats'. There are many notable events on a lake's calendar, the duckfly, the green Peter, the late-night murragh, the loveable daddy; but only the mayfly in full swing can provide the sort of bounteous feast irresistible for even the mightiest of trout. These monsters have long since settled for a life on the bottom, choosing from a menu more suited to their demeanour but this sudden top-table spread tempts them upwards. Begrudgingly, they surface and displaying an arrogant ennui, swim slowly up and down, over and back, in straight lines, cynically mopping up the arachnid stew as they go. For any fly fisherman, this is the Holy Grail; this is where my mates would be.

I knew that in recent years, Russell and Brendan had rented an old caravan on the north shore of Lough Arrow for the month of May, so this is where I headed confident that even if the business of fishing left Jacky perplexed, she would surely be awe-inspired by this natural spectacle. The lads were infamous around these parts and their humble abode easy to find. As we pulled into the clearing, there was Russell on all fours, brushing his teeth in the lake. Looking up, he beamed us his characteristic smile, greeting us as though we had just gone for the paper; ours being one of these precious friendships that simply picks up wherever it left off. Brendan, still emerging from his sleeping bag, presently stuck his head out the door of the caravan. Rather like the mayfly itself, Brendan always managed to end up looking dapper and colourful regardless of his starting point.

Introductions were made and soon we would have Jacky casting her first ever fly. We were however still on Donegal time here. Ablutions completed, we had to fetch an outboard engine from Jonjo's shed opposite. This inevitably involved a wee chinwag with Jonjo himself. Fuel for the outboard had to be acquired from Patsy's over on the East Shore. Another important and not-so-wee chinwag ensued. The boats had to be bailed of water, rods prepared, new casts tied, flies chosen, greased etc. Finally, just as it seemed like nothing else could get in the way of our departure, another car screeched to a halt just shy of the old caravan.

Unlike our pristine little Ford, this vehicle was clearly not a recent rental but the kind of unidentifiable hybrid-brand, built from old wrecks in one of the backyard garages so prevalent in this part of the world. For the most part, Donegal life is conducted in a glorious daydream, outside of the car. Once inside, these laid-back people become crazed racers. This particular driver vaulted from the hot seat and flashed us a wide grin, his pearly whites gleaming from within his rugged good looks. A spaniel sat on the passenger seat and the back seat was stuffed with coats, waders, bags, guns and rods.

"Bet you didn't expect to see me lads! Are ye's coming or going… I'm feckin' starvin!"

It seemed for all the world as though Mad Max himself had landed in this remote scene or at the very least, Mel G. struggling to get out of character; neither scenario was in fact the case. This was George, not of the jungle perhaps but certainly a convincing lookalike. George had managed estates in Ireland and Scotland and was a ghillie to the rich and famous. If Princess So-and-So wanted to catch a salmon or Sheik What's-his-Face dreamed of shooting a stag, George was the man to see to it. He had represented Ireland at the Olympics in the marathon, archery *and* rifle shooting. A wee fly wasn't going to cut it for a ravenous bear; our oars would remain dry while the full Irish was prepared.

As it turned out, George, who was currently hanging out down in Co. Mayo, was only in the area for twenty-four hours on business and had called by on the off chance that the lads would be in residence and fancy an evening at the local. Much as I liked George, I was quietly relieved when he went on his way. I wanted myself and Jacky to have Russell and Brendan to ourselves and anyway, we could find out a bit more about George later in the day. The magic moment finally arrived, and it was decided that Russell would take me to a favourite bay of his further up the lake whilst Brendan would kindly look after Jacky a bit closer to home. As the day quietened into an evening lull, the whole place went crazy. Millions upon millions of flies relinquished the relative safety of the canopy of trees lining the lake's edge and created a dancing veil before gliding down onto the water. Such profusion attracted not just the fish but all manner of birds, happy to gorge themselves on this annual feast. The lake was literally carpeted, and the trick was to single out a feeding trout and try to drop your fly in its path, somehow making it that bit more enticing than the ones next to it. A magical evening was spent at the heart of this spectacle of nature. On our return to dry land we found that Jacky had landed two beautiful brown trout, both about two-and-a-half pounds in weight. The first one had been hooked with her very first cast ever... she was a natural!!

Upon arriving at the pub, we found a bit of a session underway and George contributing vocally, as best he could. We took our seats and Jacky ended up sandwiched between me and George. Pleasantries dispensed with, we moved on to more general conversation. Brendan, who over the years had admirably taught himself the tin whistle and more recently, the uilleann pipes, was fully joining in on the music and Russell had been cornered by a couple of anglers eager to glean what insider information they could from the great maestro. This left us three. George's particular accent and the speed of his delivery would have made this intercourse quite challenging at the best of times but what with the din of the music and so on, poor Jacky didn't stand a chance. George would say something or ask a question, Jacky would look at me for a translation, then she would answer. One memorable line of interrogation went something like this:

"So, what sort of music do ye play?"

"Classical."

"Oh... is that Van Gogh and them boys?"

"Ah... yes, that's right."

"Aw, that's real music. And what instrument do you play?"

"I play the cello."

"Is that one of them bucks you put between your legs and saw wi'a yoke?"

We decided more Guinness and a couple of chasers was probably the best way of getting through. Though I've never had the pleasure of George's company since, he kept us thoroughly entertained that evening and presented us with what is surely the most colourful and succinct description of Jacky's chosen profession.

Jacky and I were happily defying all the odds, combining work and pleasure. The only fly in the ointment was the anarchic state of affairs the UK had got itself into, politically. Unable to stomach this bitter pill, we decided to look further afield, in an effort to escape, find solace and learn a new language into the bargain. In 1989, we bought an old ruin in France where we would live for the next three years. It was a picture postcard of a place with a bewitching courtyard and a sizeable orchard. The only habitable space however was the tiny apartment, which consisted of three small rooms etched out of a corner of the vast barn. One room had an ancient fridge and an even more aged device masquerading as a cooker placed dangerously close to the portable plastic shower; this was the kitchen/bathroom. Another had little more than the mattress we had transported from London, strapped to the roof of our trusty Saab. We nearly took off heading out the A40, which might have mercifully cut down the nine-hour journey time, but it wasn't to be; despite its heritage, the old Swedish warhorse stuck to its task and the macadam, ferrying us safely to the delights of the Poole/Cherbourg crossing and beyond. This mattress was then placed on pallets to avoid the inevitable results of the non-existent damp course. We erected state-of-the-art shelving using bricks and planks of wood we found lying around, a discarded aluminium clothes rail served as our wardrobe and completed the picture. The third and final space was furnished with bits and pieces from those wonderful bric-a-brac places you find in rural France; our dining table, more of those magnificent planks of oak balanced on cider crates. It was that basic, but we were happy there.

Friends, Anya and Jonathan for example, often came to stay; where they slept, I have no idea. We made new friends too, some expats but also many of the locals became close, we did our utmost to integrate and they took us to their hearts. Everything about our life there was illogical, but we were young, in love and searching for adventure and a life outside the quartet. We made cider, calvados, bottled our own wine, entered the local fishing competitions and became quite useful at *petanques*. We learnt how to restore (well, partially) a house in French, how and when to harvest *pleurotes* and how to order a morning coffee in a farmer's kitchen and still be able to drive home. We spent many hours sitting in our cramped quarters gazing out at the dilapidated scene before us, daydreaming of what we could never afford. We seriously entertained the notion that we could have a private airfield out the back by only losing a few of the apple trees. We nearly killed ourselves planting a huge beech hedge using saplings from a nearby wood (information gleaned from our trusty neighbour) only to find that this planting bizarrely coincided with another neighbour's acquisition of a pair of donkeys. These delightful beasts had been installed in the adjoining field within hours of our handiwork getting completed. Our hedge didn't even make it through the night.

It was such a romantic place however and seemed to me to be the perfect setting for us to seal our relationship. I decided that I was going to pop the question after a tour of Japan when we had a bit of time off. In the hotel bar after the last concert in Osaka, I was casually chatting to Ian about whether or not he was thinking of getting married at any time when Jacky suddenly arrived and came in on the conversation. I, desperate to throw her off the scent, started doing down the whole concept, strenuously undermining the validity of such an archaic structure in today's society. This only served to enrage Jacky and a frightful row ensued between us on the matter, Ian very wisely bowing out for a welcome cigarette. Not imagining Jacky's reaction, I'd foolishly backed myself into a corner. The problem was, I didn't want to give up on my plan and anyway, with nerves as raw as they were, now was not the time for surprises. We went our separate ways that night, angry and unhappy and spent most of the long journey home sulking and quiet.

Thankfully, we just about managed to put a brave face on it in time for our arrival back at the ancient farmhouse allowing me to perform the old 'down on one knee' routine. I wasn't so slow, figuring that the poor girl would be jet-lagged and not thinking clearly, I seized the moment, and so there on those ever-so-evocative fifteenth-century outdoor stone steps, Jacky said yes. We got married the following year in the local church and among the one hundred and fifty guests were fourteen bridesmaids, all nieces below the age of sixteen; we had to draw the line somewhere! The weather was glorious, and the party lasted many days; days filled with food, wine, sport, music, laughter and fun, all of which my parents missed. They didn't show up; getting on a bit, I guess.

Whilst living and working together poses many problems, for me they pale into insignificance next to the alternative, spending inordinate amounts of time away from your loved one. After three years in rural France, Jacky and I would return to live in North London and, in time, be blessed with two completely gorgeous and adorable daughters, Holly and Celia.

38

The Girls

I find it curious how, amongst Jacky's and my numerous siblings, only two did not have children of their own. Furthermore, I'm not even sure if those two took that decision or if that's just how things panned out. It's true, none of them put in the shift our parents had, no one approached the dizzying figures of nine or sixteen but it's interesting that their unusual experience in that regard didn't put them off completely. The effect on me seemed to be twofold. On the one hand, from an early age, I was driven in my pursuit of a mate. There was never a doubt in my mind that I wanted to spend my life with someone else; to forge a super-close, lifelong relationship with another being was a clear goal. Alongside this burning desire, however, was the absolute conviction that I did not want kids. I had spent much of my young life surrounded by my brothers' and sisters' endless wains; why would anyone choose to do this to themselves? These snotty little beggars needed constant attention; life as you knew it was over. Then there was the issue of adding to this already grossly overpopulated planet of ours. I couldn't come up with a single good reason for procreation.

Luckily, in Jacky, I had found someone for whom not having children simply wasn't an option; so we compromised and had kids. I presume the reason no one tells you about what happens when your own baby is born is because the feelings are difficult to explain and well-nigh impossible to believe. Though not everyone reacts in the same way, essentially, I instantly fell in love. I became totally besotted with this weird little slimy ET-like bundle.

On the 23rd of April 1995, a miracle took place. Jacky gave birth to Holly. Meticulously planned to coincide with a rare lean patch in our diaries, the timing happily meant that the little darling had to be conceived at the Dartington Summer School; no more fertile place on these shores, let me assure you.

Towards the end of a textbook pregnancy, we decided to grab a couple of final days of freedom before the impending lockdown. We jumped in the car and followed the sun, ending up on the beautiful Dorset coast where we managed to find a room in a typically English country hotel overlooking the sea. Little did we know that our schedule for the next two days, of long walks and spicy food, was a perfect recipe for inducing childbirth.

Though everyone had confidently told us that first babies always come late, at 5am on the second night of our stay I was awoken by Jacky in a bit of a state. This was it; it was happening. Jacky's waters had broken and here we were in the middle of nowhere. We decided to cut our losses and head for home, only we were not going home. I had the drive of my life, seventy-five minutes from Corfe Castle to the Whittington Hospital on Archway, Jacky with her feet through the windscreen, me with my foot through the floor. No sooner had we arrived at the natal unit than the contractions stopped. Instinctively considerate, Holly had put off her arrival so I could enjoy United beating Burnley 2–0.

Poor Jacky, who had worked right up to the wire, was back travelling and giving concerts within a couple of weeks of the birth. Mike wouldn't entertain the idea of giving concerts without her, so, with no other means of employment, our only choice was to get back to work. As for me, well, if maternity leave was out of the picture, paternity leave was a concept yet to be envisaged. Like all parents, I will never forget that drive home from the hospital, so unlike the drive to the hospital. Hazard lights on permanent, 10mph maximum, shouting and screaming like a mad person at all other drivers, cyclists, pedestrians, pigeons… anything moving was a danger to new life. Then the walk up the path and closing the front door behind us.

"What on earth do we do now?" said I to Jacky, genuinely terrified.

You feel so alone and helpless.

"Why didn't anyone warn us about this!?" I used to always say.

Problem is, no one can prepare you for it, it's just a life experience that you have to negotiate for yourself.

Holly was four weeks old by the time we got to introduce her to my mum. When you're grandchild number forty, celebrations are tempered somewhat by familiarity. Even on Jacky's side, the jubilation was pretty low key, yet here, Holly was only number fourteen. My mum did teach us one invaluable lesson, however. We arrived there carrying the wee mite that we'd been carrying for every minute of her short life. We were hardly in the door when Mum got out a blanket, stretched it out on the living room floor and ordered us to "Put that wain down."

The thought had never occurred to us. It was such a simple plan, but it worked a treat.

Sheer heaven, we never looked back.

Some early, work-related memories of that first year with Holly were for example, her first long-haul flight. How strange it was to actually be those people at the front of Economy with the baby in the flight cot. Being a doting parent, right up to the moment you go on stage and returning to that state the moment you come off, is exhausting. Jacky was amazing, I don't know how she did it, given that she had the extra drain of having to feed the baby. Though every concert was much the same in that respect, I recall one particularly taxing one, live to radio from the Palais des Beaux Arts in Brussels, a programme that included Beethoven's Op.135, Bartok No.6 and the premiere of a monstrous piece by a guy called Luc van Hove, which near enough finished us off.

Arriving at Paul McCartney's Mill Studio to record the quartet he had written specially for us and having Paul whisk Holly up in his arms and take over nanny duties. He was amazing with her, so natural and lovely. I remember us asking his advice, seeking consolation that we were doing the right thing, bringing our baby everywhere with us.

He totally reassured us, urging us not to change anything, saying, "It's the best education a child can get. Much more important to keep them close." This, from a family man whose children are an example to us all, was welcome news indeed.

By the time we landed in Seville for a Shostakovich Cycle over one weekend, Holly had been to twelve countries in as many months. This would have been just another day at the office for us except for the fact that our usually super-dependable manny, Mark Morgan, had mislaid his passport and couldn't travel, leaving us with five minutes to find a local replacement and teach her the ropes. Added to the nightmare was that Holly was running a fever and not feeling at all well. We coped; we had to.

This was our new life, a life on the road with a child. It's all the paraphernalia that's the real killer: the pushchair, the feeding stuff, the changing stuff, the endless changes of clothes, the toys. Then there's the cello! We would arrive at an airport; I'd hire the car while Jacky got the luggage. Get to the hotel/apartment, I'd go shopping for essentials while Jacky checked in and got organised. We'd all go to the hall; Mark would look after Holly while we rehearsed. Then, we'd take her to the park or something in the break, getting back just in time to change and get on stage. We would feed and change her etc. during the interval and when the concert was over, we'd all go back to the room, where we'd put Holly to bed and cook ourselves some dinner, while Mark went out clubbing. Suddenly, playing a few quartets was like a day off.

Jacky was soon making it clear that she wanted to add to our progeny. One child did not a family make. Holly's transition from ET into the most perfect baby ever to draw breath was almost instantaneous, and I, thoroughly content and absolutely enchanted by our one child set-up, shamelessly tried using her perfection to my advantage.

"But why do you want to mess with what we've got. How could we possibly improve on this!?" was my line of protest.

Jacky gave birth to Celia on 29th June 1998.

Once again, we were blessed, inasmuch as darling little Celia came along perfectly to plan… well, nearly. Towards the end of that pregnancy, Jacky developed a complication that was dangerous to both mother and child resulting in the consultant insisting she be induced asap. Though not thrilled at the idea, the consultant agreed to her doing one final concert on condition that we go straight to the Whittington immediately thereafter.

Under normal circumstances, we would have followed the consultant's advice and cancelled the concert, but that particular date was with the Crouch End Festival Chorus. It was not the sort of programme where someone else could have stepped in, consequently, we would have been letting down a great many people. We premiered a piece by Paul Patterson for quartet and choir and, in the second half, played Crumb's 'Black Angels'.

I'm guessing it was this traumatic experience that led Celia to decide, "OK, I'm outta here!"

Despite being well short of the due date, Jacky started having contractions as we played the last notes, ending up prostrate on the dressing room floor after the show. We, well I, jumped in the car, for Jacky it was more of a forward roll into the reclined front seat and headed north towards the hospital. No sooner were we on the road than the contractions stopped, and Jacky began to instantly complain of hunger pangs. It was a balmy summer's evening as we tootled up through Angel and soon, we were relaxing in a pavement cafe with a bowl of pasta and a glass of red, enjoying the second half of a football match. It was World Cup fever and Celia, much like her sister before her, had thoughtfully postponed her arrival till after the game.

We got to the hospital around midnight and though they did begin the induction process, not a bundle of laughs by the way, Celia was now clearly signalling her intent, and having taken our final bow on the Barbican stage at around 10pm, she was safely in our arms by 3am, mother and child in rude health.

We nearly lost our little treasure when, at sixteen days of age, she contracted a deadly virus. She spent two weeks in intensive care during which time she left us many times, only to confound the doctors by miraculously returning each time. This is not an experience I would recommend. Ultimately, it was her own grit and determination to cling on to life, and a huge slice of luck obviously, that saw her through.

Considering this trauma, we were thankful that Celia's first year turned out to be very different to that of Holly, as unusually most of our work was in the UK. The touring soon kicked in again however and we battled forward, five going mad, not only in Dorset, but in a myriad of far-flung places, from Parry Sound to Invercargill.

I'm a great believer in the notion that kids appear in this world with their characters already formed. If you take abuse out of the equation, they seem to plough their own furrow and frankly, all you can do as a parent is to provide the best example you possibly can.

Take our two. Holly attended her first concert in Zaragoza, aged two. We played a programme that included Schonberg's extremely dense Fourth Quartet. She sat there completely enthralled, only taking time out to gesture at noisy audience members to "Sssh!!"

From that moment she has been a regular at our shows and even now, as a grown woman, never misses an opportunity to come along.

Celia on the other hand, despite having had all the same chances, is only recently coming round to the idea of sitting through two hours of her parents scratching away. Though both of them play instruments and would, I'm sure, say that music was probably the most important thing in their lives; they are very different people, thank goodness.

Labelling kids is clearly a big mistake and our two girls continue to surprise us as they adapt to life, but I think it's fair to say that Celia, as a child, was a tad more difficult to deal with than Holly. Where Holly was generally more accommodating and understanding of the pressures we were under, her little sister didn't give a monkey's. That's not to say she wasn't also loads of fun to have around.

As part of one of our 'Children's Shows', we were performing a piece called 'Anna and the Moods' for narrator and string quartet, at the Sydney Festival. The narrator was a flamboyant TV personality who really camped it up and insisted on having arguably the most opulent chaise longue I think I've ever seen, in cerise, purple and gold.

Holly and Celia had, as usual, joined us for this trip and were in the audience with some local friends of ours who had a little girl about Celia's age. I thought it would be a laugh to organise a simple game during the show in which I would ask a fairly obvious question about something that was happening on stage. Celia's mate, who had been tipped off, would raise her hand and I would choose her to give the correct answer. When it came to the crucial moment however, the wee thing had fallen asleep and I was instead faced with my own little darling, jumping up and down, arms in the air, grinning from ear to ear. What could I do? Naturally, I pointed to her, she gave me the right answer, *amazingly,* and then skipped to the side of the stage to pick up her very special prize; one of our CDs. As I handed it to her she gave me a huge hug and bellowed out in an unnaturally loud Hollywood-style voice, "Thanks Daddy!!"

Never work with children or animals, as they say.

Around this time, I had started up a chamber orchestra in Derry. It was great fun and we did several concerts over a two- or three-year period till the inevitable lack of funding meant it ground to a halt. I enjoyed conducting, indeed it was my conducting which got me the closest thing to a compliment from my mum when, after the first of the orchestra's concerts she said to me; "Well, I didn't know you could dance!"

Rare as they were, coming from her, I'll take what I can get.

One programme I dreamt up consisted of music from the *Fantasia* films and was shamelessly aimed at entertaining our two girls. Halfway through Shostakovich's 2nd Piano Concerto I was a tiny bit taken aback when I felt a strange tugging on the seat of my pants. Spinning round, I was confronted, not by the one-legged tin soldier, but by Celia, who had left her sister entranced by the music, made her way undisturbed to the stage and was now gesturing to me that *she* would like to try this conducting lark. Though charmed by the action I was concerned the poor soloist might get distracted and lose his place. I conjured up as fierce a glare as I could muster, sending her off on all fours under the piano where she remained for the rest of the piece, conducting away from her prostrate position. Needless to say, she once again stole the show.

Meanwhile, our nanny was earning more than us but we had always imagined losing one of our incomes if we were to keep our little family together, come what may; frankly, a small price to pay for what we gained.

39

Doire Revisited

We recently bought an Irish hideaway, way up there in an area they call God's Country. It's true as well, God does hang out up there, every bit as much as everywhere else. Not dressed up in displays of power and wealth but quietly understated and infinitely natural, within and without us all. The girls love it there, having spent many a happy summer holiday in that area, but I wouldn't be there if it weren't for their enthusiasm. I'm gradually settling in, allowing the passive beauty of the place to overtake uncomfortable memories. It's an amazing release to be able to speak normally, without affectation, and not be judged as an outsider. It's a joy to interact with the locals, my people, their generosity of spirit and effortless camaraderie encourages my natural tendencies in that direction, making me feel less like an imposter and consequently, more relaxed. Donegal was recently voted 'the coolest place on Earth to visit' (nothing to do with the weather!) by *National Geographic* magazine, and I reckon they weren't far wrong. 'The Wild Atlantic Way' was chosen as one of the most beautiful drives on the planet; here again not something I would argue with. But why am I telling you all this, it's really a dreadful place with nothing to offer. Stay away!

The Brodsky Quartet continues to thrive and is currently closing in on its fiftieth anniversary. Soon after I joined, we had a final bash at international competitions. Though not something we were best suited to, these efforts proved very successful and were well rewarded in that they helped open up Europe and the Far East. In the forty-eight years since, we have gone on to play over three thousand concerts in more than sixty countries and have recorded in excess of seventy CDs. We have had the good fortune to work with some of the most celebrated musicians on the planet and I remain constantly in awe of my colleagues, Jacky and Ian who started this crazy gang as children and whose exemplary devotion keeps it alive and wondrously wacky today. Being a part of this group has afforded me such a rich and varied life. Whilst my playing and that of the quartet remains paramount, my role as the ideas man, the programmer within the group, has allowed me to dream and be as creative as I can be.

In 2013 Derry was awarded the European City of Culture. No, not Culchie… Culture. This shows you how things have changed. When I left in 1976, Derry was a glorified car park, countless bombs having razed much of it to the ground. Now, with the advent of peace and some care and attention, it has become an impressive place once again, a place to be proud of. Back in the '90s, BBC NI did a TV show about people who had left Derry to pursue a career in classical music, it came as quite a surprise to me that I was found to be the first one to have done so. For the purposes of the show, I starred as the elder statesman, the trailblazer of my dreams.

Paradoxically, this tremendous success for Derry coincided with the regrettable demise of its Chamber Music Society. This was the organisation that had not only hosted my debut with the quartet, but had also invited me to give a recital upon finishing my studies at the RCM. Aside from my playing, this was no ordinary viola recital, I arrived home to a bit of a hero's welcome, my ugly mug was plastered all over town, on every lamppost, in every shop window; the concert, which was in the main hall of the Guildhall, was completely sold out, filmed and attended by the great and good of the county. In return, we later introduced a very successful string quartet course that lasted for many years before, as with the Music Society itself, money got in the way, or rather the lack of it, causing the whole thing to collapse.

What a shallow world we're busy creating. Jacky reminded me the other day that, back in the '70s, with only two TV channels to choose from, you could watch programmes starring Andre Previn, Lenny Bernstein, Isaac Stern, heck you could regularly sit in on performances of contemporary music with The Fires of London and Peter Maxwell-Davies. Nowadays we're treated to an endless supply of no-hopers, skating, dancing or baking fucking cakes. Then there are the people who, in more respectable times, would maybe have been tolerated in the shower, behind closed doors, being let loose to embarrass themselves in public in front of a panel of washed-up halfwits. The worst of it is that this crassness only serves to undermine and cheapen the hard work, devotion and brilliance of all those extraordinary people who do these things properly. Mediocrity is becoming acceptable, our standards, moral and otherwise, are falling, as we slip further and further right towards a world ruled by narcissistic bullies.

Whilst not wishing to dwell on the past, what I find sad is the glaringly obvious truth in all this. Would we, the people of Derry and beyond, ever have reached this vastly improved state we now find ourselves in with only peaceful means? How long would we have had to wave our little flags, painted with slogans no one bothered to read? How many verses of 'We Shall Overcome' would have echoed out over the Bogside before anyone listened, took responsibility and actually did something remedial about the insufferable apartheid that was going on in their very own backyard? I guess, after nearly a millennium of abuse, this sort of treatment just becomes accepted as the norm, only this time, they misjudged the fervour, the resolve, the tenacity of the irritating, downtrodden, forgotten people beyond the pale.

The more I travel the world, the more I find truth in that saying, 'a little education goes a long way'. I see beauty everywhere, often camouflaged because it's not necessarily what we're used to, but it's there. Why are we obsessed with isolation and order? Why not open up, embrace variation and maybe learn something? Instead, we find ourselves hurtling towards this despicable future, like so many sheep off a precipice, all based on lies and a complete lack of information. It's a future I find almost unbearably depressing and one I will do my utmost to avoid. A future brought about by a bunch of hare-brained twats who spent rather too long closeted away halfway down the M4. We're heading back to a freak-show of tattooed, overweight, sunburnt geezers who enjoy a piping hot cup of Maxwell House with their *Daily Mail*. It's going to be fish 'n' chips or heartburn pies all wrapped up in St George flags. God save us, never mind the Queen. What was once the greatest empire on earth has charted a course from naval exploration to navel gazing.

Ironic to think that Dublin will be the only English-speaking capital in Europe. The capital of a country which is doing its best to learn, throwing off the shackles of its brainwashed past and creating an inclusive society more focused on peace, love and understanding, than exclusion and fear; whilst to the unhappy north of that great country we still have the likes of these Neanderthals, who dress up like a car crash and go out on the wrong date every July to celebrate the winning of a proxy war, a war they only won because of the financial backing of the very pappy of the group they most detest, the Catholic Church. I mean, it's embarrassing isn't it?

Now they've sold their gold, their water, their prestige motor cars and industries, their very soul for goodness' sake, the British have chosen to close the door.

Never mind.

"Have you been to a Harvester before?"

Perhaps you'd prefer a visit to a Wetherspoons; you'll have to take the kids with you because there will be no one prepared to look after them. This will involve strapping them to the spare wheel of your Morgan. Once at your destination, you'll be invited to PYO fruit and veg before entering the establishment to enjoy a self-service buffet, washed down with warm local beers and wines accompanied by Andrew Lloyd-Webber classics on a loop. Before paying your bill, as part of the character-building experience, you will be invited to clear away and wash up your dishes (this potential indignity may be avoided by simply binning them for a small surcharge).

An English person once said to me that although NI is apparently part of the UK, perhaps because it's on a different island, it doesn't feel like part of it, and certainly not the cities. I think there's a lot of truth in that, Derry or even Belfast don't get used in general vernacular the way say, Glasgow, Edinburgh or Cardiff, Swansea do. Make your minds up guys, are we included or not? The need for that old DUP vote is a bugger isn't it.

Something that probably didn't harm Derry's bid was the fact that its famous walls would be celebrating 400 years of existence. Built in 1613 by various livery companies within the City of London, the two cities have an intricate relationship to this day, our continuing headache with that confounded name, a product of this time. A London mayor once told me that the City of London is forever being approached by other cities from all over the world with requests for twinning their city with the City of London. The reply is always negative because the City of London is already twinned, with the City of Derry. The latter's formidable walls, one mile around to reflect the Roman walls of London's Square Mile, are over forty feet high in places and a real feature of the city, yet, because of the war, they'd been closed off and I never got to walk those impressive battlements till I was forty years old.

I don't think it's melodramatic to suggest that I suffer with survivor guilt. So many of my compatriots paid the ultimate price to achieve what we have today, and it is only through their extraordinary sacrifice that I can safely return to my home town with my family. I console myself with the notion that I have gone about the fight in a different way. I've chosen to go out into the world and in my own small way, try to be an ambassador for Derry. I have mingled with our tormentors, killed them with kindness, forged countless friendships with those beautiful people and hopefully, once or twice along the way, caused them to question their country's actions towards their neighbours. The world is such a complicated place and few of us seem to have learnt from past mistakes. There are still countries raping and pillaging their neighbours, trying to get their hands-on stuff that doesn't belong to them. There remain many places where you can still be strung up for your beliefs, nay, for taking the name of a god in vain. Closer to home, some of the worst behaviour I have witnessed has been that of my own dear siblings. Don't come to me with that 'blood is thicker than water' bullshit. One has to be so careful going around pointing fingers without in-depth knowledge of your subject. It's beyond sickening to know that we are covertly busy selling arms to countries that we are openly busy creating sanctions against, or that the IRA, RUC, UDA and MI5 were all in bed together.

Regardless of these depressing thoughts, I had a strong urge to come up with some way of marking Derry's City of Culture year. In many ways the resulting idea was served up on a plate.

The city itself was the starting point, then the anniversary of the walls, coupled with the fact that Derry's name (Doire in Gaelic) means oak grove, got me thinking about how a neighbouring tree will, in time, bring down any wall. How the branches of said tree will naturally spread out over the wall, built to keep in and keep out, in a kind of a 'goodwill gesture'. This simple image, in the context of my home town, seemed to say so much. If we are to mature and grow, we must reach out, show understanding, and break down any walls in our path.

It was around this time that we took a family holiday to the USA and Canada. During our stay in NY City we visited the magnificent and deeply moving monument to the Twin Towers disaster, Ground Zero. This is a huge site with a lot going on but the general gist of it is:

A spanking new edifice, the same size as the original North Tower but with a spire taking it to 1,776 feet (the year of the American Constitution) and a park with two stunning pools where the old towers stood, on the perimeters of which are inscribed the names of the victims. The centrepiece of this park is a Callery Pear Tree, or 'survivor tree', and my, how this specimen has lived up to its billing. Excavated from the depths of the North Tower's rubble, it was charred and broken but found to have one tiny limb clinging on to life. A beautiful plan was set in motion. Though not expected to survive, it was cared for, potted up and sent for safe keeping to a nursery in the Bronx where it confounded all expectations by literally returning from the dead only to be uprooted and badly damaged once again, this time by Hurricane Irene. Somehow, it clung on for dear life and now the 30ft tall arbour occupies the central spot of this Remembrance Park, a powerful reminder of the tenacity of life against all the odds.

In this spirit of looking outwards, we decided to pair Derry with other similarly walled cities, in order to internationalise the idea. Given how many walled cities there are across Europe, I was fortunate that my old friend, Ian Richie, was at that time the director of the City of London Festival, the obvious second port of call on this journey. Ian is a wonderfully erudite and free-thinking man. He immediately took to my idea and together, over a couple of years of seemingly endless brainstorming, we brought the idea to life. I could never have managed it without his brilliant insight and unerring support.

The resulting piece, which we called 'Trees, Walls and Cities', was a song cycle for quartet and voice, inspired by Schubert's magnificent 'Die Winterreise'. I gave each composer a little motif from the Schubert and we encouraged them to use this in some way in their contribution. We were joined by the stupendous Lore Lixenberg, and together, commissioned eight composers from Derry to Nicosia, asking them to collaborate with writers or writings from the opposite side of their particular wall, and create a song. The whole work was pulled together musically by the extraordinary human who is Nigel Osborne. Nigel wrote a beginning and an end to the cycle and also managed to merge the songs so that it didn't feel too disjointed. We gave the world premiere in the City of London Festival on 24th June 2013. This evening was not only the culmination of an epic journey for myself and Ian Richie, it provided a spectacle that I have never witnessed before or since, ten composers taking a bow together on the same stage. We went on to perform the piece in the representative cities, planting a symbolic tree of commemoration wherever we went.

For the most part, these seemingly worthless gestures go virtually unnoticed. This is clearly not Live Aid, but I do think such ventures are massively important; to use the obvious analogy 'mighty oaks from little acorns grow'. Years of work and an enormous input from a great many people to generate one piece of music. A dozen concerts to not many people, a CD no one will listen to. It's nevertheless the attitude that's vital as we negotiate this bewildering journey we're all on. Every single, positive, caring action we carry out, every tiny effort we make is huge and our collective example far-reaching; but be prepared, it takes resilience. Remember, no good deed ever goes unpunished.

It's anyone's guess why we're all here. Where have we come from, where are we going, what's real and what's, well actually, what even is 'real'? How many 'sliding-door' scenarios do we unwittingly negotiate every single day?

As I mentioned before, "You're so lucky to be doing something you enjoy for a living" is an observation we musicians are often confronted with. I concur that being able to play something like Haydn's 'Seven Last Words' is a privilege, but never underestimate the work that has gone into getting to that level and the constant struggle to stay there. Much of the slog is mundane and repetitive, the performances, which carry their own nightmares and demons, are only ninety minutes twice a week or so, the hard graft takes place behind closed doors.

Like in Andre Agassi's wonderful book, *Open*, when he hooks up with Steffi Graf and they both admit to 'hating tennis'! Of course, these two legends of that great sport do not hate it, but they have experienced it at the highest level from a young age, they know it from the inside out and had what you might term pushy parents. There is a strong argument that those of you who perhaps have a less creative job but can go and listen to the Haydn or watch Wimbledon, especially if you can play an instrument or a sport, have got the better deal. I cannot pretend that I was born to be a musician; that said, it is a life I wouldn't trade for anything. I never thought of playing an instrument till Bridget stuck a violin under my chin, even then, it wasn't my driving force until that visit to the orchestra. I had never heard of a string quartet till I got to college yet, within moments of playing in one, realised this was what I wanted to do for the rest of my life. Not all life journeys are mapped out the same, one can get from A to Z in many different ways if one is open, perceptive, hardworking, understanding and loving.

I am proud to have come from Doire, the oak grove, but I am also a thoroughly committed citizen of the world. I am a tree. Let's all be trees, not walls.

Acknowledgements

I would like to thank Peter Florence and Louisa Young for their invaluable advice; Brian Viner and Andy Ford for their words of wisdom; Adam Kuper for listening to my endless nattering on the subject and Declan MacManus for his heartwarming response to the book and, by the way, for spotting the title!

My thanks also go to Adeena Grubb for brilliantly bringing to life the cover I had in my mind and to Joe Shillito at Matador for expertly guiding me through the publishing process.

For most of my adult life, people have been saying to me, 'you should write a book'. It wasn't until I sat down to write that book, the one about my adventures in the Brodsky Quartet, that this one sneaked up on me. I owe every word in these pages to my precious family; Jacqueline, Holly and Celia. Without their perseverance, I would never have started; without their patience and endless encouragement, I would never have finished and without their being, there would simply be no point in the exercise in any case. Thank you.

 Matador

For exclusive discounts on Matador titles,
sign up to our occasional newsletter at
troubador.co.uk/bookshop

Milton Keynes UK
Ingram Content Group UK Ltd.
UKHW020615041123
431893UK00011B/496